T0285635

Searching
IN ST. ANDREWS

Finding the Meaning of Golf During the Game's Most Turbulent Summer

Sean Zak

TRIUMPH
B O O K S

Library of Congress Cataloging-in-Publication Data

Names: Zak, Sean, author.
Title: Searching in St. Andrews : finding the meaning of golf during the
  game's most turbulent summer / Sean Zak.
Other titles: Searching in Saint Andrews
Identifiers: LCCN 2023051940 | ISBN 9781637273326 (hardback) | ISBN
  9781637273340 (epub)
Subjects: LCSH: Golf—Scotland—St. Andrews—History. | BISAC: SPORTS
& RECREATION / Golf | TRAVEL / Special Interest / Sports
Classification: LCC GV984 .Z35 2024 | DDC 796.35209412/9—dc23/
  eng/20231117
LC record available at https://lccn.loc.gov/2023051940

This book is available in quantity at special discounts for your group or organization. For further information, contact:
  Triumph Books LLC
  814 North Franklin Street
  Chicago, Illinois 60610
  (312) 337-0747
  www.triumphbooks.com

Printed in U.S.A.
ISBN: 978-1-63727-332-6
Design by Nord Compo
Page production by Patricia Frey

*To Grandpa, the golfer, and
Grandma, the writer*

Contents

Prologue

There's a video on my phone from the summer of 2022 that really says it all. Within the borders of the screen is a different world. It's 9:47 PM there, in St. Andrews, Scotland, and for just a few minutes the sky is holding on to that periwinkle blue. The sun has already dipped behind us, but there is only one direction for us to go. There are three holes left in this silly match.

It's July 26, nine days after Cameron Smith took a Claret Jug–sized bite out of Rory McIlroy's soul when he rallied to beat him in The Open. Four hundred yards ahead, whatever remained of the sunset reflects against the windows of the Old Course Hotel like little nightlights steering us toward the finish. It is too dark to play most sports, but to golfers, "twilight" lasts much longer. We've switched out the white balls we'd been using for their yellow cousins. We need all the help we can get.

Whenever I watch this video—it's just nine seconds long—I am reminded of how bewildered I felt recording it. Not because of the enchanting surroundings—I had grown accustomed to St. Andrews delivering when the sun goes down. I was bewildered by this tornado of a human in front of me. He weighed maybe 150 pounds and stood all of 5'9". He was taller on his right side because there was a hospital boot wrapped around his right foot. He had broken it a few months earlier but had clearly grown tired of sitting at home. His daughters told their dad not to push it, but he didn't listen. They also wanted him to stop smoking, but here he was with a heater between his lips.

Rich Halliday told me he was from Hawaii, and I suppose I had to believe him. He wore a white cap and a blue quarter-zip over a striped red polo. His grey chinos were tucked neatly into that hospital boot, which was adorned with stickers like a teenager's diary. A mini Scottish flag was affixed to the Velcro strap. If that wasn't enough of an aw-shucks appearance, his woven belt was too long and flopped about in the air off his hip. He had introduced himself as Rich on the 1st tee, and as the day progressed, he engraved it in my memory, referring to himself by full name exclusively.

"I'm Rich Halliday, baby," when he buried his par putt to win the second hole. "I'm Rich Freaking Halliday," when a 30-footer for par rolled in on No. 5. Was I being punked? The putts kept dropping.

Mr. Halliday and his pal Andy were acquaintances of my newest St. Andrews friend, Pete Couhig, and had bumped into him earlier that afternoon in the clubhouse at the St. Andrews Golf Club. Pete and I had planned on sitting in the bay windows of the club that look out over the 18th green, downing pints of Tennent's, talking (European) football, and wagering a few pounds on the folks finishing their rounds in front of us. But Andy and Rich had two spots open in a 6 PM tee time on the Old Course. We'd be the last group on the course, an opportunity you just don't pass up—I don't care who you're playing with.

After about three hours and 45 minutes of getting Rich Halliday-ed, I found myself needing simply to capture the man on camera. He made the same, rigid move at the ball, lurching his body up off the ground at contact, his skinny legs locked straight, abbreviating his follow-through for no other reason than lack of flexibility. His toes grazed the turf through the gap in his boot and his driver delivered another annoyingly smooth cut into the fairway.

"Thaht's in the bon-kur," Andy said.

Halliday had pirouetted on the tee before his ball came back to earth, holding his palms to the sky like some sort of magician saying *I did it again.* And with a name like Rich Halliday, he could probably sell out a theater in Vegas. If his naysayers hadn't spoken up, he might have even bowed. I shook my head as I stopped the recording.

"Fuck youuu, man," he replied playfully.

No, fuck *youuu*, Rich Halliday.

How.

In the hell.

Is this guy tied with me?

I was dumbfounded. Not pissed off. Not irritated. Mostly just staggered and riled up in that internal, ultracompetitive way golfers can be when they know they should be playing better. When we convince ourselves that, yes, we are playing the dumbest game ever. I felt like I was at the state fair shooting 12-foot jump shots on those abnormally tight rims and the basketball just wouldn't go in. Rich Halliday was the carny who elbowed me out of the way, tossed the ball through the hoop, and turned to say, *You think this is hard?* I was getting pipped by a man who was getting progressively drunker, louder, and more creative with his two favorite words.

"That's what Rich Halliday *does*," had been ringing in my head since he nullified my birdie on 9 with one of his own.

The torment in my gut was what golf—and its random stream of characters—does to you. And in a somewhat sick way, it was exactly what I hoped for when I booked a ticket to Caledonia. An uncomfortable shape-shifting of what I thought golf—and even specifically, *my golf*—could look like. Maybe what it *should* look like.

For years it was destined that the golf world would storm into St. Andrews—a town of 18,000—and host the most significant tournament in decades. But just as quickly as the private jets arrived, they'd be taking off again. Only I would stay behind, by design, in my new home away from home, lapping up the leftovers. I would see anticipation and culmination and expiration. But then what? I'd be there when the Home of Golf got back to being itself. There would be no greater portrait of what golf *is*—no greater indication of what matters—than what I'd find in St. Andrews during those weeks. Somehow it looked like Rich Freaking Halliday, and I loved that.

Chapter 1

The Why

I t's a distant memory now, but not hard to remember. Complex times are never hard to remember.

We were 18 months into a global pandemic, and optimism had slowly been beaten out of me. Case totals were ascending once again. Vaccine hesitancy was buoyed by additional requests for booster shots, and infections would soon peak like never before. Omicron made it dangerous to just…attend a wedding.

It was mid-November 2021 and temps were falling too. It was the end of another Chicago golf season and the beginning of "don't leave the house without three layers" season. My fully remote life is idyllic in the summer—windows open, nature's soundtrack pouring in, daylight that lingers forever. But then winter arrives and the walls seem to creep inward a little more each day.

A week earlier, I had made myself newly single for the 12th, 17th, or 27th time, depending on which of my friends was counting. If one thing didn't seem right, the whole thing wasn't right for me. Call it "red flag hunting." Living with no strings attached goes a long way for a traveling writing career, but it also prompts a special type of questioning at my age. I was 29 staring down 30. Angst bounced off the walls of my chilly, one-bedroom apartment. *What was I looking for if this one, a really good one, wasn't the one?*

I had worked for one company since college, and *GOLF Magazine* had been good to me. But was it...*fulfilling?* Was golf writing filling up my tank? How about a *life* in golf? Would I be happiest burrowing further into this niche sport and all its complications? That's the way my brain works. Contentment doesn't feel right. You must go *deeper*. My 19-year-old self would have said, *Hell yeah*. My 29-year-old self had questions. And if you have to ask the question, don't you already know the answer?

Round-number ages do this to us. We analyze where we've been and try to determine how rosy it will be where we're going. Was everything you pursued in your twenties worth it at the start of your thirties? Once-foreign jealousies arrive. *Was I jealous?* Friends who slaved through grad school were now reaping major rewards. CPAs became equity partners. Fellows became surgeons. Some of them were *founding* companies. Their work starts to feel more impactful. It feels important. More important than writing about a silly sport where people chase a little white ball around a field. The rewards feel more permanent, too. Houses, cars, *second* houses—*gasp!*—children. Family. It's all connected.

I wondered if what the studies said was true—that you'll change careers seven times in your life. I had severely overstayed my welcome if that was the case. And when I looked at the upcoming golf calendar, it felt like we were flipping the vinyl record over to play the same album once again. We'd go to Augusta with some storylines and then we'd go to Oklahoma with a couple more and then we'd go to Boston and visit another old-timey East Coast country club. The names and faces were mostly unchanged. The questions would be too. The men would play for a lot more money than the women. The diversity of the game would continue down its rich, white path. Sameness can comfort people, but in this case it annoyed me. You definitely don't save the world writing golf stories, and even if I wasn't trying to save the world, I was trying to *feel* some sort of reward for my commitment to it all.

I speak with a heavy dose of privilege when listing these first-world problems, but when one feels helplessly single and annoyingly bereft of work excitement, and both Mother Nature and a wildly infectious virus are telling you to stay indoors, *be* indoors—never leave!—the waning days of my twenties were not promising anything exhilarating about my thirties.

Thus, Thursday, November 11, followed the same arc of my increasingly typical Thursdays. Work from 8 AM to 4 PM, force myself into a 3-mile run through Lincoln Park, and whip up some chicken and rice before that night's streaming content of choice: a Golf Channel documentary titled *St. Andrews: The Greatest Story Ever Told*. I popped two bags of popcorn.

The St. Andrews doc had been recommended to me for years now. It was green-lit back in 2018 and filmed over much of 2019 and 2020 before the pandemic made life weird for everyone. Watching it felt like a reprieve not only from the static, indoor life we'd grown conditioned to but also from normal life as well. This doc felt like vacation. The charm of St. Andrews, known as the Home of Golf, was served in abundance through the screen. There's the librarian, the bartender, and the university historian each describing the role they play in this golfy version of Disney World. It felt like a targeted ad campaign when the film opened with Midwestern accents. A buddies' trip from Eagle River, Wisconsin—three hours from where I grew up—was wide awake at 4:30 AM, spending their night on the pavement, eager to secure a pass to this golf course they'd dreamed about.

The doc was about more than golf. It delved into layers of society—the elites and the working men and the sporting export they could all agree upon. It explained how rabbits impacted the local economy. It explained the legend of St. Andrew himself and how his namesake village reached the brink of destruction during the Scottish Reformation. And how the University of St. Andrews once seriously considered moving away from…St. Andrews itself. This doc tells you a lot of things, but what it told me was, *Yeh, you've been to St. Andrews. You've played the links. You've had yorr Guinness and yorr Tennent's, aye. You think ye know the Auld Grey Toon? You think ye know golf? You don't know anything.* I was a bit shook watching it. I thought I knew the depths of this game as well as I needed to. I had certainly passed the 400-level seminars. But there were 600-level classes waiting for me across the Atlantic. Maybe even a 900-level doctoral dissertation to explore. In order for me to decide if a life in golf would be fulfilling, I needed to spend a season studying abroad. It had to be the summer of 2022.

This was more than a one-town thing. The entire surrounding county, known as the Kingdom of Fife, and the rest of Scotland was preparing for a celebration. The Open Championship, an event twice as old as the Super Bowl (and then some), was visiting St. Andrews in mid-July. The best golfers on the planet would congregate there for the 150th Open, an occasion for which locals had been waiting seven years, since the last St. Andrews Open. I had to know what it looked like when a town of 18,000 contorts itself to host hundreds of thousands of visitors. If the Masters, held annually in April, is golf's Super Bowl, then an Open held in St. Andrews is like golf's World Cup. I paused the doc halfway through and began scheming.

I texted Laurie Watson, a dear friend and head of engagement at the St. Andrews Links Trust, the non-profit that operates the golf courses in town. He would be a vital piece to this puzzle. I texted Graylyn Loomis, a buddy who attended the University of St. Andrews. As a former golf trip planner and local property owner, he would be my logistical guide. I texted Max Vander Wyst, a close friend and unofficial Chicago golf deputy. Leaving Chicago behind just as summer begins is lunacy, but it would give Max the best reason to stop talking about that Scottish vacation he wanted to take and actually *do* it.

"I think I want to live in St. Andrews next summer," I wrote. "Write a book. June 1–September 1. Quit your job and join me if you have the stones!"

"Dude it would be an absolute dream," Max replied. "I'd even help you write it."

I guess convincing Max wasn't the issue. Convincing my bosses would be the harder part, but since you're reading this book, you can trust the pitch worked. Their demands were simple:

1. Don't do *less* work.

2. Be available on East Coast hours (a five-hour difference) and cover the game as you normally would, just abroad.

They'd pay for my flight, but I'd be on my own after that. In exchange for my commitment to the excursion, they could package my work to sponsors, the modern journalism way. It would be 90 days in the Home of Golf, writing, researching, videoing, podcasting, and just...*living.* Breathing it in. Enrolling in Course Architecture 601 and making my own version of a St. Andrews documentary. If I returned home and my doc wasn't any good, okay then. Maybe a life in golf isn't it. At least you started your thirties with a home run swing. The immediate sensation of setting a new target felt good.

Only on my 30th birthday, 162 days later, did summer in Scotland begin to feel real. I wired $799.50 to the Bank of Scotland on April 22, the equivalent of £600. The funds would be taxed and directed to the account of a lady named Lorraine whom I met via email. She was always responsive, but her grammar wasn't perfect. Lorraine had sent some iPad photos of a tiny 1-bedroom on the south side of town. It seemed legit. The $800 was good enough for two weeks' rent. She told me that was a bargain. I brought only the essentials I could fit in one travel golf case, one suitcase, and one backpack. Computer equipment, golf clubs, running shoes, and golf shoes. Some rain gear, some cold gear, the white Nike cap Scottie Scheffler had gifted me, and, for some odd reason, four pairs of shorts. (I figured summer in Scotland was like summer everywhere.)

On the date of my departure, May 31, many hallmarks of the pandemic remained. I wore a hunter-green facemask around the airport, a press gift from Augusta National. It was 9:45 PM in the international terminal of John F. Kennedy Airport—my layover from Chicago. Gate B26 was filled with weary travelers who kept empty seats between themselves and strangers. Different gates had different rules because different countries had different Covid rules. The U.K. was kind toward American travelers, thank goodness, because a fifth wave of infections was sweeping through the Midwest and I was battling all the obvious symptoms. As much as my mother worried about me living abroad, it was healthier for me in a two-square-mile Scottish town six time zones away. After four negative tests, I finally felt assured I wouldn't become Patient Zero in a tiny Scottish town.

What would America look like three months from now? I had no way of knowing. But there were comforting signs at the gate. A trio of buddies signed their receipts at Brooklyn Brewery and then donned their "Scott's Crew" hats—a surefire bachelor party. One of them began rehearsing his swing in the hallway. If party-hungry 20-year-olds pile onto jetliners headed for Ibiza, the clientele leaving New York for Edinburgh is just as obvious: 50-year-old, rich white dudes with a penchant for spending their money on logoed hats and quarter-zips. Riding on that golfy flight is a bit like playing the license plate game we use to pass the time on long car trips. *Was that winged emblem Baltusrol or Olympic Club?* You're surrounded by insignia. I strapped myself in and texted my family four emojis: two Scotland flags and two peace signs. *See ya!*

Just as the jetliner reached its cruising speed and before I could cue up a rom com, an antagonist entered my inbox. A fledgling golf tour called LIV Golf, long rumored to have goals of arresting the pro golf ecosystem, finally publicized the field of its first event. "Free agency has finally come to golf," said Greg Norman, LIV's commissioner, in the press release. "This is an opportunity to start a movement that will change the course of history by bringing new and open competition to the sport we all love."

My stomach lurched, and not from turbulence. LIV employed all the confidence of a Silicon Valley savior complex but had spent the previous three months overpromising and underdelivering. Internal documents were leaked. Sign-up portals were underdeveloped and faulty. Not to mention their ticketing scheme was going to bankrupt any modest golf fan. In February, inflammatory comments from Phil Mickelson exposed much of the greedy inspiration that attracted him and other pros to the league. LIV was backed by money from Saudi Arabia, and Mickelson was covertly using it as an opportunity for leverage against the PGA Tour. He wasn't getting everything he wanted in pro golf—mostly, he sought a bigger piece of the money pie, greater control of media rights, and for top players to hold more power in how the Tour was structured. He clearly wasn't alone, but he was the lead man in this struggle and stumbled in epic fashion. When golf headlines CNN and the *Washington Post* and the BBC in the middle of February, it's rarely a good thing. LIV nearly floundered right then and there. The stacked field of pros playing at the Genesis Invitational that week all denounced LIV, declaring it not a viable competitor to the PGA Tour. Rory McIlroy spoke for them all, saying LIV was "dead in the water."

This field of names in my inbox was decidedly *not* dead in the water. Dustin Johnson, one of the 10 best golfers in the world and one of the 30 greatest players of all time, had joined. Sergio García, Louis Oosthuizen, and Martin Kaymer were among the other major champions on board. Twenty-six of the top 150 in the world were linking up, arm-in-arm, to make a statement. This was an entity the PGA Tour did not want to exist. LIV was bankrolled by the Public

Investment Fund (PIF) of Saudi Arabia, a gigantic dispensary the Saudis had grown from the modern world's dependence on oil. The Middle Eastern country represents a lot of things to the world, and some of them are reprehensible. The Kingdom has banned gay marriage, treated women like second-rate citizens, and jailed and even reportedly killed dissidents who speak out about its regime.

As part of what the Saudis call Vision2030, Crown Prince Mohammed bin Salman Al Saud directed the PIF to diversify the country's assets as the world around it reduced its addiction to oil. Golf, and sport, became an obvious target. On one hand, this is business, and pro sports are a nearly undefeated investment opportunity. On the other, it's something more sinister: a practice many call sportswashing. Take that pile of oil money to sports and let it distract from the atrocities of the past and current regime. Bring the greatest athletes in the world in association with the Kingdom. Literally bring them and their events *to* the Kingdom. Develop Saudi Olympic teams. Infiltrate the football world. Convey the idea that the reputation the Saudis want is one deeply serious about sport, which makes so many people…happy. The PIF invested in Formula One, Newcastle United Football Club, global boxing matches, massive snooker tournaments, the Spanish Football Association, etc. They weren't going to buy an NFL team. (At least not soon.) Rather, the investment would be in places ripe for disruption, the structures of which were particularly susceptible. I love money and you love money, but pro golfers *love* money. Even for some pros, who have made more than they could ever spend, the idea of deriving some untapped value from their skill set is significantly stronger than any concern about where it's coming from.

So…where did I sit on this whole mess? Wait. Was it even a mess? Was I so holy that I would refuse a 10x salary increase were I in their shoes? My pride says yes, but my bank account may think otherwise.

I had better get my thoughts straight, and quickly. Did anyone else on this jetliner to golf heaven know that the golf world had been turned on its side? I typed up the news story straight as could be for GOLF.com. Only 42 of 48 guaranteed spots had been announced. Curiously, Mickelson wasn't among them, but I had a hunch he would be soon.

Using whatever battery life remained within my eyelids, I stared out the window at the pillows of clouds. This flight was the first leg of a golf odyssey, focused on understanding the sport at its very core. It is rooted in humility, honesty, tradition. It might be the most meritocratic sport on earth. I was intent on tapping my needle into the game's central nervous system and appreciating it like I never could in tree-lined middle America. I was keen on starting a new chapter of my life from the most wholesome golf place in the world. Literally, from a street called Golf Place. And before I could even fly over the eastern edge of Maine, new questions swamped my psyche. *What is it going to be like in the home of golf when some of the game's biggest names decide they'd rather be paid by Saudi Arabian oil profits? Will the ripples extend to Scotland?*

I was going to find out soon enough. LIV's first event was scheduled for June 9, just 10 days away, outside of London. That's just a train ride from St. Andrews. But did I even want to go?

Chapter 2

Where Am I, Exactly?

What did Americans do to deserve this luxury? That was the question I pondered as I silently snaked through customs. Lucky visitors to Scotland with U.S.A. and Canadian passports are escorted to a special, expeditious aisle while others wait in the growing queue to the left.

I placed the passport photo of my shaggier, 22-year-old self facedown on the reader, and seconds later two glass doors ahead of me parted. I was free to roam the United Kingdom however I pleased. It all felt deviously simple. Around the corner was a shuttle driver named Colin I had arranged to lift me to St. Andrews. He held an iPad with my name on it and a surprised look, as I was much earlier than expected. If we hustled, Colin said, he wouldn't have to pay for parking. We made it just in time.

If Colin's demeanor was a cocktail, I would have labeled it four parts curious and one part suspicious. After all, I looked far too old to be an undergrad at the U of St. Andrews. (I always told myself with a clean shave and a haircut I could pass for someone pursing an MBA, but that was becoming less and less true every day.) And even if I *was* enrolled there, I was arriving on June 1, just as all the students were leaving. I was arriving alone, too, my destination nowhere near the hotels or bed-and-breakfasts adjacent to the Old Course. During a quick panic back in the parking lot, I had declined Colin's offer to ride shotgun, which further surprised him. (Blame Uber for normalizing empty front seats.) For a man who typically packs his van to its brim with six or seven golfers and their luggage, my backpack and two bags were an unusually light trip for him. I could feel Colin's gaze in the rearview mirror, waiting patiently for me to initiate conversation. (There are few things Scottish people hate more than silence.) He broke in with the most natural question: "How lang yeh herre fohr." My answer raised both his eyebrows. "Ninety days, actually. Now until September."

Colin understood that my golf job could bring me to St. Andrews for a month leading up to The Open, but he couldn't fathom what I would write about when it was all over. Frankly, nor could I. I would have to make some friends to stretch this work-cation the full three months. I figured Colin could be my first pal. Add up all the trips to and from the airport and Colin is introducing a couple thousand visitors to the Auld Grey Toon, as St. Andrews is known, every year. He's their first tour guide, replete with bar, restaurant, cafe, and grocery recommendations. "If yeh want a good meal," he said, "try the hot bahr at Morrisons. They've goht everything."

Conversation 1 had already delivered. But the eye-contact tag we were playing in the mirror was not helping me appreciate my surroundings. Between Edinburgh, the nation's capital, and St. Andrews, its golfing capital, is a 50-mile introduction of rolling hills, crops, and countryside. Even the highway signs feel eco-friendly, colored green, brown, and yellow. Every 10 minutes another quaint town arrives to distract you, home to anywhere from 1,000 to 40,000 people. There might be a stoplight or two, but the real inhibitor of pace is the street parking. Stationary vehicles jut into the lanes on either side of the road, bottlenecking traffic from each direction. Evading the parked cars (and their side-view mirrors) serves as good practice for the rural stretches, too, because there is no shoulder in this country. Rather, if it exists, I haven't seen it. Americans live with a shoulder surplus. But in Scotland, your car is always one club-length from a plot of farmland fenced in by hedges or stone walls built who knows how long ago. Shuttle drivers are an inexpensive way of maintaining your sanity fresh off a redeye. Colin turned the countryside into a blur. *If this van has a brake pedal, he sure hasn't touched it.*

We'd had an inauspicious start, but Colin and I really hit our stride when we started talking European football, which was the news of the day. The Scottish national team was hosting a World Cup qualifying playoff that night in Glasgow, about 90 minutes west of us. If the Scots won, they'd take on Wales four days later, and the winner of that would face the plucky Americans in November.

"We are the only country in the world pullin' fer Scohtland tonight," Colin said with a laugh, hinting at their opponent—Ukraine, now three months deep in a conflict not of its own choosing against Russia. I assured him he was correct.

By the end of our 70-minute trip, any remaining suspicions Colin had involved my safety. He could tell I was excited about my summer ahead, but he wasn't so sure about my residency plan. We pulled into the cul-de-sac parking lot of Allan Robertson Drive, which is as far as Google Maps will take you. He looked uneasy. "You sure?" *I guess so?* If this wasn't the place, I at least had 10 hours before nightfall to figure it out. Directly ahead of us was 56 Allan Robertson and off to our right was, oddly, 44 Allan Robertson. In between was nothing more than a sidewalk that meandered out of sight. The place I was looking for—48 Allan Robertson—was apparently only accessible by foot. This sidewalk access was new to me, the Midwestern middle-class man, but it is a defining trait of residences in St. Andrews. All over town, tiny alleyways weave between backyards, front doors, patios, and parking lots. They're nothing more than four feet wide, and if you know them well, they become shortcuts that chop minutes off your ETA. If you don't, you will get lost. Many a visitor hath been scorned on circuitous stumbles home after a few Guinnesses.

I dragged my belongings down the path and up to what appeared to be the front door of 48 Allan Robertson. Colin peered around the corner. The instant I rapped my knuckles on the door, it flung open.

"Hahlo!" she said, basically leaping through the doorway and onto the sidewalk. Lorraine! My queen. Colin waved happily from the parking lot. I was someone else's problem now.

To this point, my only interactions with Lorraine were periodic emails. She and her husband had recently downsized their house in the most literal fashion: turning an underused, corner living room into a guest flat with all the fixings needed for a short vacation. Their two children had graduated from high school and moved out, so they built a permanent wall and quartered off that living room to make some extra money on the side. Everyone in town was renting out their places for Open week, and they wanted a piece of the pie, too. One of Lorraine's friends had rented to Tour winner Billy Horschel for $25,000 that week. Five bedrooms goes a long way when the entire family wants to tag along.

A simple woman in her fifties, Lorraine represented a particular subset of St. Andrews native. Like Colin, she was not a golfer, but also like Colin and like so many of her neighbors, Lorraine props up the St. Andrews experience in her own little way. She runs a private laundry business out of her backyard, and one of her most important clients is Kingsbarns Golf Links, located just south of town, one of the 100 best golf courses on the planet. Once a week, every week, a couple sacks of long, white Kingsbarns-branded bath towels arrive at the back patio. A day later, they're twirling around on the clothesline, drying in the wind. A day after that, someone from Kingsbarns scoops up the fresh linens and they're drying off visiting golfers in a matter of hours. Rinse and repeat. Lorraine has lived here for decades. Businesses like hers help make St. Andrews *go*.

Lorraine led me down the sidewalk around another corner and down another paved path unlatching a wooden door into her backyard. To the left was my glass-door entrance, and on the right was her house. This was how I would enter my one-bedroom flat all summer long, ducking under the clothesline. For the equivalent of $1,550 a month in rent, 400 square feet wasn't much, but it was mine. I didn't ask her about the peculiar display case that housed dozens of elephant figurines.

My new landlady explained how to operate the electric tabletop stove she purchased for me and then shared the most important information yet. "Whenever yeh need yer clothes cleaned, just toss 'em out on the porch. Eleven pounds per load, I'll have them folded next day." Not two hours since landing in Scotland, I had already acquired a Scottish mother. She had outfitted my mini fridge with half a dozen eggs and a glass bottle of milk, delivered to her front door straight from the local dairy farm.

She couldn't conceal her maternal instincts. "I'll get out of yer way," she said. "I'm sure yer tired."

This would become a hilarious trend to me. Whenever I looked tired, and even sometimes when I wasn't, Lorraine would tell me, "Shonn, ye best get some sleep." She sounded exactly like my mom back in Wisconsin, and often, she was correct. But on occasion she'd say it at 10 AM after a full night's rest, absolutely jolting my confidence for the day.

When she pulled the sliding door shut, I lay down on the full-sized bed. My toes hung off the end. This was home for the next 90 days. Home *and* work, actually. Eat, sleep, read, write, lounge, yoga, cook, podcast...all of it was going to happen right here. But most importantly, I was *in* St. Andrews. Outside my bedroom window was a dilapidated playground with two swings, a 10-foot slide, and a teeter-totter. They had all seen better days, but at least this was a neighborhood, where children play and dogs are let off their leads. By the end of summer, it would feel homey enough. I shut my eyes for two hours. It felt like 20 minutes.

That nap was like a first night's rest in a hotel. You wake up unsure of your surroundings. It takes a few seconds to remember, *Oh, yes. I live in Scotland now.* I grabbed my camera and crossed paths with Lorraine on my maiden voyage through town.

"That tree ye see over the house," she said, pointing to an arc of leaves peeking up over the shingles. "That's where the bus will pick ye up. Take ye anywhere in town in five minutes."

"Oh, thank you," I said. "But I'm very much a walker."

It was the path of least resistance—not literally, as the trek is mostly uphill—but I didn't have any British pounds in my wallet and wasn't sure my American credit card would be any help on the bus. My goal for the day was to simply get acclimated. Get some steps in, make sure I was still tired enough to sleep through the night, and understand exactly *where* the Old Course was. I needed to learn which of these sidewalks were going to be *my* sidewalks. In this part of town, many of the houses are literally strung together, sharing walls. You could Jason Bourne your way across 11 rooftops from 41 Allan Robertson to another house 100 yards away on a completely different street. But I'm not Jason Bourne. On the ground, all these houses look the same. You'll find stretches of 10 homes in a row, all facing the street, all slightly askew, all sporting cream-colored facades and russet rooftops. Hell, Jason Bourne might even get confused.

St. Andrews can be disorienting for a newbie even though it's just two square miles in size. The key streets are simple. They've been the key streets for hundreds of years. There's South Street and North Street—they came first—and in between them is Market Street. They run mostly parallel to each other and make up the commercial center of town. All three intersect with City Road—one of the main arteries that extends all the way through Fife—which brings you within pitching distance of the Old Course.

I couldn't help but laugh as I reached City Road for the first time. Between the Aldi grocery store and a Volkswagen dealership was Tom Morris Drive, named after Old Tom Morris, the father of modern golf. If we unwound the strings of time, the earliest reason why I was summering in St. Andrews was Old Tom, for he established how golf courses should look and play and that standardized courses should be not 10, not 12, not 22, but exactly 18 holes. But there his name sits, on a blue-and-white street sign, two feet off the ground and 10 feet from a brand-new Volkswagen SUV, exactly like Old Tom always imagined.

I couldn't look *more* like a tourist, with my golfy quarter-zip and a camera hanging around my neck. At some point, word of mouth was bound to pass on the fact that a writer from the biggest golf website in the world was visiting for the summer. I would say yes to every golf invite and force myself to get comfortable drinking alone at the pubs. I promised myself I wouldn't wear earbuds unless I was in my apartment. I would relish the freedom of no expectations, doing everything I *wanted* to do and almost nothing I didn't. Everything would be at *my* pace—the walking pace. Uber doesn't exist here.

On most summer days St. Andrews is alive but unhurried. College towns are like that when class isn't in session. Students and professors and visitors mill about with distant deadlines. Nothing *needs* to happen today. Patrons exit the bookstores and immediately crack open their purchases on the first bench they can find. Most of the pubs spill outward onto the sidewalk, a prime place for people-watching. The vibe is no different at the intersection of Golf Place and Links Road, which creates the far east corner of the Old Course. That's where everything *really* slows down. Husbands and wives halt their strolls to watch strangers hit tee shots. Undergrads spread out picnic blankets on the hill behind No. 18. It's all a bit dreamy. The closer you get to the Old Course, the more varied the accents become. French, British, American, Australian, Kiwi, all venturing to Golf Mecca. Tomorrow's players plop down on the steps behind the 1st tee and visualize the score their shots will weave together—the same steps Jack Nicklaus sat on as he signed his scorecard in the 1964 Open. It adds to the lore of St. Andrews that 18-handicaps begin and end their dream rounds in front of a thirsty audience and also in front of the Royal & Ancient Clubhouse, home to the international governing body of the game. Make a par, you'll hear claps. Make a birdie, it's a full round of applause. Miss the grass for the pavement and you'll hear about that, too. Old Tom Morris' great-great granddaughter, Sheila Walker, lives next to the 18th green and spends many summer evenings in a chair near the windowsill, surveying the action playing out below. The passage of time in golf is always linked to this intersection.

I had been here once before, four years ago, when an Open was held up the coast at Carnoustie. I'm not sure what I was expecting, but I was delighted that almost nothing had changed. The green-and-white fence that borders the course seemed to have a fresh coat of paint. It has been there for more than a hundred years. The auburn Hamilton Grand hotel had been turned into luxury condos, but its white Victorian spires still tower over everything. When something is made so perfect and over time it remains so perfect, you trust it will forever be *so perfect*. But things change. The only differences now were the massive grandstands erected along the right side of the opening hole and the golden behemoth scoreboard looming above it. The scoreboard made me oddly nervous. The good kind of nervous. Six weeks from now it would be filled with names, numbers, and significance. The elements of history. Whoever chose the combination of navy and gold as that R&A's color scheme deserves annual royalties. The way those scoreboards contrast against the grey skies and wheat-colored turf is perfectly striking. They impose. They command your attention. They taunt you into thinking about the future. They seem to have a sense of life, even if they're just a maze of wood and hard plastic, with zero meaning until golf shots are played.

Today at the Old Course, Day 1 for me, featured one of the oddest scenes of the summer. A flight of 60 influencers assembled by Hugo Boss—a major sponsor of The Open—had taken over the afternoon tee times. Models, actors, comedians—even rapper ScHoolboy Q—were playing, all decked in beige and black, posing for golf-adjacent photos and videos here on the most sacred turf in the sport. Their reason for being there is so obvious it hurts. They have…followings. Millions upon millions of internet fans.

It's such a weird thing, this influencing. From where I watched, some of the Boss bunch were golf lovers—like the sweet-swinging Kathryn Newton, actress of *Big Little Lies* fame, who played golf in high school. (Her swing is better than mine and probably better than yours too.) ScHoolboy Q, a rapper from South Central Los Angeles, has talked at length about how the sport changed his outlook on life. He makes you feel *good* about the game and what it can do for people. Aligning your brand with these golf-junkie celebs makes sense. But in the process of pursuing them, marketing teams get hasty. They've landed millions of eyeballs, but they want millions and millions more. And so on this special Tuesday in June we had a soccer-star-turned-TikTok-personality sprawled out on the turf for a calendar-worthy photo shoot. We had Spanish actors faking the most generic fist pump on the 18th green. We had parkour athletes doing flips over the Swilcan Burn (a move that stewards of the St. Andrews Links Trust did *not* appreciate). The entire influencer squad would dine at the Rusacks St. Andrews, one of the more sought-after reservations in the game. It was a tornado of beige, black, and white. That was Boss' color scheme of 2022. A small group would even spill out into the town and party with students into the night.

Ultimately, proceeds from this "event" benefitted UNICEF, so who am I to judge? But it all just feels a bit goofy —this overzealous way of stirring hype around your brand by viewers this is the way to #BeYourOwnBoss—especially at one of the most revered golf courses in the world. Hugo Boss literally issued a press release saying, "The event introduced the game of golf to a new generation," which felt like an offensive overreach. They dressed up 64-year-old golf legend Sandy Lyle as chic as ever so he could ask a bunch of TikTokers, "Are you ready to Boss the course?" Boy, is that silly. But golf rarely ever leans in to silliness. Maybe that's the point. Maybe golf needs to be sillier? What eventually made its way to Instagram were half-smiles, deep blue eyes, and captions drunk on enthusiasm. If this was what Golf, capital G, needed to survive for generations to come, I wasn't sure I was gonna stick around for it.

I knew what I needed, and that was dinner, so I watched Newton finish up the 18th, snapped a photo of the grandstand on 1, and headed to the Pilmour Bar, a lesser-known enclave beneath the Ardgowan Hotel on North St. I had eaten my first St. Andrews meal there back in 2018, and I ordered the monster mac 'n' cheese burger once more, reminded again that meat served pink is not on offer in the U.K. At 5 PM, there was just one other soul in the joint, a bartender in her early twenties named Surrey. She wasn't born in Scotland, but she had developed just enough of an accent to make you wonder. Like Colin and like Lorraine, Surrey was not a golfer. She was a student living in nearby Dundee, 15 miles up the coast, covering a shift for a coworker. For an hour, it was just the two of us, conversing about everything from Beyoncé's greatest hits to how different this bar would look in six weeks.

"I would make reservations for dinner now, if you can," Surrey said. "Last Open, people were literally selling their seats at the bar for 20 pounds to people waiting outside." This really was the calm before the storm, in more ways than one. North St. had no bustle that evening.

Surrey guessed everyone was home eating angsty dinners ahead of the World Cup qualifier. After scarfing down my burger, I grabbed a can of Irn-Bru, a Scottish delicacy, and retraced my path home down City Road. By the time my head hit the pillow, football fans in every other country were thrilled. Ukraine wins, 3-1.

Chapter 3

Getting Acquainted

The battle was lost the night before. I had not closed the blinds tightly enough before bed and now it was 4:30 AM on Day 3 and sunlight filled the room. I stared at the ceiling, restless. This country seems to have an unofficial ban on air conditioning, which takes some getting used to. Lorraine neglected to include a fan in my flat, so cooling my bedroom required cracking the window, the final link in a chain of annoying factors that would normally be no issue if not for Scotland's noisiest residents: the seagulls, who were having a *ball*.

Visitors have long suggested there are more gulls in this country than humans, and you think they must be joking. But upon arrival you realize it might actually be true. *Death, taxes, and seagulls.* Audacious, criminal seagulls. Locals warn you about eating sandwiches outdoors. The gulls notoriously cannonball onto unsuspecting diners, stab at their paninis, and make off with whatever they can grab. (It even happened to me later in the summer, at a cafe on South Street, when out of nowhere two webbed feet smacked down on my dome, spun me a new hairdo, and snatched half of my bacon roll without even saying *thank you.*) Seagulls feel as inevitable as the sun rising, partly because they are actively squawking before it rises. Admitting defeat, I laced up my running shoes and set out in pursuit of a story at the Old Course.

The Old Course is the game's North Star in both design and aesthetic. It sits atop the family tree as an ancestor worth emulating, especially in terms of access. Earning a tee time on the Old is attainable, for sure, but in a few very specific ways. Like tickets to a Taylor Swift concert, a round there can be purchased far above face value. Dozens of tour companies offer access to the Old through country-wide golf packages, which start around $5,000 a person and, pending your inclination for helicopter rides, can quickly grow up to $25k. Without the Old Course included, those trips would be pointless. But *with* the Old? Many consider them priceless.

Similar to T-Swizzle tickets, a round on the Old can be acquired via lottery. Every day the St. Andrews Links Trust hosts an online ballot where locals and visitors alike can enter their names and handicaps in hope of snagging a reservation 48 hours in advance. The odds of being selected, like any legitimate lottery, are not great. During the height of summer, the Old Course sends groups off in 10-minute intervals beginning at 6:40 AM. The last tee time is 6:30 PM, making about 70 foursome slots during peak months. Most local golfers get precedence with their annual Links Ticket, which, for about $400, allows them to play as much golf as they'd like on the seven courses in town. It remains the greatest golf deal on the planet, and locals make the most of it, reducing the number of times available to visitors. Maybe 5 to 10 percent of ballot entries are successful for non-locals. Ballot entries must include two golfers, implying that when the ballot has been drawn, the only spots leftover are unfilled singles or doubles.

Thankfully, unlike concert tix, despite everything you just read, you can *will* your way into a tee time. You just have to sacrifice some sleep.

I jogged the hills of City Road shortly after 5 AM, in search of these sleep sacrificers, reminded by my legs how much I hate morning runs.

But on this day I was distracted by how dormant St. Andrews was at dawn. The only business open was the Shell petrol station—one of just two fuel stops in town—and that'll remain the case for the next few hours. Most of St. Andrews sleeps in. If you want coffee before 8 AM, get it at the gas station or brew it yourself. I ran past the quiet pubs, turned onto Golf Road, and met a brutal headwind. A chilly breeze off the North Sea brought tears to my eyelids. I paused at the West Sands Beach—1.25 miles from where I started—to find the tide up about 200 yards, waves crashing against the embankment, blowing mist into the air. My face often becomes a red, overheated mess when I run, so the sea spray was refreshing, but it had to chill the bones of the crazies huddled outside the Old Course Pavilion.

About a gap wedge from the beach, a throng of sorry souls leaned against the tiny building for warmth. They had reached the final half hour of an overnight gauntlet, and you could see it on their broken faces. Mother Nature had set the thermostat to 45 degrees. The group was frozen in place by both the wind chill and the rules. In pursuit of a singles tee time, one arrives at the pavilion and earns a corresponding place in line. Seated on the pavement in front of me were nos. 2 and 3, a father and son who showed up at 8 PM, 9.5 hours ago. Nos. 4 and 5 were two buddies in their sixties who arrived a half hour after them. They were glad they did, too, because the line grew and grew every half hour, eventually snaking around the building, in the direction of the sea spray. Everyone was behind Jordan, and they knew it. He set his bag against the pavilion at 7 PM, thus earning the first available tee time.

I couldn't help but think of those Wisconsinites who opened the St. Andrews documentary, their giddy excitement basically daring me to come here seven months ago. The bedless beauties in front of me now—about 30 in total—were their golfing brethren. If there are open spots on the tee sheet, they get slotted in, one by one. Ballot winners from out of town who signed up a twosome or threesome have no choice but to accept strangers into their group. Local links ticket holders, however, reserve the right to show up with a twosome and decline any additions to their party. Them's the rules. (Thankfully, this rarely happens.)

The unspoken code for overnight guests is to stay within a reasonable proximity of the pavilion. You may relieve yourself in a nearby bathroom, but only on an expedited round trip. You can practice putting on the nearby putting green, but mostly you plop down and waste away the time chatting with fellow golf sickos. (It's worth noting: the Links Trust isn't in love with this system—a night on the pavement isn't exactly good for sexagenarians—but they've been unsuccessful in brainstorming a truly equitable system.)

I approached the pavilion beaming off a runner's high and received very little glee in return. Queuers 2 and 3 were on the course side of the building, shielded from the wind. They had kicked off their tennis shoes and squeezed into sleeping bags, laid out on top of yoga mats. The only part of them visible was their smiles. Nos. 4 and 5 laid next to them and eagerly flashed me a thumbs up as I snapped a pic. These were grown men grinning like children, straining for comfort on the cobblestone, steps from the most famous golf course in the world. They were bundled up like little golfer burritos inside white comforters they smuggled from nearby hotel rooms. Housekeeping would have to deal with the dirtied duvets. No. 9 regaled the group with his travel stories from Ireland. No. 13 shivered on the other side of the building, his shoulders wrapped in a hotel bath towel.

Everyone was a bit curious about Jordan, an athletic kid in his mid-twenties with a ball cap pulled tight on his head. He paced around to keep warm, not saying much to anyone, rolling a few putts on the practice green. His tidy carry bag was filled with hickory clubs—a telling sign of a golf hipster. A black and white HOME OF GOLF towel hung over the club heads. It looked brand new.

You'd have to be a golf cuckoo to spend a night outdoors hoping for a tee time, but you'd have to be extra cuckoo to do it alone. You'd have to be extra, extra looney to do it on behalf of someone else, but that's what Jordan was doing. Around 5:40, a 12-year-old named Philip and his father appeared, just in time. Philip was from Virginia and was competing in a nearby junior tournament. Jordan was the generous family friend who agreed to fly across the Atlantic to caddie for him. "A free trip to St. Andrews would be worth it," Jordan told me, even if he was carrying clubs most of the way, rarely swinging them. Standing in line all night long was his idea.

Shortly after 6 AM, staffers from the Links Trust opened the doors to usher my new, frigid friends inside. Jordan backed away from pole position to let Philip squeeze in, earning a round of applause from the fathers in line. "Jordan, that is the most generous thing I've ever seen," No. 9 said, urging Philip to thank him. The Old Course tends to incite hyperbole. (*The best round I ever played; The best putt I ever hit; The most generous thing I've ever seen.*)

I sympathized with those numbered 18 or higher. They were unlikely to earn what they had woken up early (or stayed up late) for, but still had to go through the motions of entering their name in the queue. On a normal summer's morning, in a non-Open year, Nos. 18, 19, and 20 probably make it through just fine. But the course was closing in 12 days and demand had never been higher. Every tee time gifted to corporate sponsors—and then regifted to people like our TikTok friends—infringed, if only slightly, on these red-eye tee times. This whole ordeal is exactly why you make backup plans as a St. Andrews visitor. Overbook your schedule with rounds on other courses in case the Golf Gods don't call your number. Otherwise, beat demand the obvious way and show up earlier. Or know someone like Jordan.

At that instant, the Old Course Pavilion was the liveliest place in town and maybe the most optimistic place in all of Scotland. Nos. 25–30 believed they had a shot, even if they were told it wasn't likely. But like the folks who spend hours outside a Foot Locker waiting for the newest Jordans or the gamers who camp outside Best Buy hoping for a fresh batch of PlayStations, there's a chosen-until-proven-unchosen belief system we could all benefit from employing more often. Dreams of swiping their credit card are merely the start. These guys were already visualizing their approach shots and how they'd lift their putters in the sky as their birdie putts drop into the hole. If my bed weren't so cozy, I think I'd start more mornings here. You couldn't have a bad day after seeing all that optimism lined up, single file.

Around 6:30, I watched young Philip ready himself with a couple tense practice swings. I asked if he was nervous.

"Oh, mmhmm," he said sheepishly, eyes wide, like most 12-year-olds prompted by a stranger.

There was no way Philip could properly understand the gravity of a St. Andrews tee time. His elders took turns stepping in to remind him how lucky he was. One jetlagged foursome with an afternoon tee time had congregated with coffee on the steps behind the 1st tee. Another ballot-winner had lost his own sleep battle, so he moseyed down to investigate the scene. There isn't a shop in town open, but there's always an audience on the 1st tee.

The first player in Philip's group was a middle-aged Arizona man who stumbled onto the tee full of jitters. A day earlier his first swing at Kingsbarns produced a cold shank, and he couldn't help but think about it once again. He had coaxed his wife out of bed to capture this moment on camera. But then he hit a thin skidder up the turf. They say there are no pictures on the scorecard, but there's also no scorecard on the pictures. All smiles.

Philip stuck his peg in the ground and calmly rehearsed a rather professional pre-shot routine before using every ounce of his tiny frame to send a tee ball down the widest fairway in the world. He was off and running, and with an official Old Course caddie on the bag. Jordan was off to his hotel room. I was off to my flat, where I devoured a bowl of cereal and the local morning news. The story of the week was Queen Elizabeth's Platinum Jubilee. With the BBC as my professor, it seemed like the biggest event in the world. And for most of the United Kingdom, I suppose it was. To the delight of news anchors and thousands of people lined outside Buckingham Palace, our 96-year-old Royal Highness was feeling healthy enough to take part in the festivities marking her 70th year on the throne. On tonight's docket was a concert at Windsor Castle featuring Queen (unironically), Adam Lambert, Alicia Keys, and more.

Through conversations with cab drivers, bartenders, and baristas, I was learning that not everyone in Scotland was a fan of the Queen, much less the reign of the royal family. Not everyone was a fan of the role Scotland plays (or is asked to play) within the United Kingdom. Sixty-two percent of Scottish voters chose to remain part of the European Union in 2016, but their fate was sealed when 15 million English voters chose to leave. England looms large, and a lot of Scots don't like it.

Watching this jubilation over the Jubilee, it was oddly nice to feel some distance from the issues of the day back in America. The Johnny Depp–Amber Heard trial. The comings and goings of the Proud Boys. The most recent mass shooting, because there are so many it's hard to keep track of where the last one happened. Shootings rarely happen in Scotland because the ownership of guns is not a bipartisan debate. There were things everyone seemed to agree upon. I was jealous of that. One of them, Landlady Lorraine told me, was that the Jubilee was at the very least "an easy excuse to spend the day drenkin'." *Get it, girl!*

After an afternoon of writing, I returned to the Old Course for the final tee time of the day. This appointment I had scheduled, but like Jordan, I would not be playing. Just watching. At 6:30 PM, it was what they call a "dark time," the last hour or so of slots that, pending the pace of play, might not finish all 18 holes before dark. And by dark, I mean, *Hopefully the town lights help you find your golf ball* dark. These late tee times are exclusively saved for Links Ticket holders and their guests, and they're the best way to enjoy the Old.

My sherpas were four St. Andrews students I met for a pre-round pint at the New Club, one of the golfing societies housed in a building along the 18th hole. There was Nico from Switzerland, Graham from Connecticut, Teddy from just outside of London, and Euan from Rhode Island. The people and places this sport brings together are unmatched. Euan was a friend of a friend and, therefore, *my* friend. I needed one. My first St. Andrews friends. These boys had it better than anyone. Graham and Euan had finished their final exams and were just hanging out in town before their families arrived for graduation. Nico and Teddy had more semesters to finish, and were thus the envy of everyone.

By Euan's estimate he was approaching his 100th round on the Old since he arrived as a "freshie." One hundred times around the hallowed ground, and it probably cost him about $2,000 total. It was a weekly ritual for this quartet to snag a dark time off the ballot, pack up their textbooks, grab their clubs, down a pint, race around 18 holes. I'd call that a dream, but they'd call it Wednesday. (My collegiate recreation was limited to intramural flag-football games on a beat-up patch of crabgrass.)

Euan told me it took him exactly 91 attempts to finally shoot under par on the Old, thanks to his tee ball on 18 clanking off one of the homes on Links Road and rolling back into play. "I almost cried when it came back in," he said. One hundred rounds on the Old Course for an American kid who loves golf. That's an education.

"Do you guys ever get…*tired* of playing the same course? Even when it's maybe the best course in the world?" I asked. The ripe 30-year-old in me wanted to know if these young'ins appreciated how lucky they were.

"I know it doesn't sound great," Euan said, "but honestly? Yeah."

I guess if you took batting practice at Fenway Park three times a week, its luster would wear off, too. Graham admitted they sometimes have to pinch themselves when they get one of those perfect dark times, not a cloud to be seen. Nights like this one, where the only noise we could hear was the wind shuffling through the long grasses. A perfect dark time. Only when we reached the 6th tee did Euan strap a speaker to his bag and dial up the Oldies but Goldies playlist on Spotify. We had Counting Crows belting out Joni Mitchell's "Big Yellow Taxi" on the Old Course.

Don't it always seem to go
That you don't know what you've got 'til it's gone.

The group stood around in silence, waiting for the signal to play ahead. Inside my head I hoped they were considering those lyrics. Joni Mitchell got it right. Before long, their 21-year-old dark times on the Old Course would be gone. A lot of us look back on that senior spring as one of the happiest, freest times in our lives. I know I do. It would've been nice if someone reminded us how good it was while we were living it. Maybe our parents did, and we just weren't paying attention. Or maybe that's just me.

I had not come prepared for how the temperature plummets on a Scottish summer night, so I hung around for a few more holes before quitting the chase around 9:15. As I made the three-mile trek back to my flat, it finally dawned on me. What I just did was exactly what visiting golfers should do—walk the course in its entirety. Not just 1 and 18; 1 *through* 18. First-timers to St. Andrews ought to tag along behind a group of golfers or even make friends with them as you provide an audience for their shots. You'll learn just enough to intoxicate the mind, like watching a movie trailer the day before going to the cinema. There are endless free lessons about what is to come. And if you're planning a night's rest outside the pavilion, the four-mile walk will help you catch some Zs.

Among my learnings:

- Fifty degrees in Scotland feels much colder than 50 degrees back home. The next time I played golf in shorts, it would be back in America.

- You won't lose a ball by playing to the left on the Old Course—only to the right. That's where the out-of-bounds line is painted, either on the turf or atop an ancient rock wall.
- However many bunkers you think there are on the 12th hole, double that. Act like they aren't there and "just wail away with driver," Teddy says. He caddies in his spare time.
- The middle-right pin on the 17th hole might be the most diabolical middle pin in the world. I could spend hours watching hopeful approach shots get rejected.
- Lastly, if you can foot the $36,000 bill for international tuition, go to school at the University of St. Andrews. People would pay that much alone for 100 rounds on the Old. Plus, you could meet my friend Nigel.

Chapter 4

Nigel Snow

Nigel Snow's silver hatchback barreled wide around the corner and onto Allan Robertson Drive. It was the afternoon of June 6, and I stood at the end of the cul-de-sac, perturbed, golf clubs lying on the pavement between my legs. My agitation was not directed at Mr. Snow, but rather the antiquated system that made me question if he was going to arrive at all. Uber and Lyft don't exist in St. Andrews, and I was realizing how much of a certified City Boy I had become.

Mostly I was unnerved that the keystrokes of computer programmers in California had rewired my brain to demand efficiency. Waiting is a cousin of the skill we call patience, and I was realizing with these very annoyed eight extra minutes that the skill had been beaten out of me. The seven years I lived in New York City began in 2013 with a first date telling me, "I'm just going to get an Uber taxi" and ended in 2020 where the act of hailing a yellow cab from the curb was a move of complete desperation. If you wanted a ride, your phone placed you in the backseat of a stranger's vehicle within minutes. But here in St. Andrews, I had stepped back about 20 years. A guy like Nigel arrives only after a string of careful negotiations.

It begins with your phone, too, by tapping something called a dial-out code into your digital keypad. What follows is a conga line of digits so long that the numbers shrink as it stretches across the screen. On the other end of the call is one of the dozen taxi companies in St. Andrews. Add them to your contacts to simplify your future dialing. When they answer, you better know exactly where you are and exactly where you'd like to go. It's best for all involved if you know when you'd like to get there, too. And how long the trip will take. Then comes the hard part. You hang up and you wait, unsure if five minutes means 10 or if 15 minutes means 25. Have you lost the skill of patience, too? Finally, cash is king, because cash is quick. Most cabbies' credit card payment systems run on cell service, and there isn't always much of that. You don't want to be stuck spinning around the parking lot searching for a connection while your train to Edinburgh rips into the station.

I recounted this sequence of steps while I waited and concluded that if Uber and Lyft want to streamline this process and take over the world of getting people from here to there, maybe we should just...*let them.*

But then there's Nigel, one of a handful of men who drive for Independent Taxis, the first company that picked me up in June and thus the first to earn my undying loyalty.

"Hah-lo," Nigel said, hopping out of the driver's seat to grab my clubs. His nasally voice fit his short, stocky build. There were fresh scabs atop his nose and above his eyebrows. You could tell he had picked at them, but they weren't healing quickly on his aging skin. He had to be north of 60 years old but was spry for his age; he moved quickly with my clubs in hand.

"Arr we off to the Deeyooks then?" he said.

I was off to the Deeyooks—also known as the Duke's Course, just outside of town. I settled into the backseat, and we lurched away at the mercy of his jerky stick shift. Over the next 10 minutes on our three-mile commute—for the price of "nine pounds, thirty"—I was baptized into what a taxi ride in St. Andrews really is: an appraisal of all comings and goings in town.

Want to know what's going on? Slide into a taxi. Want to know where the locals drink their Tennent's? Ask a cabbie. Want an explanation for why there are so many…*mothers* in town? This was the first weekend of three consecutive weeks of graduation, Nigel told me. The wealthy American parents who sent their children to school abroad had arrived to see what those international tuition checks were actually worth. Graduates from 2020 and 2021 had their ceremonies postponed due to Covid, so each class had a week to themselves, back-to-back-to-back. Twenty straight days of festivities.

Nigel took my silence as a cue to teach me about life as a student at the first university founded in all of Scotland. He explained the May Day Dip, an annual tradition where students party through the night on April 30, keep warm by campfires on the West Sands Beach, and eventually sprint into the North Sea at dawn. Many of them do it fully naked, wearing nothing but a smile, all in the name of washing away their academic sins ahead of final exams. Every school has its traditions, we agreed.

Nigel then told me all about the less-nude ritual of academic families. First-year students—known as "freshies" or "freshers" but definitely not freshmen—are adopted by two upperclassmen (often a dad and mum) who help ease their way into campus life. Things we all were curious about as 18-year-olds: where the best coffee shop is, the quickest route between academic buildings, and, perhaps most importantly, how to carefully manage binge drinking. The relationship culminates in what is known as Raisin Weekend in mid-October with a presentation of gifts—academic children typically gift their academic parents a pound of raisins—a scavenger hunt, and a massive foam fight/party on the college lawn. (This trumps anything we did at UW–Madison, maybe by a lot.)

Nigel urged me to inquire around campus about the Graduation Ball, which was coming up. It was the hottest ticket in town, he said, and if I flirted just enough, he figured I could score a rare invite. I loved how immediately confident he was in me. There was a ball for every graduating class, and every graduate gets a plus-one. "They can bring *anyone*," Nigel said, raising his eyebrows in the rearview mirror. He thought I had good odds.

If that was any inclination of where Nigel's mind wandered while he ushered people around town, it was no surprise then how my initial ride with him finished. He left me at the Deeyooks with his business card and perhaps my favorite quote of the summer: "Agh, there so many, many gerrls out an' lookin' grrreat. Of course, as a married man I don't ever look," he said with a wry smile. "But it seems they wear less and less clothes every year."

Nigel had officially secured my business.

I found myself calling Independent Taxis all summer long. They employ seven cabbies, but every time I rang, I hoped to hear Nigel's voice on the other end. His answer always came in a flash, as if pausing between words was illegal. "Indapendentoxis!" he'd shout. When I shared the pickup spot, there was always a burst of pep in his voice: "Ah! Is this Shonn!?"

With Nigel, I never knew what was coming, and yet I knew exactly what I was going to get: 12 minutes of hyperactive conversation. A simple *yes* is replaced with a cadence of, *Yo, yeh, yep. Aye, aye.* It's either a factor of a slight stutter or that Scottish war on silence. I was getting 12 minutes of his sharpest attention and perhaps a lesson about town. Nigel was my own academic father.

While I walked home one evening during Open week, I saw Nigel's cab approaching the intersection. We locked eyes as he made a hard left turn, and he nearly wrecked his car as he thrust a waving hand out the window. I grew up in a small town where honking horns meant someone you knew was driving by, rather than someone behind you is getting impatient. I missed that. Weeks later after an infuriating round at the Deeyooks—where I ran out of golf balls on the 10th hole and promised myself I would quit this stupid game altogether—it was Nigel who answered, like a fairy godfather ready to distract me with the silliness of life.

"Maybe get away from yer golf for a day or two," he said. "Maybe yuh need a coupla drenks.

"Shonn, maybe yuh need a FEW drenks."

I was not in a talking mood that night, and he realized it, but Scottish people (as established) are allergic to silence. "Well, I've been doing lots of exciting things," he said before narrating every detail of a trip to the Burntisland fair with his five-year-old grandson. Nigel is not a golfer, so he didn't have time for my moping. When he's not on grandpa duty, he gets his kicks through seasonal trips up to the Scottish Highlands. Those scabs on his face came from a mountain biking accident, yet another indication that I had severely underestimated him on first glance.

To ride in Nigel's taxi is to open a St. Andrews almanac. You learn something every time. Like the hottest temperature Nigel ever witnessed in St. Andrews—31 degrees Celsius, or "a night fer sinking a few berrs." The Scottish term for bumper cars? Dodgems. The British term for the hood of a car? A bonnet. And what about that trailer park on the southeast side of town? That's a *caravan* park, he corrected me. Most of the owners live on the west side of Scotland, near Glasgow, but vacation here in Fife because it doesn't rain as much. At least that's what he thinks. He'll always tell you what he thinks.

I write about Nigel not because he is some revelatory character who changed the trajectory of my summer. I never secured a ticket to the Graduation Balls. I also didn't drown my golf sorrows at the Dunvegan, as he suggested. I acknowledge Nigel mostly because he's commonplace in the Commonwealth. He's unassuming but fundamentally interested in everyone who rides with him. He represents the type of normalcy behind a wheel that, if you ride in the back of a lot of Ubers and Lyfts, you could just as happily avoid interacting with.

Modern traveling presents so many Nigels on our path, and we either embrace or eschew them. If you happen upon a poster in Italian, Google can translate it instantly. No need to ask for help. *The New York Times* insists we pay with plastic while abroad rather than chasing down foreign currency, because everyone knows Monsieur Mastercard. Life is easier that way. But that doesn't make it better.

During one ride, Nigel wondered aloud, "It's probably different here in northeast Fife den oh-ther parts of the world. Us using arr radios and all. Oh-ther companies it comes up on derr screen, ya-kno."

I do know. Had Uber fully succeeded in its dreams to take over the globe, it would have ruined a bit of what makes this part of the world great. The storytelling. The lessons about our surroundings. The sharing of intel. The sharing, period. When Independent Taxis is inundated with requests, rather than strain the system and rush around for every last pound, they pass those riders off to other taxi companies in town. An informal *You scratch our backs, we'll scratch yours.* Competing brands in America could never.

I thought about Uber and Lyft every time I rode in Nigel's car. I thought about how transactional and ironically silent the ridesharing experience can be. I know the driver's name and they know mine, as our phones ping each other constantly, but we won't share more than a few words. I thought about the dozens and dozens—maybe hundreds?— of times I've told friends that my preferred ride-share is exactly that: a shared ride, nothing more. As little communication as possible. The path of least resistance.

I also thought about how golf presents a macro version of these opportunities all the time, and how I approached it much the same. When playing alone, I preferred to *stay* that way. When playing quickly, I'd rather skate on through a group of strangers than link up. When asked to fill out a foursome, I tended to spend another hour on the range or skip a hole to race ahead. I was the first to explain how the experience of golf is entirely about who you play with, and yet golf with strangers felt like an ominous blind date where you have just one thing in common.

After that first ride with Nigel, I had lived in Scotland for a week, and my inbox was humming. My DMs were brimming with invites to the best courses in the country, and some of the best in the world: Carnoustie, North Berwick, the Old Course, Cruden Bay, Panmure. Woe is me, right? If I was going to get the most out of this summer, I needed to rewire my brain *against* convenience. I needed to lean in to the strangers around me. Journeys with Nigel were just the start.

Chapter 5

The First (and Only) LIV Golf Draft

We waited as long as we possibly could to make a decision. I was in St. Andrews, begging my bosses to approve a trip to London, where I'd cover the first LIV Golf Invitational, but this was a trickier assignment than most. Most of the golf world was unsure what to do with the Saudi-funded rival golf league that had hastily upended the status quo. Equipment brands weren't sure if they should honor their contracts with LIV golfers. Television networks weren't sure if they should even admit that LIV Golf existed. And media companies like ours, well, we had our own advertisers yanking banner ads off any webpages that featured LIV content. Internally, we discussed the implications. If the biggest golf website in the world simply shows up, does that mean this league is relevant? And if so, how relevant? Do we want to make this thing relevant? Do we have a choice?

There was no choice. I shouldn't be picking a side. My role was strictly observational. This was not my doing, but rather the decisions of some restless golfers and financial leaders of a foreign entity. I took a lot of comfort in the fact that people more important than me were going to decide how it all moved forward. I just needed to be there taking notes.

Finally, on Monday evening of tournament week, merely hours before the first press conferences in LIV Golf history, I secured the green light. I jumped on the first train for London, a 9:22 AM straight shot from Leuchars Station to Kings Cross. Five hours and 27 minutes later I had completed one of the longer trips you can make via train in the U.K., about the same distance from New York City to Raleigh, North Carolina.

Unable to reach the course in time for the initial press sessions, I set my sights on the LIV Golf draft, a truly novel concept on a novel golf tour. The draft was always going to be one of the juiciest pieces of the LIV puzzle: pro golfers staring down other pro golfers while they draft the *other* pros seated right next to them. In such a genteel sport, where the sound of loose change in someone's pocket can send a golfer on a tirade, the idea of a draft was intoxicating.

If this were really going to be team golf reimagined, we would want the creation of these squads to matter, and perhaps to see some animosity or rivalry manifested in the process—the things that carry storylines in other sports. LIV was promising a legit snake draft, where the team drafting last in the first round drafted first in the second round. And it was not just a draft where players' names are selected off a big board, but a draft *party* buzzing with VIPs—wives, girlfriends, coaches, and families mixing about with players, event staff, and even fans who had paid top dollar to see it all. For its debut season, LIV promised draft parties would take place during each tournament week, at some ritzy establishment, serving as a hype track for the weekend days to come.

LIV's communications staff had touched base weeks earlier, hopeful I could attend. (If media attends, that means it matters, right?) They offered to fund my cross-Atlantic flight *and* my accommodations in London, even offering me a spot in the pro-am. Invites like these are popular in the golf world, where trips and gear are tossed around in exchange—at least that's the hope—for positive coverage. It's an unwritten, unspoken agreement that creates very murky borders for journalism ethics, and was a good reminder of what we were dealing with: a start-up. LIV Golf wanted press. They needed press. And they were willing to pay for it—and there's no way I was the only one receiving an offer. (For obvious reasons, the answer was *no thanks*.) But if there was any group of people who would be dubious of LIV and its Saudi Arabian backers, it is those in the same profession as Jamal Khashoggi, a *Washington Post* journalist who was critical of the Saudi government and was murdered at the Saudi consulate in Istanbul for openly criticizing the Kingdom's limitations on women's rights, its relations with other Middle Eastern countries, and, importantly, how it quelled free speech among its citizens.

It's not exactly clear when, but in the days preceding the draft, LIV pivoted from being pro-media to *prohibiting* media. It wasn't explained to the journalists at the golf course, many of whom asked to cover the event, but you could literally see the indecisiveness on the walls at the draft party. Signs at each doorway displayed a legend of colored wristbands for security to monitor. Commissioner Greg Norman's wristband was grey. Orange bands were guest services, red bands were for security. Black bands were players, white bands were captains. There were 10 distinctions in all, and media wristbands were yellow, but no yellow bands were handed out that night. I can't say definitively why a league thirsty for media coverage suddenly got skittish about reporters covering its draft, but based on that morning's press conferences, it wasn't surprising.

During the first set of LIV pressers, there was a battering of questions about Saudi Arabia's human rights record. Players were asked about their decision to take "blood money," and the potential to be banned from the PGA Tour or—even worse—miss out on major championships. Every player had received strict media training and talking points to adhere to whenever Saudi Arabia, suspensions, or money was brought up.

Louis Oosthuizen spoke first, a bit surprising from the soft-spoken South African, but he was emboldened by two shiny new sponsors on his chest. Oosty had sported a UPS logo on the front of his apparel for more than 11 years, ever since he won the 2010 Open Championship—in St. Andrews, no less. But here in June 2022, that deal had suddenly died. Same for Lee Westwood, another LIV commit, whose relationship with the shipping company stretched even longer.

Oosthuizen raved about the chance to do something different. Dustin Johnson raved about the team golf format and how it would be "great for the fans." They were both talking on message. Graeme McDowell followed suit, if only for a few minutes, but eventually, his sensibilities snapped and he said the quiet part out loud:

"We are professional golfers. If Saudi Arabia wanted to use the game of golf as a way for them to get to where they want to be and they have the resources to accelerate that experience, I think we are proud to help them on that journey using the game of golf and the abilities that we have to help grow the sport and take them to where they want to be."

These answers were truly the first of their kind, and even if they mostly lacked nuance, they were the first chance for players to explain *their* side to this story. McDowell's story, even if he didn't seem to realize it, is basically a word-for-word definition of sportswashing. That he was willing to say it out loud and invoke the country's name and imply misgivings was more than we were getting elsewhere. Almost immediately G-Mac was roasted online for this transparency, but the whole act of this press conference was worthwhile. The British press is notoriously harsher than its American counterpart, but there is at least a baseline level of respect between the two roles at play. We ask the questions, they answer. The rest of the world is the jury.

Two hours later, at the end of the second presser, an AP reporter named Rob Harris pleaded with LIV staff to get one more question in. LIV had promised 30-minute press conferences but was wrapping this one around the 25-minute mark. When Harris' request wasn't granted and Kevin Na and Co. began to leave their seats, Harris leapt from his own, confronting players at the dais. He shouted a question about "blood money" as players awkwardly retreated from the podium. Security confronted him and promptly removed Harris from the media center, an ordeal that was wiped from LIV Golf's archival video. Fellow writers explained later that Harris' actions were toeing the line if not blatantly crossing it. But even as he was allowed to return minutes later, an unintentional statement of sorts had been made from Day 1: a writer was dragged out of LIV Golf's media center. Details of the incident whizzed across social media.

The draft hovered in the wake of this. Anyone on the guest list had exactly one afternoon of LIV Golf coverage to react to. The sacrificial players who had faced the initial interrogations were off the hook, at least until Thursday. The others were learning what they were in for, literally, over cocktails. Sergio García dipped into a yogurty hors d'oeuvre as he soothed Jane MacNeille, the LIV staffer who met the brunt of Harris' fire. García told her not to worry, "There are just bad people in this world." The irony of his words was clearly lost on him. This Day 1 checkpoint was clearly a safe space for everyone, especially without media crawling around. Everyone there *wanted* to be there, at RD Studios, a boxy, state-of-the-art event space in Central London. It had opened just weeks before LIV arrived.

From the outside, the setup felt conspicuous. Event security extended about 100 yards out from the gate, along the fences of a DHL shipping warehouse. It felt odd that this flashy new league was launching in an office park next to a Bestway, the British equivalent of Costco. The VIP guest list was about 10 pages long and included everyone from Lee Westwood to Claude Harmon to Eric Trump (though he did not attend, best I could tell). My name was not included, but because I had been friendly with LIV staffers in the weeks and months before, I had secured one of two media invitations. LIV's own media skittishness made me wary, partly because the other invitee didn't show. I knew I could get an exclusive story that would be the envy of the press room. There is seriously nothing better. But it would be granted by a brand I didn't know what to think of. Again, if a major golf media institution is there plucking shrimp from the seafood spread, doesn't that look like LIV relevance? I convinced myself I'd see something few others would ever see. Journalists live for that stuff, so I went along for the ride.

When LIV first launched its ticket service in late April, access to events like this one was also for sale. A one-day grounds pass to the tournament went for $85 and hospitality seats for $310. But VIP access to the draft party could be had for $1,500. Sticker shock aside, the business plan made sense. Push all your high-priced LIV golfers into the same room, hand out free drinks with lobster rolls, and fans would pony up to rub elbows with their favorite pros. Only LIV was struggling so hard to get people to simply attend the tournament rounds that it was essentially giving tickets away for free with discount codes. If they couldn't get fans to pay $85 to watch the golf, $1,500 to watch players get drafted was out of the question.

Given the price tag, it was no surprise that the first draft was overly gaudy. Upon arrival guests posed for photos in front of a LIV banner as if this were the Academy Awards. And in fairness, they were walking along a 200-foot red carpet toward the action. Various props were located nearby, with LIV's logo emblazoned everywhere: on director's chairs and megaphones and a radio studio sign lit up in red reading LIV ON AIR. "Golf, But Louder" was the official slogan, and this was as visually loud as it gets. I trailed behind 20-year-old, uber-talented amateur David Puig, who had arrived just days after competing in the NCAA Championship at Arizona State. He wore an untucked white button-down over some blue jeans and Stan Smiths. We walked down a narrow corridor lined with fluorescent lights and overstaffed by workers in formal attire. House music thumped from a room around the corner, where disco lights flickered in every direction. It had the feel of a European night club, which made even more sense when I found myself chest-to-chest with a bouncer protecting the official draft room, dubbed Studio 54. Tucked back in the corner, deep in the belly of RD Studios, most of the guests gathered in a room named The 19th Hole. That's where the disco lights streamed from, calling you inward.

In just a few months of existence, LIV had established an impressive knack for spending its Saudi money, but settling for The 19th Hole—the most cliché name for a golfy bar setting—showed it clearly lacked in creativity. This rectangular cave was packed shoulder to shoulder, if for no other reason than it was physically small: just 3,150 square feet, with a central bar around which the guests mingled. Chase Koepka, the kid brother of world-famous Brooks Koepka, was the first pro I spotted, milling around in an untucked dress shirt. Claude Harmon was next, one of the game's most popular coaches, peering down at his phone while a bartender mixed him a drink. Ian Poulter and Graeme McDowell had cleaned up into cocktail attire. On the far side of The 19th Hole was the most decadent spread of British seafood I had ever seen. Smoked salmon plucked from the nearby River Severn, about 100 miles west. Tuna tartare served with shallots and sour cream. (I salivate once again just writing about it.) LIV was putting on a party and doing the specifics *really well*.

The irony in this room may not have been clear to everyone in attendance, but it was to me. Yes, there were major champions and Ryder Cuppers and some of the greatest golfers on the planet. Also among them were completely innocuous gents like Wade Ormsby wearing loafers, Phachara Khongwatmai dressed in a polo, and Ian Snyman rocking wire-frame glasses and washed blue jeans. In about 40 hours, they would be competing against single-name golf icons—Phil, Dustin, Sergio—but in this setting you'd confuse them for somebody's cousin.

Around 7 PM, 30 minutes before the draft was to start, I finally bumped into one of those single-name icons. Dustin Johnson was in a cheery state, being the single entity that breathed life into this league when he signed on the dotted line at the deadline, on May 31. He wore a blue blazer over an untucked, light blue dress shirt, a white pocket square jutting out the breast pocket. The kind of uniform only a man with endless self-confidence can really pull off. DJ may not have won best-dressed, but no golfer on the planet makes a blazer and jeans look as good as he does. He accented it all with a bottle of Peroni dangling between his fingers.

Johnson ventured directly into the conversation I was having with MacNeille and was happy to chat to her about his recent vacation to the Bahamas, the hole-in-one his brother made at Baker's Bay, and the fishing he did in the run-up to LIV London. But shortly after we shook hands and I introduced myself, something flipped in his demeanor. Johnson said he recognized me, which felt genuine, but he suddenly seemed rushed to leave the convo now that a media member was in front of him. We've worked on plenty of magazine projects together in the past; I wasn't here to present some gotcha question. I playfully asked if his face was a bit sunburnt from all that fishing, but he didn't take the bait. Maybe the low lighting was playing tricks on me. Either way, what started as a pleasant convo quickly ended when Johnson darted off to find another Peroni. A few minutes later the main doors of Studio 54 flung open and about 250 people moseyed in.

At the front of the room was a wide stage, about the size of what you'd see on Broadway. The first three rows of seats were reserved, mostly for the undrafted 36 players and their plus-ones. Seats in the second row, third row, and every other row in the room were the basic kind you'd find sitting around circular tables at a corporate retreat. They have a certain squareness to them, with a metal frame and hard plastic backing. The seatback has a little give but sitting in them comfortably only lasts for so long. The chairs in the first row were very different. They were round and wide, with convex armrests that made them feel even wider. The seats weren't canvas cushions like the rest of the room. No, these were black leather, with gold nailhead trim lining every edge. In any other scenario, these details would stretch beyond what is acceptable storytelling. But this was no normal scenario. In a word, the first-row chairs were…royal. First Class. This is where the important people would sit—several LIV executives and their plus-ones. Greg Norman, LIV Golf's 67-year-old CEO and front man, was situated near the center with his wife, Kirsten, on his right. Two seats to his left was reserved for Majed Al Souror, the head of Golf Saudi and recently appointed director of Newcastle United Football Club. (Months earlier, the Saudi PIF had purchased an 80 percent ownership stake in NUFC, our first sign that Saudi sports ownership is not a fight exclusive to golf.)

In between Norman and Al Souror's seats, literally front and center, was a white placard that read in all caps: RESERVED HIS EXCELLENCY. That designation, of course, was for Yasir Al-Rumayyan, the managing director of all those billions of dollars in the Saudi PIF and close confidant of Mohammed bin Salman, the Crown Prince of Saudi Arabia. Suddenly the elegant chairs made more sense. All of this pomp—the happy golfers, the giddy spectators, and the lights and glitz and glamour—was a show for the Saudis. Asking one of Saudi Arabia's most powerful men to sit on a grabby, canvas cushion was not going to suffice.

As the crowd settled into position and those royal seats were filled, the lights quickly dimmed, just like in a movie theater. Showtime.

Gigantic rectangular screens lit up at the front of the room, beaming out a 110-second mix of strobe lights, colors, beats, optical illusions, avatar golfers, tees flying at you, and a sequence of five flashing words.

Whatever

you do

don't

blink.

You didn't want to. At any second the room was completely dark, and the next completely illuminated. From the back of the room, the strobes silhouetted the still noggins of the crowd. Grey, white, and black golf balls clanked into each other to fit in the screen frame, as if they were ping pong balls in a lottery machine. LIV may have goofed on The 19th Hole, but the graphics team was crushing it.

"Isn't this *amazing?*" Jane MacNeille asked, nudging me with her elbow. I hadn't given an ounce of reaction yet. It *was* amazing. After months of anguish and indecision, this was a sudden dose of reality, and I truly felt the hype. Ten days earlier, I didn't even know who would play in this tournament, and suddenly it felt like a marquee event. If I had woken up from a two-year coma to find captain Dustin Johnson drafting teammates into a cash-soaked shootout in the middle of major championship season, I would have thought, *Holy shit, golf got really cool.* Only I hadn't been comatose for two years. I knew all the context for why this was in front of me. It's flashy as hell, and it has some uncertain intentions.

When the video lifted, two hosts took the stage: Kirsty Gallacher and Shane O'Donoghue. A carefully worded script had been loaded onto teleprompters in front of them, but their main job was guiding the draft to fit the "Golf, But Louder" motto. Gallacher started quickly, telling the audience that, yes, it is okay to get up out of your seat and be loud during the draft. They wanted to inspire the sort of viral reactions you see from New York Knicks fans during the NBA Draft. The audience didn't really know what to do. The loudest anyone got all night was intermittent shouts from a well-lubricated member of Wade Ormsby's team. "Kah-mon Wade!"

If I was confused by anything at first it was O'Donoghue's presence, for no other reason than he seemed like a straight shooter, and nothing about LIV Golf was straightforward. I was just surprised to see him so all-in from the jump. Night 1 of Event 1 of Year 1 in an ultra-controversial endeavor. But the explanation came later in the night when Shane reminded the room that he was the host of a show called *Living Golf* on CNN. Over the previous 12 months, the show was sponsored by, of all places, Golf Saudi. Their money had been good to him already. If some is good, more is better. That could suffice as the entire thesis for LIV Golf.

Before any captains were announced or selections were made, an original, 23-page run-of-show called for a speech from Yasir Al-Rumayyan, the most important man in the room. Three-hundred and forty-eight words were spelled out on the document, including these two sentences of interest:

"From the outset, we focused on enhancing golf's ecosystem. This isn't nor has ever been an aggressive takeover bid of world golf."

The word "ecosystem" would come to dominate legal documents and statements from governing bodies all summer long. The second sentence, I felt, was one that would have found its way into lawsuits, too, had it been delivered. Whether or not this was a takeover bid of world golf, it was definitely aggressive. But for some reason, Al-Rumayyan's speech was removed from the script and scribbled out in red ink. Instead, Norman took the stage, delivering his own speech exactly as it was spelled out in the run of show. "The future of golf starts Thursday," Norman said to the packed room. "And there's no looking back."

I wondered how much bloviating I would have to parse through. Norman was laying it on thick, gushing about the innovation he was bringing to the sport and labeling the players and caddies the "first-movers at this historic moment in time." At the end he thanked his

Saudi supporters and told the entire room, "LIV does not exist without any of you." Then he stuck his fists out to each side and raised them in the air, flexing his biceps like a gladiator and letting out an awkward cry: "LET'S GOOO!"

Let's go, indeed. Twelve of the best golfers in the world had been standing at each side of the room, split into lines of six, now partially illuminated by the glow from the screens. These were your team captains, standing in reverse order of their world ranking and in the order by which they would select players. It dawned on me in this moment just how rarely we prop up golfers as celebrities, introducing them to truly raucous applause like other pro athletes. They looked a bit awkward, though, dressed in differing levels of attire. Maybe it's fitting we don't treat them as pop-culture heartthrobs. First on the right was Graeme McDowell, the 2010 U.S. Open champion, and first on the left was Peter Uihlein, the 2010 U.S. Amateur champion who had struggled to establish himself atop the pro game. Fourth in line along the right side stood Phil Mickelson, in the flesh. Finally, I felt it. That anticipatory, only-three-hundred-people-are-seeing-this kind of eagerness. I don't know why it felt like a surprise to see him—he had been announced as a final addition to the field just a day earlier—but part of it was certainly because he was making his first appearance since taking a voluntary leave of absence after his true motives for joining LIV were put on full display in February. Mickelson wore black pants and a black leather jacket, his long hair slicked back. After 30 years of being clean-shaven in the public eye, he sported a prickly beard. This was a different Mickelson.

I could feel the anticipation build in front of me. As soon as Gallacher began introducing Mickelson, phones shot into the air. Whether it was capturing Phil for the first time in months like a bunch of thirsty paparazzi, seizing a pic of peculiar golf history, or just grabbing a photo to remember the night by, this was the moment everyone cared about.

"Now please welcome to the stage HyFlyers GC," Gallacher announced. "With a name like HyFlyers, their identity has to reflect a team in flight. Powered by its winged logo, this team will be hoping they live up to their name and soar above the competition at the LIV Golf Invitationals."

(Mickelson's team was promised to fly high. Fireballs GC was called "anarchic" and for younger golf fans. Dustin Johnson's 4 Aces were billed as golf's greatest magic trick. With a completely blank slate to work from, LIV chose its team names like it named its bar, in the cheesiest manner possible.)

As Mickelson climbed up on stage and posed for photos with Norman, a trend started to reveal itself. Gallacher introduced him with only one set of credentials: six major championships, the most of any LIV golfer. No one in this room had done more on the PGA Tour—or done more *for* the Tour—than Mickelson, who won 45 times in the last three decades, good for eighth best all time. But you weren't going to hear those two words uttered during this description. In fact, you weren't going to hear "PGA Tour" mentioned once all night. And you would have to strain to find those words written into any formal communication from LIV Golf all year long (that is, until litigation between the two brands began). LIV was not going to imply any added relevance to the Tour by citing it during its own proudest moments. So on draft night, Sergio García was labeled as "a major champion with 36 career victories." Ian Poulter's career was introduced as "19 professional victories."

"That's a cool lookin' look for Phil," O'Donoghue said as Mickelson got comfy at a desk on the far left side of the room. "It's his birthday next week, folks. June 16, and he shares it with Old Tom Morris. How about that for a little bit of history?"

Dozens of video producers scurried about, capturing the content we'd see on YouTube and Twitter the next day. In front of each of the captains was an iPad with team names and logos on the screen. It was impressive tech, in a way, that Mickelson could scroll through the remaining players available while García made a selection 50 yards from him. Suspenseful music played over the speakers as captains were given exactly 54 seconds to lock each selection, part of LIV's undying commitment to the roman numeral LIV. Only most captains didn't use the iPads. A production staffer wearing a headset chased around the room with a physical list of players on a clipboard. Captains pointed to the names on the list, and soon enough that name was read across the teleprompters in front of Gallacher and O'Donoghue. On paper, that's how a draft works—a genuine draft. But this wasn't a totally genuine draft.

In front of Louis Oosthuizen were two things: a list of players available and a reminder: Charl Schwartzel is already on your team. He is your second-round pick. Branden Grace is also on your team. He is your third-round pick. When the hosts pan to you for those picks, please—please!—don't select anyone else.

Earlier in the day information trickled out on social media that there were really only 31 players available to be drafted, not 36, as the format had promised. Oosthuizen's Stinger GC was basically already assembled, pre-arranged by South African friends who wanted to play together. Screw the draft. The same went for Ian Poulter's Majesticks team, which was assembled again by friends who wanted to play together—screw the draft. Sam Horsfield, Lee Westwood, and Laurie Canter were already locked in on Poulter's team, so he didn't have to make a single pick. This is, of course, how you end up with an unknown like Hennie Du Plessis as one of the first 12 players chosen. Chaos actually arrived much sooner than that. McDowell snatched Bernd Wiesberger with the first pick, and then after a bit of deliberation, Uihlein selected Hideto Tanihara. It was a sound pick, by all accounts. Only it quickly became clear that Kevin Na had expected Tanihara to still be available at No. 10. Na clearly wanted to assemble a team of players of Asian descent and had communicated to the other captains that he wanted the Japanese Tanihara to join his Iron Heads. Uihlein didn't get the memo.

Players glanced awkwardly from desk to desk. Uihelin was laughing and Na was panicking. A long, pregnant pause was maintained by the two hosts. Everyone in the room was confused. "There's a bit of deliberation going on," O'Donoghue said. "We're not entirely certain what happened with the computer. But these things happen, folks. This is LIV Golf, this is live TV, it's live golf. And so if something has to change, we'll figure it out." He was right, something did have to change: the second overall pick.

As innocent as this was, the ordeal served as LIV Golf's first hiccup with a draft it was marketing as totally genuine. Na ended up selecting Richard Bland with his second-round pick, 15th overall, and by the time the teams were announced to the public, the first-round snafu had been rectified. The first LIV Golf trade had also taken place: Tanihara for Bland, straight up. Nothing else. Another seat-of-their-pants adjustment.

Most of the captains' intentions had already been widely known to LIV staffers. MacNeille, sitting next to me, already knew Sergio García was going to draft Spanish amateur David Puig. It was clear Talor Gooch was going to select Hudson Swafford, rising to bear-hug his buddy after taking him ninth. The most genuine part of the draft may have come from Dustin Johnson, who admitted he knew so few players in the room that he was using a cheat sheet made for him by an equipment rep from TaylorMade. With plenty of partnerships roughly in place, and the frivolity of whether Mickelson would choose Chase Koepka or Andy Ogletree, the rest of the draft went off without a hitch. The crowd was never going to be anxious about who might earn the draft rights to Sadom Kaewkanjana, so it went by rather quietly, too. Each pick earned the requisite amount of applause, waved on stage for a few seconds, and then went to sit next to their captain. The graphics were great, the production was great, and the milestone for LIV felt very real. The hosts did their job.

"They have built it, and they have come," O'Donoghue said when it was over, a perfectly hokey sign-off for the night. Every player and team was called on stage for photos with Norman, who passed out logoed hats for each of the newfangled franchises. Some captains conducted interviews with producers as the after-party started in spirit. Wait staff began circling the room with gin-based cocktails made special for the event. Turk Pettit yanked his new Niblicks GC ball cap down tight around his head and posed for a pic with his girlfriend. The photo would later find its way to Instagram with the caption, "Big Draft Energy."

"I like that hat, baby," McDowell said to his 23-year-old, baby-faced teammate. "It looks good."

"Yes sir," Pettit replied with a smile. "All week."

All week, for sure, but not all year. Not all summer. As novel as this draft was, it had meaning, but it didn't have weight. LIV announced that it would have drafts at each of its events, which greatly underpinned how "good" Pettit looked in Niblicks green. If this was golf imitating other sports, the value of signing young Pettit to a franchise was nonexistent. His time on the Niblicks lasted all of four days, as he would become a member of Cleeks GC at the second LIV event (and even change teams again before the third event). This league was adjusting on the fly, but should I blame them? How much should I let expectations impact my view on things? *Did I need to hold it against them? Did they have to thump their chest so much?*

Another sign came from Richard Marsh, a man I met earlier in the night. On paper, or rather, LinkedIn, Marsh was the group strategy director for Performance 54, a golf marketing company. In reality, he was introduced to me as one of the lead contract negotiators, and despite hiding behind a director title for P54, he was one of the top straws stirring the drink for LIV. Marsh used to be the CCO of World Golf Group, who first launched the idea of a rival tour years ago. It didn't happen then, but now it was—and it was hard to imagine there was a busier phone than his over the last two months. "You must not be getting much sleep these past few weeks," I said, trying to make the kind of small talk that incites some juicy detail. "Nope," he said, stealing a sip from his cocktail. "This is just the beginning."

I met Majed Al Souror, too, the head of the Saudi Golf Federation. Like Dustin Johnson, he seemed happy to chat and shake hands, right until the moment I explained what I did for work. I asked him about Newcastle's prospects in the Premier League now that he and the PIF were involved. "Just wait until next year," he said, before turning to another conversation.

I met James Costigan that night, LIV's head of event security, a gruff man who had been plucked from Augusta National. This sent my curiosity sky high. You don't leave Augusta National unless you've got one helluva job offer. I guess that's what this was. Costigan was just one of many industry veterans LIV had recruited to join its enterprise. Slugger White, who retired from the PGA Tour after 40 years as a Rules official, jumped back into action to do the same job for LIV. I didn't want to guess how many digits were in his salary. He scooped up a fellow ex-Tour official and began assembling a staff with others from the USGA and PGA of America sections. Ari Fleischer, former White House press secretary, was brought on exclusively as a consultant to aid LIV with its early, thorny press conferences.

Seeing this all-star staff with my own eyes, LIV started to look like a jigsaw puzzle slowly shifting into order. Even more clarity regarding LIV's intentions would arrive in the following days. After posing for a few photos, Mickelson received one last spurt of media training that night before heading off to bed. In 12 hours, he would face the press for the first time in more than four months. I was exhausted but so enlivened about the weirdness that was to come.

Chapter 6

LIV London

When Philip Alfred Mickelson takes the stage, golf writers perk up. On top of being one of the finest to ever swing a golf club, he's long been one of the game's greatest talkers, too. In press conferences, you can often tell what type of mood he's in, and what's been circling around in his brain.

Mickelson has used his time with the press to lead all-out assaults on course maintenance and tournament setups. He's torched Hall of Famer Tom Watson just 20 feet down the podium from the man himself. He'll wax on about muscle stabilization, the power of vegetables, and California's state income taxes. If a harmless question allows him to spin a yarn, make yourself comfortable. He'll go for minutes on Russian ballerinas.

His unpredictable nature filled the LIV press room with purpose on June 8. When he walked in just before 9 AM, there wasn't an empty seat. Everyone had hurried into place long before the doors swung open. Mickelson might be emboldened, I thought, grabbing the mic two or three hours before anyone in the States would be ready to react. He might continue holding his tail between his legs, bashful that his

59

desire to fracture the payment structure of pro golf had been laid out nakedly for the whole world to see…and by his own doing. He could be strictly concise, only answering the question he'd been asked (a Tiger Woods staple). He could go long and circumvent the topic. Never has there been such anticipation for a Mickelson presser. And never again will there be another like it. He was a different man.

For starters, that beard—mostly dark with a tinge of grey at the corners of his chin—looked much better in the daylight than it did in front of the keylights from draft night. He wore aviator shades and offered the room the softest, no-teeth smile as he sat down next to Chase Koepka, Justin Harding, and Ratchanon "TK" Chantananuwat, the three men he drafted to the HyFlyers 12 hours earlier. His apparel was all black, layered with a dark grey vest, matching the villainous outfit from the night before. More important than anything, it was bereft of the logos we had come to associate with Mickelson. (These sponsor logos can seem meaningless at any point and then feel like glaring, removed tattoos at another.) KPMG and Workday both sacked Mickelson as an ambassador, while Callaway announced it would "pause" their 18-year relationship. In their place, the only logo on his person was…his person: a silhouette of a leaping Mickelson stitched into his chest, each of his limbs spread wide as he celebrated his first major victory back in 2004. It was an ominous token of the loneliness he must have felt for the next 25 minutes.

Mickelson faced a barrage of questions relating to his sudden reappearance after more than four months away, led by Dan Roan, a steely reporter from the BBC. "A few months ago, you were reported as describing the Saudis as 'scary,'" Roan said. "What did you mean by that, and if they are that scary, why are you here given that they are bank-rolling this tournament?"

There's an art to asking questions, and Roan perfected it. No one else in the room could answer it but Mickelson. It followed up on his own phrasing and was simple in nature. The best questions are simple in nature. Why are you doing what you are doing? The response could go in any direction, but it would have to address why Mickelson went dark to begin with. His answer was 110 words, but if you saw it in complete sentences, like most people would when they stirred to read about it online, it looks very different from the calculated and careful way it was uttered.

Well, certainly, ahh—

I've made, said and done a lot of, ah, things that I regret, and I'm sorry for that and for the hurt that it's caused a lot of people.

Ahh, I don't, ahmm—

I don't condone human rights violations at all. I don't think, I—nobody here does, ah, throughout the world. I'm certainly aware of what has happened with Jamal Khashoggi, and I think it's terrible.

I've also seen the good that the game of golf has done throughout history, and I believe that LIV Golf is going to do a lot of good for the game as well.

Ahhm—

And I'm excited about this opportunity. That's why I'm here.

Mickelson was asked a variation of Roan's question a handful of times. What about the "leverage" he was hoping for against the PGA Tour? What will it mean for his legacy? In the past, he was quick to tell a story or share his sharpest opinions and biting jokes. But this Mickelson paused after every question, assessing them internally for as much as 10 seconds before spitting out an on-brand answer. This had to be the only press conference in golf history where a subject felt compelled to say "I don't condone human rights violations" four different times.

Mickelson declined to say anything about the PGA Tour. He did not want to comment on a possible suspension he could face or whether he was already suspended. He urged reporters to ask just one question at a time, which is entirely within his right. It's just the kind of defense mechanism that expedites a presser toward its finish in a much more efficient manner. We didn't need a linguistic analysis of this deposition to see that something in him had changed. The golfing entertainer had zapped himself on the third rail, brazenly exposed greedy interests, and then evolved into a brick wall as the public quickly realized it.

People do this all the time, I told myself. Greed runs rampant in pro sports. Was Mickelson's version particularly egregious? Probably. It was also just playing out in slow motion. We waited four months for these answers, and when they arrived it felt like a podcast playing at half-speed. Opinions on the matter would fly around much faster.

As I watched from the fourth row, I didn't feel bad for Mickelson. This was his own doing. I just felt bad *about* him. This was a man I had affectionately nicknamed Uncle Phil, because he seemed like America's favorite golfing uncle. There was always some sense of deviousness to the way he acted, but it often made him a tragic hero—stirring a mix of sympathy and antagonism from fans. We love the emotions he's made us feel. The bewilderment and disappointment and vulnerability. He could do things with a golf ball that most Tour pros could only dream of. He explained golf shots with the exactitude of a NASA scientist analyzing liftoff conditions. Mickelson literally spent part of his 2019 Thanksgiving weekend texting me about his special six-day coffee and water fast and how it would change my life. He called me a week later and yapped about reading 50-year-old Russian studies about health and wellness. He always had something to say. But right now he didn't. And what he did share didn't feel entirely truthful.

Sports reporters face a concoction of half-truths, quarter-truths, and full-truths all the time. Athletes are encouraged toward deceit in the name of maintaining a competitive edge. But they're human. The delivery is often a tell. Are the canned responses presented smoothly?

How long are the pauses? And do they come mid-sentence or after complete thoughts? Wait a second—are there *any* complete thoughts?

The staccato, deliberate way Mickelson discussed Saudi Arabia and his new bosses felt revealing. But so was the demeanor flip in the middle of the presser. One reporter laid out and asked simply, "What have you done the last four months? No one has seen you." Mickelson grinned and looked down at the floor for a beat before peering back up with a serious face.

> I have had…
> [pause]
> an AWESOME time.
> I have had a four-month break from the game that I have not had in over three decades. I've had an opportunity to spend time with my wife, Amy—a bunch—and travel parts of the world and spend time at a place we have in Montana skiing and hike in Sedona. What a beautiful place that is.
> It's given me time to, ah, continue, some of the work and therapy I've been working on in some areas that I've been deficient in my life. It's given me time to reflect on what I want to do going forward.
> What's best for me. What's best for the people I care about.
> And—
> This is an opportunity that allows me to still have golf in my life, but also have a balance where I can be more present.
> I can be more engaged with the people I really care about.
> And that is—that is why when I think about being a part of LIV Golf, I feel so good about it.

The Phil who talked about his wife was forthright. He was smooth. He pressed reset on his vibe, if only for a few moments, when he could think about attending his nephew's little league games. It felt obvious that he was going to struggle with some aspects of his golf life moving forward. And the brief respite of looking back on some rare non-golf moments helped him speak freely once again. It may have lasted just 76 seconds before he was asked about his future on the PGA Tour, but it felt important.

As an introduction to LIV coverage, this ordeal was oddly comforting. My own angst about LIV Golf wasn't unique. Every writer in the room had serious questions about the operation and knew there wouldn't be a straightforward route to getting them answered. It would require questions today, tomorrow, and many days after that. After 23 minutes and 26 questions directed exclusively at Mickelson, Ari Fleischer politely reminded the room that there were other golfers at the podium, which drew a laugh. Phil was the showman whom LIV had paid. He was the loose-lipped freewheeler whose words nearly shut down the enterprise in February. Staffers told me how that shitstorm put a hold on everything for most of a month. (Then more investment arrived.) He was the one with the largest signing bonus—a reported $200 million—and this was finally his time to make good on the investment. To hit the shots and make the putts and smile all the while.

He did exactly that all afternoon, playing in the pro-am alongside Yasir Al-Rumayyan, his excellency from those royal chairs on Tuesday night. They played on an empty golf course at Centurion Club, another oddity that made this feel like a tiny club championship. Tournament staffers were still hard at work peeling wrapping paper off everything on campus. As far as a tournament goes, this thing looked the part. Nearly every open stanchion was emblazoned with *LIV, LIV, LIV.* The tour logo floated in the water hazard on 18. LIV Golf was on flags flying in the sky and on the flags cut into the greens. It was printed across caddies' chests and on TV towers and tee markers and trash receptacles. The marketing team was not strapped for budget. Brand mottos were everywhere, too.

Golf, But Louder stretched out 100 feet wide across a walkway bridge.

Don't Blink in font size 10,000 next to bleacher stairwells.

Welcome to the Future on a metallic sign in the Fan Village.

Part of this was futuristic, for sure. During my first spin around the grounds, I ducked into Club 54, a VIP balcony area that overlooked the practice range. The massive space was completely empty except for a robotic vending machine that spun around the room like an over-caffeinated R2-D2. It had two creepy cartoon eyes and stood about four feet tall, carrying mango sodas and cans of Heineken. Yes, it was also branded with the LIV logo. If you didn't grab what you wanted when it drove by, just wait; it would be back in a few minutes.

Club 54 extended from the range, through a private dining area run by a Michelin-starred chef, over the putting green and most of the way to the Fan Village, which is where it seemed LIV had spared no expense. On Wednesday afternoon, the village looked like a movie set, with scaffolding and huge recycling containers everywhere, production staffers hustling it all into place. On one end was a stage worthy of a music festival, which is where LIV would commence its Après Golf dreams. On the other, a 100-foot "Crazy Putt" competition—make it from deep, win a prize. In between was a dizzying mall of activities, attempting to be all things all at once. There was an eco-friendly station where patrons could ride a bike to create reusable energy and buy clothes made from recycled ocean plastic. There were four simulator hitting bays—standard for the golf crowd—and The LIV Food Market, which was flanked by classic, red England phone booths for the local aesthetic. There was a face paint station, playground equipment for children, and bean bags strewn about for lounging parents. Near the mini golf course stood a 15-foot-tall *Terminator* skull statue with glaring robot eyes. The "Metaverse Tent." LIV had even commissioned video game artists to custom brand a *Mini Golf* video game, in which players raced around in as little time and as few strokes as possible.

You could have paid me Greg Norman's salary and I would have never imagined coding LIV logos into a video game.

Twenty-four hours later, the village would be covered by workers dressed in costume—temp carnies, if you will—to encourage even more fun. But four days from now, where was all this stuff going to go? Does the 30-foot LIV Golf tee just get recycled for parts? Or does it get shipped across the world to the second event, in Portland, Oregon? I could see it being donated to a playground somewhere as a balance beam. But does the 10-foot-tall LIV Golf ball become anything but firewood?

Back at the clubhouse, a dozen construction workers rushed through a last-minute addition on the patio. I thoroughly doubted they could get it done in time, but when you host a LIV event, it seems, things spring into form overnight. When 11 AM struck the next morning, all was complete. Only 20 fans or so waited for the gates to open, but before long a swath of spectators gathered at the range, watching intently as Mickelson warmed up. Phil was in grind mode, wearing all black once again. He was one of just two players on the range, tending to his swing path with a Trackman and his burly 6'4" coach Andrew Getson. A drone occasionally hovered on the ground in front of Mickelson as Sia's "Cheap Thrills" blared over the loudspeakers, a perfectly ironic song ahead of the most expensive tournament in the history of this sport. *Baby, I don't need dollar bills to have fun tonight.*

Richard Marsh, the main negotiator I had met Tuesday night, stood about 30 feet behind Mickelson and chatted with his manager, Peter Davis. Marsh excitedly shared the newest LIV hype video, which had just gone live on Twitter. It was named "Evolution" and was paired with a starring voiceover by Dennis Quaid. Everything was moving very quickly now. LIV's tentacles had extended all the way to the father from *The Parent Trap*.

"Evolution can be uncomfortable," Quaid said at the end of the two-minute clip, "but we love this crazy game enough to try. So join us, because the future we see is bright. The future of *golf* is here."

I had been standing close enough to hear Marsh and Davis chatting about the format of the team championship scheduled for later in the year at Trump Doral. That was 4,500 miles and 142 days from now, but if money were truly no issue, there was no doubt we'd get there. I was clearly standing too close, because in a matter of moments I was ushered by security to the other end of the range. All that did was position me perfectly for the silliest scoop of the week. Mickelson completed his initial warm-up around noon and began his march to the putting green, right past where I stood. Sewn neatly in grey thread on his black vest was another logo: Augusta National's. The three-time Masters champion had shown up wearing the most recognizable golf logo on the planet on the day he was publicly stiff-arming the PGA Tour. When he packed his suitcase from San Diego, this was the one vest he chose? And when he woke up that morning for the first round of the rest of his life, he never stopped to consider the message he was sending? I could barely believe it. I snapped a photo and raced back to my laptop to pull the file from my camera.

Golf fans searching Twitter back in the States found it to be extremely entertaining breakfast fodder. An hour later, I received a text from a communications director at Augusta National: "Enjoying your trip???" We had clearly struck a nerve.

ANGC is veiled in almost everything it does, but hearing from them on this day was no coincidence. When I gave a purposefully vague answer, a more focused response arrived: "Keep me posted on any outfit changes by Phil."

Noted! (But also: Don't kill the messenger.)

It's an extremely esoteric thing, but it takes a special level of DGAF to slap an ANGC logo on the space that other brands in golf were sprinting away from. But that's where we were in the waning hours before LIV Golf's first tee shots, and it became a theme of the day— extremely odd, maybe purposeful posturing.

Mickelson held the benefit of playing from the 1st tee in this experimental golf event. LIV's invitationals were shotgun starts, where every player begins at the same time, just on different holes, at the theoretical sound of a shotgun. This is common for CEOs in pro-ams or for your grandpa at his club's member-guest, but not in professional tournaments. LIV promised it was for a good reason—everyone playing at once meant the entire field would have the same playing conditions. No one could bitch about playing during a chilly, windy morning while the sun came out for the other half of the field in the afternoon. All that meant for the 45 players not in Mickelson's group was they'd be starting elsewhere. Some poor soul was going to have to leave the practice range and travel a couple miles just to get to their starting position. This is hardly the wackiest aspect of LIV, but imagine Steph Curry being yanked from warm-ups just to take a lap around the arena right before tip-off.

The first poor soul was Ian Snyman, the 386th-ranked player in the world, who strolled off the range and into a nearby roundabout 37 minutes before his tee time. That's where LIV had staged 25 London Black Cabs they hired for the week as an ode to England's capital city. All the cabbies had to do was pledge their availability and slap a "Don't Blink" decal on their vehicle and they'd be paid much better than if they were driving around the Big Smoke all week. These drivers had it *good*, and they knew it. They showed up Tuesday for their first test drive through the grounds. They performed another run-through on Wednesday and were grinning as a group when I asked about their duties. During tournament days, all they had to do was drop players off at their starting holes and pick them up five hours later. They had complete freedom to do whatever they pleased in between. "It's like we're on holiday," one told me.

Hundreds of fans had packed in around the 1st tee. The music thumped even louder now. The electropop hit by Zedd and Selena Gomez bellowed out of every speaker on property: *I want you to know, that it's our time.* Dustin Johnson meandered quite anonymously through the crowd and ducked under the ropes onto the 1st tee. Scott

Vincent did the same. Mickelson was treated the way almost all champions are when returning from controversy—with the loudest ovation yet. He and DJ were interviewed on the 1st tee. Vincent was not. Greg Norman was, of course. This was his show, and the Shark was welcomed like the founder of a Silicon Valley startup who just received Series B funding. (In many ways, he had.) Another extravagance appeared above him—nine prop planes from 50 miles north had made their way to Centurion, hired by LIV to circle the grounds and commemorate the occasion. While that expenditure tore up the sky, a more flamboyant one traipsed around at sea level. LIV had also hired the London Fanfares, a marching band of trumpeters who "celebrate the Best of British Pageantry" by dressing like the Queen's Guard with bright red tunics and obnoxious black bearskin hats.

The Fanfares website hails their product as "the most impressive way of drawing your guests' attention to your function's key moments." The first tee shots in LIV's history felt like a key moment. So the Fanfares played their 14-note ballad, nicknamed "Flourish 2" on their song sheets. "This is historic," one fan whispered to his buddies. "It feels like we're watching something big." I had to agree. Johnson stuck a tee in the ground and ripped a 3-wood over the corner. Vincent took iron next. Then Mickelson swung long and loose on a driver up over the corner of the trees. LIV Golf was off, and if you weren't distracted by the "British Pageantry," you'd think you were watching any old golf tournament. For a few minutes, at least.

There were typical white nylon ropes lining each hole, held up by thin metal poles. This is the standard. The only problem was there were only a few marshals to manage them. Of all the things LIV had indulged on, they overlooked the number of volunteers it takes to calmly keep humans on one side of a thin strip of nylon. They had spent so much time convincing people to be amped up that they didn't totally prepare for the moment when they would be.

By the time a crew of media members sauntered up to Vincent's place in the fairway, a couple dozen spectators had slipped under the ropes and blended in alongside LIV execs and TV cameramen. They walked around phone-first like a group of 14-year-olds at the mall. It reminded me of the draft from Tuesday, when heads turned and phones were thrust upward as Mickelson walked by. People were feeling some weird sense of privilege to be there seeing sporting history of the most bizarre kind. They wanted to capture it. The panicked face of Mickelson's security detail said it all. This could not be good. But also, could it? It may have been impossible to avoid the thought of who was bankrolling this event, but I was having fun with the novelty of it. The same thought from the draft party kept rising in my head—if I had been comatose for the last two years and woken up right here in the middle of the fairway as reigning PGA Champion Phil Mickelson flipped a wedge inside 15 feet while ticketholders roamed wherever they pleased, I would have thought, *Okay, Golf! At least somebody is trying to inject some fun into this sport.* Perhaps I had grown a bit bored by the staid PGA Tour product safeguarded by executives in Ponte Vedra Beach, Florida.

PGA Tour HQ was well aware of the proceedings. Right around the moment Mickelson had tapped in for an opening par, the 17 players in the field with Tour membership status of any kind were suspended by Tour commissioner Jay Monahan. The reason: they had played in an event held at the same time as a PGA Tour event without earning a conflicting event release form from the Tour. This was how the PGA Tour had long maintained profitable media rights for its collective of about 250 members. If you can promise TV networks and event sponsors that *your* product will be the premier product that week, your product is automatically worth more. If you allow players to move about freely on and off your tour, your product is automatically worth less. Knowing that this day was coming, Mohanan and the PGA Tour refused to grant conflicting event releases to the players who had applied, and once any of them hit a single shot on the LIV tour, suspensions were in their inboxes. Monahan sent notice to those players and their representation, but he also sent a note to his entire membership who stayed "loyal."

"These players have made their choice for their own financial-based reasons. But they can't demand the same PGA Tour membership benefits, considerations, opportunities, and platform as you. That expectation disrespects you, our fans, and our partners…

"I am certain our fans and partners—who are surely tired of all this talk of money, money, and more money—will continue to be entertained and compelled by the world-class competition you display each and every week, where there are true consequences for every shot you take and your rightful place in history whenever you reach that elusive winner's circle."

I stood about 20 feet from Mickelson as I read Monahan's letter. Phil had no idea it had happened, but he had to know it was coming. Phones began buzzing across the property, and you could hear fans along the rope lines discussing the hammer that had been struck down. I ask you, reader: Do you know how many players have *ever* been suspended by the PGA Tour? This is the sporting league that goes by the nickname "the Class Acts Tour" for how proper, traditional, and polite everything is. Dustin Johnson failed a drug test for cocaine in 2014 and the Tour went so far as to deny the reports of his suspension, calling it strictly a "voluntary leave of absence"—the kind of leave you take when you know you're going to be suspended anyway. Mickelson's leave felt similar in hindsight. Without diving into the history books, just know the PGA Tour does *not* do suspensions well, nor does it do them often. But in a matter of minutes after LIV golfers hit their tee shots, their Tour careers had been effectively frozen. And with another 4.5 hours of absolute bliss ahead of them on the course, this quickly became the weirdest golf round of 2022.

The brilliance of a shotgun start is, for reporters at least, completely undone by the shotgun finish of 48 players all returning to the scoring tent at the same time. We wanted to ask every single one of them their thoughts about a suspension, but LIV players were all over the map. Lee Westwood posted up by the scorer's tent and could barely be bothered to care. "You know, no longer a member of the PGA Tour, so why would they be worried about me? I've resigned."

Fair enough. Graeme McDowell stood at the podium a couple hundred feet from him and admitted that he expected the suspension and had resigned his membership about 30 minutes prior to teeing off. It was "an abundance of caution" that would put him "in a less litigious situation" moving forward. Everyone knew what was coming down the pike for LIV Golf and the PGA Tour: a lawsuit or two or four. Standing 30 feet away from McDowell, Ian Poulter held court with the European press. "You know when you feel you haven't done anything wrong and you feel you want to promote the game of golf for what the game of golf really is? Yeah, I would be incredibly disappointed if it turns out that way."

He then left us with one ominous thought: "I would appeal, for sure."

Recapping the day for GOLF.com was a delicate exercise. What was real and what was strategic bluster? The suspensions and overall lack of concern from the players. The threat of lawsuits and tactical resignations. This wasn't exactly chess. It was more like *watching* chess. Thinking you know what each side was silently thinking. The fact that Mickelson changed to a new vest *without* the Augusta logo a couple holes into his round. Was that purposeful? Sergio García was pleading for us to understand how important family time was. But was it so important he needed to surrender his PGA and European Tour careers for it? It was still too early to judge what was truth and what might be lies, but LIV wanted to move forward. From our desks you could feel the thumping beats of a James Bay concert kicking off in the Fan Village.

With every passing day, LIV gained momentum. More fans arrived on Friday than Thursday and then even more on Saturday. No one really seemed to care who was winning. Slugger White managed his way through LIV's first rules dispute with a gentle touch. White had retired in early August at 71 years old but was wooed into Norman's league just three months later. "I didn't want to do nothing [in retirement]," he told me. "Did I want to do this again? I don't know. I kind of got tired of chasing rental cars and airplanes, but with the schedule—it's a great schedule. We've only got eight events this year, but it's not week after week after week without a week off. It's been good." With the right offer, you can pull an old man back to work.

The biggest crowds followed the most popular players, no matter the fact that Johnson and Mickelson were getting waxed by Charl Schwartzel, who hadn't won a tournament in six years. Three more PGA Tour members—Bryson DeChambeau, Patrick Reed, and Pat Perez—each popular in their own, polarizing ways, phoned in to the broadcast to pledge their commitment to LIV's next event. The plan was for DeChambeau and Reed to announce their commitments jointly, I was told by a LIV staffer, but the latter requested to be announced solo.

As the weekend progressed, I became increasingly fascinated by Norman's role. He wasn't doing any press. LIV was purposefully helping him recede to the background. When LIV's golfers were suspended by the Tour, the response came in a generic statement from the league, not from Norman himself. And yet, each day he made himself more visible on-site. He made a point to be on the 3rd tee with Mickelson and Johnson on Day 2, promising fans, "I've gotta see my guys off." He joked with DJ about how Dustin could become assistant commissioner, but added, "We don't wear suit and ties. No jacket, no ties at LIV." Before the final round, I followed Norman around the 1st tee as he did everything a campaigning politician does—pressing flesh, posing for photos, swooning volunteers and fans and even his own wife. He pulled Kirsten in for a look at the tablet technology LIV used to track live player locations during play.

"They don't do this at other tournaments?" she asked.

"Oh, no," Norman replied, shaking his head. Augusta National and the PGA Tour would beg to differ. But Kirsten was impressed.

"Don't you want to be competing?" a volunteer asked Norman.

"Yes, of course I want to be competing!" the 67-year-old said, referencing the $25 million prize fund.

You couldn't blame Norman for being so boastful. He had dreamed about this moment. Not a soul on property was going to fact-check him. Instead, spectators treated him like the disruptive leader he believed he was, lurching over each other to snap selfies as Shark and his security detail forged through the crowd. I tailed Norman with my inside-the-ropes badge as he ducked onto the quiet driving range and cruised by Club 54. I wanted to see if perhaps he'd have time for just two questions, now that his dreams had become some sort of golf dystopian reality. But I never got close enough, and was halted when I saw a lone golfer still hitting balls in the center of the range. If every player was supposed to be on the course starting at the same time, who was this kid?

His name was Shergo al Kurdi, an 18-year-old Jordanian pro with the Golf Saudi logo stitched into the front of his hat. He was the 1,751st-ranked player in the world, but LIV had snatched him up as their first reserve. He'd be treated like anyone else in the field—all travel expenses were paid for player, caddie, family, etc.—but would only compete in the event of emergency. He was technically *in* the field until Mickelson committed at the 11th hour.

"I don't care what [Mickelson] said—you know, scary motherfuckers," his father, Musa al Kurdi, told me. "People make mistakes. When a legend like that arrives, you stand down."

Musa stood watch, arms crossed as his son grinded. They had come a long way in this game, even if Shergo was still just a teenager. Father caddied for son a lot of the time, his tanned skin and grey hair indicating many days in the sun. Shergo was doing everything he was supposed to do. He took the invite from LIV and acted like a pro's pro, practicing for every hour that the competition was taking place. His dad beamed with pride. Shergo was already the best golfer from Jordan and the first from the Middle East to make a cut on the DP World Tour. When Shergo was just 16, he had become the first Middle Eastern golfer to earn world ranking points. LIV officials told him he'd be in the field in Portland, no problem. Just come along for the ride. His swing was strong, succinct, and pure. It looked like Rory McIlroy's, partly because Shergo's frame was similar, maybe an inch taller. But Shergo's idol was DeChambeau. They had met at the 2021 Saudi International, when Al Kurdi earned an invite as an "international rising star" and DeChambeau earned an appearance fee as a top-10 player on the planet. DeChambeau took a liking to Al Kurdi and offered some speed-training lessons, helping boost his ball speed from 173 mph to 180 in just 10 minutes. Musa's thoughts on Bryson: "There isn't an ounce of arrogance in him."

Musa's thoughts on LIV were similarly stilted. At one point he saw a little too much pessimism in my eyes and squared up to me, tapping me on the arm as he made his points. Clearly, I needed convincing. "You *gotta* admit, this is cool," Musa said. "This is pretty cool."

And like the boastful Norman, why shouldn't he feel this way? The event that his son met his idol at—which led to various texts and DMs between the two—was sponsored by the Saudi PIF. This LIV event, of course, was funded extravagantly by the PIF. Their flights from England to Portland in a few weeks would be paid for by LIV, which is completely funded by the PIF. If Shergo could just stay in the field—and not get bumped out by additional LIV commits from the PGA Tour—he would receive $120,000 at worst. That was the last-place share of the record purses and more money than he had made in his entire career.

It took a while for me to focus on anything other than that image of father and son on the driving range. The tentacles of LIV Golf were extending much further than just this tournament. Much further than I think anyone properly understood. They had invested $300 million into the Asian tour and were creating feeder invitationals that could eventually graduate players to the Megabucks tour. If there was money to be had and places in the field, some pros somewhere were going to pounce on it. Even if it meant flying across the world to western Oregon to simply hit more balls on the range in front of Dad.

After 10 minutes I let the Al Kurdis be and retreated to the media center to watch what was ultimately a Charl Schwartzel coronation. He led by three after 36 holes and never relinquished on the final day, earning an absurd $4.75 million in the process—more money than he had made in the previous four years. (Feel free to think about your own annual salary and earning *four times that* for a week when you felt on top of your game. It must be nice!) Hennie Du Plessis, the fourth and forgotten man of the Stingers, doubled his career earnings when he finished second. Branden Grace, yet another Stingers member, tied for third.

In the moments immediately after Schwartzel's win, it was Grace who raced around the 18th hole in pure jubilation. He hugged teammates, their caddies, LIV staffers, and friends and family. Everyone affiliated with the new league was there on the 18th fairway. Together they had reached a checkpoint where they could finally let loose and breathe. Grace saved the biggest bearhug for Marsh, who had helped recruit him to riches he had never experienced before. (He had just won $2.025 million.) Grace was pulled up on stage for the closing ceremony and handed a massive bottle of champagne, the contents of which would soon be in the air. Also on stage was Norman, triumphantly bellowing out to the fans, "Over the years, for 27 years, there's been a lot of obstacles put in our path. There's been a lot of dreams that have been tried to be squashed. But they couldn't squash us."

The loudest quote of the night came when Al-Rumayyan grabbed the mic and told the crowd that a perfect score of golf—one round of 18-under par—was 54 strokes. If any LIV golfer ever carded a 54, Al-Rumayyan would add a preposterous $54 million bonus to their winnings. That got exactly the rise out of the crowd that he hoped for. And hey, I chuckled, too, if only because I knew this was akin to Quicken Loans promising $1 billion to whoever can fill out a perfect bracket during March Madness. No one is shooting 54. It's not going to happen. But for a few moments everyone visualized Al-Rumayyan signing a life-size cardboard check for $54,000,000.

This was the way this week should always end—the perfect Rorschach test. However you viewed the money and the distribution of it—particularly the seeding of it—was how you tended to see LIV Golf. On one hand, it was making a 10-figure investment into the sport. On the other, the intentions seemed mischievous. Players were benefitting, no doubt. Saudi Arabia was benefitting, one would think, by association. But golf fans had just watched the status quo be splintered in two. There's a reason the XFL crashed when it tried to offer *more* football. There's a reason why conference realignment tears at the hearts of college sports fans. Change comes quickly, and it doesn't often leave a good taste in everyone's mouth. But hey, the players were getting Paid—capital *P*—and a very common refrain began circling everywhere in golf: Wouldn't *you* take the money? LIV's schedule would unleash $255 million over eight events, and they already had hopes for 10 events in 2023, then 14 events in 2024. Players had been instructed to keep contract details private, but in an honest moment Dustin Johnson leaned in to share with me that his deal was for four years. LIV was not going away.

About a half hour after the Stingers doused each other with champagne, they sat in front of the press one final time, smiling and sticky. Schwartzel was asked about earning such a fantastic paycheck but from such a controversial employer. For the first time, players were informed that families of 9/11 victims had begun planning protests of the league. Fifteen of the hijackers on 9/11 hailed from Saudi Arabia. Schwartzel sat and considered the question for a heavy eight seconds.

I have never, uhm, ahhh—

Where the money comes from is not something that I, ah, uhm, have ever looked at playing in my 20-years career, you know. I think if I start digging everywhere where we played, uhm, you could find fault in anything.

Yeah, I—you know, it's a question there that's just hard for me to answer it because it's really rhetorical at the end. We can argue this all day long.

I earned about four hours of sleep Sunday morning after filing my story at 2:30 AM. As I waited for the train back to St. Andrews, I did what any competitive journalist would do: read the work everyone else had written. It's a dangerous game that often leads to imposter syndrome but seems worth playing in the name of improvement.

My search began and ended with Kevin Van Valkenburg, a senior writer for ESPN. We spent a couple evenings together that week desperately searching for anyone willing to take our per diems. Work ended late and most every pub closed at midnight, so we probably spent more time walking from one CLOSED sign to the next than we did actually drinking beer. But it was those convos that served as inspiration for this very book. For the first and probably last time in my life, a waiter showed me a slab of cold, raw meat *before* it was cooked, asking for my approval like they do with the first pour of bottle of wine. (Thank you, Wright Thompson, for the recommendation of Macellaio—aka The Butcher's Theater.)

KVV is a former journalism professor and an award-winning sportswriter. An hour or two talking shop with him will make you a better writer. Probably a better person, too. Then you read his work and acknowledge that maybe you were better off in those innocent moments before doing so, because the sportswriting competition wasn't so much a competition at all. I had covered LIV Golf's inaugural event exhaustively—my eyes were red and dry from the pollen and lack of sleep. I did a damn good job, too. My bosses were happy, which made me happy. But I was exclusively focused on the grounds of Centurion Club. KVV looked elsewhere.

He talked with Lina Al-Hathloul, whose sister, Loujain, was an activist who had long campaigned for improving women's rights in

Saudi Arabia. Loujain advocated for an end to the male guardianship laws that required a man—often a woman's father or husband—to determine when and how women could do simple things like drive, travel, or get married. Her efforts caught hold and inspired others to call for changes to Saudi law, and eventually, women over the age of 21 were allowed to travel without the permission of men. These changes were sworn in in 2019 and championed across the country, but only after Loujain and other activists had been captured by Saudi officials in 2018 and charged with terrorism in 2020. She was imprisoned for nearly three years and reportedly tortured throughout. KVV spoke with her sister within one year of Loujain being set "free." In this case, Saudi officials ruled that "free" means a personal travel ban and sanctions against speaking with media.

She has nothing to do with golf but everything to do with Saudi Arabia's public image. LIV was obvious connective tissue, Lina argued, between those two things. "It's gross. It's inhumane," Lina told KVV. "It removes all the humanity of Saudi people. It's really used as a façade for the regime to pretend like they're opening up. I don't want to say it's about sports. It's about the use of sports. You're basically using famous people to cover up what is happening in the country, to pretend that they're having reform. It's about players repeating the narrative of criminals."

KVV spoke with Lina, who now lives in Brussels, exclusively on an encrypted messaging service because she feared being tracked and kidnapped herself. Capturing this reality, the other side of the coin, felt vital to understanding the messaging of pro golfers. When they used phrases like "growing the game" on a platform made possible by ruinous people, what did it say about everyone involved? Myself, spectators, capitalism, Bryson DeChambeau. It was the kind of reporting that demands readers look through a 30,000-foot lens. And it was a sound reminder for myself: you can only spend so much time focusing on what's directly in front of you.

I picked up my reporting pride with a vanilla latte and hopped on a train at Kings Cross for a charming, six-hour journey back to St. Andrews. The route rips through blue-collar English towns and flashes by the locales that Americans recognize from the names of English football clubs. Peterborough, York, Newcastle. That last one was a sweet connector for the week, too. Newcastle United Football Club was purchased by the Saudi PIF in October. Both Majed Al-Sorour and Yasir Al-Rumayyan became directors of the 140-year-old football club instantly. No questions asked. The club had gone winless in its first 14 matches of the season but has ascended like no other club in English football since, earning their way into the Champions League. Money goes a long way in sports uncapped by salary restrictions. There was no such restriction in golf.

With billions of dollars to play with, you can buy so many things. You can buy Phil Mickelson. You can buy Dustin Johnson. You can buy all the accoutrements needed for historic photos and the hype videos voiced over by a golf-nut actor from Texas. You can buy broadcaster Arlo White away from working in soccer and convince him to cover a sport he's never worked in before. You can buy a three-night mini concert series and the rights to a rich man's golf course for a week. You can buy a platform on which Saudi leaders can thump their chests and make outlandish promises about perfect golf rounds.

You can buy your way into headlines and thus the public conscience, though you have no control over what the headlines actually say. You can buy the curiosity of fans, but only at first. You can buy the future of Bryson DeChambeau and Patrick Reed, but you can't buy an exciting finish. Golf doesn't work that way. The money can't urge magical ballstriking from Sergio García or a torrent of birdies from Talor Gooch. Money goes a long way and yet it only goes so far. Far enough to show that this sport could be bought, and not necessarily with the cleanest intentions. Which only meant that golf itself was now, in a way, up for grabs. The overwrought clause that PGA Tour stars long used so they could be choosy with their schedule—calling themselves "independent contractors"—was finally being taken dangerously seriously. LIV Golf had some contracting work for these golfers to do, and step one was reneging their contracts with the status quo.

I don't know why I felt compelled to do this, but during the train ride I sent an email to an agent who reps some of the biggest players in the game. "Avoiding LIV feels like 1000% the proper move," I said. Why? It all just felt...dirty. It felt shortsighted. It felt like a dangerous alliance to slide into, regardless of the money. Reputations were at stake.

The agent, of course, was very interested. So were some of the biggest coaches in the game. One of the most famous coaches on the planet slid into my DMs looking for a rundown on everything I had seen. Photographers, Tour pros, caddies—everyone wanted to know how it might impact them when LIV would make landfall in the States. That was just two days away now, at the U.S. Open at Brookline, just outside of Boston. If Mickelson and gang weren't already on their way to Massachusetts, they would be soon. I needed a cigarette, as they say, which for me was just a run. I needed a run. I dropped my bags on Allan Robertson Drive and set out for the landmark in town I knew best. Two miles to the West Sands Beach, a cooldown walk on the sand, a peek at the Himalayas putting course, and then 1.5 miles back home. All may not have been well in the golf world, but all was well at the Home of Golf. I leapt over the Swilcan Burn that day, just not as smoothly as the TikTokers from the week before. You're really not supposed to do that. (It's quite the long jump, anyway.) The folks at the Links Trust aren't keen for it. But it was a weekend where rules were being broken all over, I told myself.

Chapter 7

Course Corrections

"Have yee found yourself a pretty young British lady yet," my high school friend Isaac texted. I hadn't, but I knew why he was asking.

I couldn't help but notice a trend in the days before I left for this trip—almost everyone I talked to forecasted that I would fall in love. And rather ominously, I'd say. *You'll meet some girl over there and never come back* was the common refrain at weddings, over FaceTime, even during my 30th birthday. My ongoing five-plus years of singledom was apparent to all. Europe, they figured, might cure my pickiness.

Isaac was prying for an update. And the truth was I actually had made an honest attempt one morning at the Cottage Kitchen, a charming restaurant in the center of town. With its wood flooring and squeaky front door, it certainly feels like you're dining in someone's cottage. They might make the best brunch in St. Andrews, and it would rank even higher were it not for the slowest service in all of Scotland. On this day, I could look past it because one worker in particular was by far the loveliest I had seen in my time as a resident. She was brunette and moved about in an unassuming and more hurried manner than her coworkers. If there was going to be a love story for me in St. Andrews, perhaps she could be on the other end of it. I waited and waited for her tardy colleague to come take my money, rehearsing a sequence of obscure lines in my head, building confidence that *now* was the time. As one Scot told me, if you're in St. Andrews, you're either a golfer, a student, or a senior. I may not cross paths with another one like her all summer.

It had taken all of 60 seconds to swipe through the entire lot of Hinge accounts in town. There weren't going to be many women in St. Andrews who 1. Were my age, 2. Caught my eye, and 3. Were predisposed to actually talk to me. She checked all three boxes, including the last one because, well, I still needed to pay. I decided I couldn't stew any longer and strode up to the desk. She turned away from the dishwasher and toward me just as I reached the counter.

"Can I, uh, pay here?" I said, extending my receipt forward.

She smiled, nodded, and began tapping my order into the system. Two scones and two lattes came out to £13.

"So, uh, weird question," I began. "Do people use dating apps here?"

Why not launch right into it? I could innocently indicate my status, and her response might even hint at hers, too. If she rattled off three apps she uses, bingo! If she pulled out her phone to reference them, even better! Regardless of her response, it would pave the way for my intended follow-up: *How weird would it be for a customer to skip the swiping and just ask you out here?*

"Oh, yeah," she said, giving me a quick once over. "There's a bunch of them. But there's not that many people that live here."

Uh yeah, I know.

"Okay, but like, which of the apps is most popular?" I pressed. "In the States, most people use Hinge or Bu—"

Wham. Just as I had pulled a credit card from my wallet, the waitress who had been oh so delinquent in serving me suddenly reappeared at the worst possible time.

"Dating apps?" She said, barging behind the register and elbowing my brunette queen back toward the dishwasher. There was barely enough room for one person behind the counter, let alone two, and she had positioned herself directly in front of me. This was her conversation now.

"Yeah, there's a handful," she continued, snagging the card reader and grabbing my Visa. "Plenty of Fish is one."

There were *not* plenty of fish in St. Andrews' sea, and her dominating presence was forcing me to cut bait. The barista I wanted to talk to was directed to clear the un-bussed tables in the back room.

"I, uhm, well I'm just new here and was curious. About, uh, what the dating scene is like. I know it's kinda, uh, graduation season."

Uh, uh, uh. *Get it together, Sean! You sound like Mickelson at his LIV presser.* She spun the card reader back to me and I tipped 20 percent because that's what Americans do. She didn't deserve it, but I was clearly shook by the sequence of events and left as quickly as possible. Operation: Woo Cottage Kitchen Brunette had failed miserably.

Impromptu dating fail aside, this was the typical morning of my St. Andrews lifestyle, and I absolutely loved it. I was in the Cottage Kitchen because to learn the cafes is to learn St. Andrews. I woke up each day, shunned the convection stove Lorraine had provided, and picked a new cafe on the map. To access them, you have to maneuver the cobbled streets and pass through quiet university quads. You squeeze down the wynds and keep your eyes peeled for hungry seagulls circling above. The cafes became cornerstones in my mental map of town.

There's the Northpoint on North St., which, according to the phrase etched into the window, is "Where Kate met Wills (for coffee)." As in Kate "Catherine" Middleton and William, heir to the British throne. The owners are not shy about the fact that a corner of the royal family tree took root in their shop. There's Taste, the student favorite, which is so small (about 400 square feet) that patrons are asked to wait outside as the coffee is brewed. There's Con Panna, which serves its lattes in tall, skinny glassware more fitting for vanilla shakes. Down the street is Munch, where construction workers wait patiently every morning for bacon rolls, a U.K. delicacy as simple as it sounds: bacon, on a roll. I preferred mine plain, though locals soak theirs in brown sauce (a tomato-based molasses and spice concoction). In the center of it all is the Cottage Kitchen and across Logies Lane its quieter sister, Cafe in the Square, which specializes in scones. Not the dry, stone-like kind you strain to break apart. The type of scone that's big as a grapefruit, warm from the oven, and covered in powdered sugar.

With the GOLF.com staff expected to work East Coast hours, my mornings became my weekends. That's when I would make a pit stop at the walk-up window at Gorgeous, grab a raspberry scone, and head out to explore campus, snap photos of colorful doors, hike along the coast to Maiden Rock, or watch the local soccer teams practice. My sleep-tracking device wasn't a big fan of the schedule, but my mind found it relaxing. I was satisfied opening my laptop in the afternoon once I had actually *done* something that morning. And around 9 PM, when the workday was done, I was done. Mentally spent. Ready to dream it away and then go someplace new when the seagulls woke me.

"Something is different, Sean," my coworker Claire Rogers said over FaceTime. "You seem so...happy."

I was happy. I felt like I had cheated the system and crafted the European fantasy world so many Americans dream about. But just as I started getting comfortable, my summer hit a snag. I had lived out a lovely Tuesday in mid-June and was about the shut the laptop for the night when…

INBOX (1)

9:47 PM—Subject line: Jim Bashleben Passes Away

Sean,

You may have heard by now, but the great Jim Bashleben passed away yesterday. I know you are a friend of his as am I. It was sudden and painless, and I don't really know much more than that right now. Started having some dizzy spells and such about three weeks ago. I was looking forward to a round with him next week at Colorado Golf Club … I wish us all the happiness Bash found and shared with us.

I hadn't heard. I was alone in my little condo and overcome with disbelief. *Whatttt?* One of my favorite golfers in the world had died at 74 of sudden cardiac arrest. One month before his 50th wedding anniversary.

That the news arrived via email made it even more staggering. We cloak ourselves in a security blanket when we're at work. That tiny red notification bubble pops up and there is rarely any alarm. For me, it might be a mindless work assignment or the photos we'll choose from for the cover story. Not an industry acquaintance emailing about a death in my golf family. How do you shut the laptop and sleep after that? You don't. I stared into the corner of my bedroom for most of an hour. For the first time, St. Andrews felt extremely far from home.

For a 30-year-old I had spent too much time thinking about death. It always seems to arrive right when life begins to feel simple, as though it's some binding course correction toward neutral. I fidgeted anxiously over the idea on my flight across the pond. *What would I do if, say, my best friend's mother died while I was golf-gallivanting in the U.K.?* I was being selfish, hopeful nothing would interrupt the summer of my dreams. And when that plane landed in Scotland, Jim Bashleben was one of the first people to text me.

"Loved your comment today," he wrote. It was about LIV.

"Lots of $$, DJ, but maybe limited options in the future. With enough $$, maybe he doesn't care.

Hope you're well and enjoying your remote digs.

Bash"

It took me five days to respond because, well, communication can be a weakness of mine. When I finally did, it took him just two minutes to reply because, well, communication was a strength of his.

"Beautiful spot, great courses," he said. "Enjoy your stay."

We met in 2008 at Horseshoe Bay Golf Club in Egg Harbor, Wisconsin. I was the 16-year-old, shaggy-haired kid running around as a bag boy. Minimum wage, plus tips. Bash was the 60-year-old early retiree, playing golf in the afternoons with his friends and watching the sun set over the lake with his wife, Debi, in the evenings. Truly living his best life.

Bag boys hustled around like Santa's elves to make sure everything was *just so* for the membership. We valeted their cars, addressed them exclusively by last name, carried and cleaned their clubs, looked after their grandchildren, shined their shoes, tossed away their trash— whatever could keep them from lifting a finger. They had paid tens of thousands of dollars (and sometimes much more) for their memberships, so some felt entitled to that Plaza Hotel pampering. Bash didn't want it. The best members don't care for it. He didn't want to be called *Mister Bashleben*. Just *Bash*. He didn't want us sprinting around to clear the putting green of golf balls left behind. He'd rather we hang out and chat so he could pepper us with questions. What we wanted to major in. Where we wanted to go for college. What our career goals were. Where our girlfriends worked for their summer jobs. Bash gained happiness from communicating with those around him. In that way, he was destined to love this game, which plants you next to friends and family and strangers for hours at a time. When the local newspaper showed up to write a story about the club, he was the member they interviewed. No one was surprised.

Rather than sleep, I dove back into the archives of my texts with Bash. He was the rare friend who was in my life *exclusively* because of golf. Were it not for golf, we would have never met. It was how we stayed in touch—him thinking he was keeping tabs on *me*, the world-traveling writer, but really it was golf that helped me keep tabs on him. He was the marshal at the Solheim Cup and the one rubbing elbows with Bryson DeChambeau when they shared the same physio. When

Covid struck, Bash was on the tail end of a buddies' trip across New Zealand—a once-in-a-lifetime boondoggle for him, his friends, and their wives. But he and Debi were in their seventies and particularly susceptible to the coronavirus. They just wanted to get home, drop the bags on the floor, and lock the door behind them, but it was actually safer to stay abroad. So they rented a villa on a golf course and played every single day. He took life in stride.

After the Bashes left Wisconsin to be closer to their grandchildren in Colorado, Bash quickly invited me and two other former bag boys to visit his new stomping grounds—Colorado Golf Club. "Meals, golf, and accommodations are covered," he said. "Just tip your caddies." He rolled out a 54-hole red carpet, ordered hats with "Caddie Bash 2018" embroidered on the back, and customized a head cover that would serve as the official Caddie Bash trophy. He wasn't competing, just officiating. Riding in the cart and catching up with his golf grandkids, asking the same questions he did a decade earlier. No other sport does it better—that generational cross-pollination of ideas and stories and goals and insights. You often don't notice it until it's over. We didn't know how good we had it.

My first invite to play the Old Course arrived during the afternoon of that crushing email. "Fancy a game Thursday night on the Old? 6 PM?" went the text from Laurie Watson, the head of engagement at the St. Andrews Links Trust. I was getting my first crack at a Dark Time. When I set out for my one-mile trek across town, bag on my back, I texted the other members of Caddie Bash: "Teeing off on the Old Course in a half hour."

"Bash will be with you!" Nicky replied immediately. Nicky's a Bash-like communicator.

Nine days earlier I had written somewhere on GOLF.com that if the Golf Gods exist, they must hang out at the corner of Golf Place and The Links, the two roads that create the 90-degree corner of the Old Course's finishing hole. That's where Old Tom Morris grew up, filling his wheelbarrow with sand from the nearby beach to create slopes and fairway humps to challenge golfers back in the 1800s. It's where he died, too, just around the corner. If Bash had anywhere to look down from, it would probably be right here.

I met Laurie on the tee a couple minutes before 6, which is the only way to really do it. Driving range sesh—who needs it? Float down the same steps as Tiger Woods and Jack Nicklaus and millions of other golfers before you, stick your peg in the ground, uncork the stiffness in your body with a practice swing—just one practice swing, too—and take your lash at it. Laurie paired up with one of his longtime friends, Steve Moore, and I was teaming with Gary Payne, the new sports editor at *The Telegraph*. What media jobs lack in their year-end bonuses and lavish salary structure, they greatly make up for with perks.

St. Andrews' 1st hole runs alongside its 18th with nothing separating the two, creating what many call the widest fairway in the world. The second cut, on any side, is often pavement. People miss it, but you shouldn't, no matter how stiff you are. I damn near missed it on this day, tugging my driving iron into the far left corner, just short of the Swilcan Burn, the most perfect hazard in the world. It snakes all the way from the North Sea, rips across the edge of the 1st green, and then continues out of town two miles into the countryside, ending on random farmland. The entire way, the burn measures maybe 10 feet wide. Just broad enough to gobble up golf balls from any angle.

With about 140 yards left, downwind, I fatted a gap wedge—fluffed it into the air in such a way that I knew it was burn-bound. I looked down immediately, seeing a crater of turf much bigger than I intended. Then I looked back up to watch for an inevitable splash. But seemingly on command, a gust of wind grabbed my ball. The breeze altered its angle of descent as it fell, planting it on the short side of the crevice with a couple feet to spare. The concrete turf hadn't received much for rain and sent my ball back upward and over to the other side, safe and dry, on the edge of the green. I wasn't even sure I could trust my eyes, but I didn't bother taking a second glance. I was standing in the way of golfers playing the 18th so I grabbed my bag and hustled up to the green, not even mentioning the incident to the group. I two-putted for an opening par, no questions asked.

The pace was sluggish that night. Every group ahead of us seemed to be grinding out a score and also posing for an entire magazine photoshoot on the Swilcan Bridge. That comes with the territory. But that's why the Links Trust feels obligated to call those evening tee times the Dark Times. The only guarantee is you'll finish in darkness, searching for each other's golf balls. Hit and hope, I say. And listen. If you're lucky, it'll be a night of the gloaming, where the setting sun streaks across the landscape in such a way that, for about 30 minutes, 10 PM looks like noon. The entire course gets caked in a golden haze, reflecting extra light off the hotel windows. Then, as the sun bends over the horizon, the light lingers in the clouds. You can see it in photos, but it must be experienced in person to properly understand the meaning of Scottish summer. When the pace gets slow, a gloaming can carry dark times to a surprising finish. We just weren't very lucky. The only lights touching the course when we reached the 18th tee were the streetlamps up the right and the Old Course Pavilion along the left. It looked like a golfy fly trap with more overnight golfers buzzing around its halo. In between the lights was the R&A Clubhouse. Our line off the tee was the massive, roman-numeral clock on its exterior.

Laurie and Steve had closed Gary and me out on the 16th hole, so it was all pride at this point. A bogey 5 would keep my score from brimming into the 90s, decidedly not how I wanted to start my Old Course summer. I found my tee shot in the center-left side of the fairway about 80 yards from the hole, now facing the same wind that guided me over the burn 4.5 hours ago. A perfect, smooth sand wedge is all it would take. A dozen golf sickos were huddled near the steps off to the left of the green. I crunched it good. Like, *really* good. Maybe too good? I imagined the big blue shot-tracer you see on golf broadcasts painting a tidy draw from right to left. At the *worst* this thing was going to fly the hole by 10 yards and leave me a putt for birdie. *Hell yeah, give those spectators something to talk ab—* DONNNGGGKKK.

Whoa, what the hell was that?

Everyone within a half-mile would have heard it. The sound splintered the air conspicuously close to when my ball should have landed on the green. But it happened way over *there*, a full 30 yards to the left, over by the R&A clubhouse. The early platforms of Open Championship bleachers were being set up, and around them stood a ring of fencing.

"HEYOOOO," shouted the huddle of players standing at the edge of the clubhouse. Their reaction broke the calm of the night even further. I guess that *was* my golf ball. "Crunching" it apparently meant a pull-draw through the wind that flew the full sand wedge number. My ball landed in the center of the R&A parking lot.

It's one thing to nearly hit someone on the course, because you've hopefully forewarned them. It's another thing to send a pellet over their heads with no warning. It's another thing altogether to do it on the Old Course, nearly sniping the R&A clubhouse in the process. You only get so many chances to play this hole, and it's just begging for a birdie. Three hundred fifty-seven yards with the widest fairway in the world. You should be able to hit this green wearing a blindfold. I tucked my tail between my legs and walked toward the *DONGK*.

When I met them, they were surprisingly giddy, not normally the vibe of golfers who recently took on shrapnel. They were laughing because they had seen something absurd. The *DONGK* was my ball colliding with a steel pipe atop the construction fencing. During any other week, this shot might've ended up on Golf Place, bouncing across the street, right up to the front doors of the R&A Museum. But the way they described it, the ball moved with a purpose—something akin to Michael Jordan's fateful ace in *Space Jam*, controlled by Bugs

Bunny's super magnet. It caromed off the steel pipe, bounced between them, then kicked back in bounds via one of those famous stone steps. It might have hit the clubhouse, but they weren't sure. But just as they grasped what had happened, they caught sight of it rolling out onto the green, 20 feet from the hole. I whipped around to find Laurie bending over on the green.

"Callaway 2?" he called out. Callaway 2, indeed.

"You're super lucky," one of my new friends said. *Ya think?*

Two putts and about six apologies later, it was an early contender for sleaziest par of my summer—among the sleaziest of my life. But it helped polish off an 88 I'll think about forever. It wasn't until late that night, after beers with Laurie at the One Under Bar, that I fully appreciated the cyclical nature of my round. It began with an obnoxious gust that sent my ball skipping over the burn and ended with an equally despicable rebound from a parking lot. Two greens in regulation, two fours on the scorecard. Had our match still been alive, I'm not sure my conscience would have survived.

Sportswriting clichés bubbled up in my head once Laurie dropped me off that night. Endless ink has been spilled about teams of destiny, bound together in response to hardship. How else would we explain the whims of randomness here on Earth? It was hard to avoid the thought. Two of the most ridiculous bounces of my golfing life took place 300 yards from each other, one day before the course would close for The Open and just four days after Bash had passed. Right at the goofiest intersection on the planet. Like some sort of course correction back toward neutral, just when things were feeling bleak. Two pars that should have been double bogeys. Coincidence, surely. Unless it wasn't. I loved not knowing.

Chapter 8

Kitchen Gossip

Eavesdropping is an occupational asset in golf writing. You need good eyes to track the ball, but what you really need are good ears to understand the context around it. You can tell the difference between a perfect wedge and a 95 percent perfect one. Or between what upset Jordan Spieth looks like and what upset Jordan Spieth *sounds* like. When his tee ball on the 72nd hole of the 2018 Masters crashed into a tree branch, I leaned in as close as possible. He growled to Michael Greller, "You have *got* to be kidding me. That barely got past the ladies' tee." For that moment, it tells you *everything*.

Early on in Scotland I was doing a lot of eavesdropping. I didn't know many people in town. The only ones who recognized me were a bartender at the Dunvegan and the server at Munch who was becoming familiar with my bacon roll order. *No sauce, please.* I did a lot of silent observing, as though I were walking around a living, breathing museum. I learned that June wasn't just a transitional month for me, but for St. Andrews as well. It was flipping from college town to golf town. A mattress company was literally replacing old mattresses in St. Regulus Hall dormitory ahead of Open Week.

Over breakfast at the Northpoint Cafe, I tuned in as uneasy parents moaned about their children who forgot to secure tickets to the graduation ceremony. I listened as those same children gossiped about how strange it was to have parents on campus. It was all rather amusing as I felt equidistant in age from graduating-senior-years-old and being-a-parent-years-old.

The pandemic may have been waning, but the effects were still ever-present. Whereas in the States we read graduates' names over Zoom, the University of St. Andrews backlogged its ceremonies. During the second week of June, 2022 grads would be honored. A week after that, the graduates of 2021. And finally, the last week of June saw the Class of 2020 walk, many of them well adjusted to life in the real world. Their parents arrived in Fife to find the same thing golfers have long known—there are only so many beds in a two-square-mile town.

Toward the end of June, I was back at the Cottage Kitchen enjoying some fried eggs on sourdough, my favorite barista nowhere to be found. The CK's backyard is enclosed by stone and ripe for eavesdropping. My ears perked up when I heard two elderly gents ask a waitress if this was the last week of graduation.

"I think so," she replied, but then caught herself. "I hope so."

Locals were ready for graduation month to be over. St. Andrews runs on golf for much of the year but on university-adjacent commerce most of the other months. And when 40 to 45 percent of the student body hails from outside Scotland, it can create a simmering antipathy from the locals when their home is overrun by youths from abroad. They have a perfect name for this mini rivalry: Town vs. Gown.

The two men concerned with the end of graduation were catching up over coffee, but by their casual posture alone you could tell they were longtime friends. They quickly switched topics to pro golf, which brought a certain pep to their voices and perked my ears even more. They were thrilled to see Englishman Matthew Fitzpatrick triumph at the U.S. Open and were still spellbound by the approach he hit into the 18ᵗʰ green. When golf history was first being written, in the early 1900s, it was a big deal when a Brit would win in America, and vice versa. Telegrams were sent across the Atlantic mid-tournament to let traveling golfers know their friends back home were in their corner.

These coffee pals were equally as pleased that Rory McIlroy hung around to congratulate Fitz in person after his victory. McIlroy won the previous week and nearly played well enough to win at Brookline, too. But his win at the Canadian Open may have been more important, as McIlroy triumphed the same week as LIV's first event, dueling Justin Thomas and Tony Finau through to the 72ⁿᵈ hole, reminding the golf world who is king after all. It was the 21ˢᵗ victory of his Tour career, precisely one more than Greg Norman, which McIlroy made abundantly clear in the interview that followed.

"His wedges at the Canadian Open," one of the seniors said. "Agh. Amazen'."

"When he's in that freewheelen' mode, Jim, no one can touch him."

"Zalatoris is probably going to win sometime, eh?"

"Oh, aye. No two ways about it."

Back and forth they went, so avid they could have been podcasting. They referenced the grandstand that had been built along the 1ˢᵗ hole here in St. Andrews and how it was grander than any they had ever seen. They noted how far the parking lot would be from the 1ˢᵗ tee and how, during the Dunhill Links Championship in the fall, everything is just so much…*easier*. "I'm looking forwahr to it, but also looking forwahr to it being over," one of them said. I was crafting a column in my head about the lead-up to the event and deemed this private convo great fodder, as though I were some golfy version of *Gossip Girl*. I got up from my seat, slung my backpack over my shoulder, and prepared to ask a passing question as I left.

"You guys certainly know your golf," I said. "I heard you talking about Fitz and Rory."

"Oh, aye! Did ye watch? Where're ye from?"

I had grown used to hearing the second question. My Midwest accent preceded me wherever I went. I explained myself—job, hometown, curiosity about St. Andrews—and figured this was the time to ask for advice only locals could offer. The underappreciated course, the bar only residents frequent. The things Americans always look past when we're staring down the Old Course.

"Why don' you just sit down," they said, basically in unison. "Have a coffee."

Scottish people are different than English folks, who are different than Irish folks, but one rule of thumb tends to apply to all residents of these golf-savvy islands—if you're visiting from America, they're going to figure it out quickly, and they're going to want your story. They, in this instance, were Ronald Sandford and Jim Rait.

"I'd love to know what I'm *missing*," I said. "I just played the Castle Cou—"

Sandford cut me off. "The Cahstle—what a wasted opport-yew-nity. Cahstle Stuart is a three-hour drive, but I'd rather do that than play the Cahstle Course in town."

What a damning review! I'd played the Castle two days earlier and found it certainly challenging. But a wasted opportunity? It was the newest course in town, opening in 2008, and clearly the most polarizing. David McKlay Kidd was given the unenviable position of designing the seventh St. Andrews course and making it fit in among the others that had been there for centuries. DMK was given a perfect plot of land, elevated up on the hills out to the east, with perhaps the best view of town itself. Maybe that's what had Ronald so incensed. Tom Doak, one of the most famous course designers in the world, infamously gave the course a rating of 0 on a 10-point scale, signifying, in Doak's words, that the course was so contrived and unnatural that it may poison your mind. Unfair and rather unprofessional as that may have been from Doak, many locals agreed.

The premise of links golf is simple: you don't need to fly the ball to the hole from the air. In fact, if you do, it'll be rejected by firm turf into some treacherous spot off the green. Links golf is supposed to allow for running the ball up onto putting surfaces via the rigid soil. The ground game, they say. The Castle's turf certainly maintained the promise of firmness, but the slopes of the greens were so severe that good shots didn't seem to be rewarded properly—only great shots. This felt like a drier, harder, Scottish version of Whistling Straits, the popular course along Lake Michigan, which is already meant to be a derivative of what Scottish golf should be. From the perspective of a senior player like Ronald, who doesn't create as much loft, spin, or speed through the ball, this course probably isn't worth his time—especially around Fife. Ronald lives just south of town near Kingsbarns, one of the best courses in the entire country. His buddy Jim lives in Kilconquhar, a town about 11 miles south (pronunciation: not kill-conquer, rather, kin-yuck-er.) If a course in the area didn't suit these two, they had an endless list of others to choose from.

Ronald had more than three decades on me and Jim probably five, maybe six. His earliest golf memory was the 1946 Open at St. Andrews, when his father brought him down to the Old Course to watch Sam Snead triumph by four. Two under par was all it took. Jim couldn't believe his eyes, he told me, watching The Slammer in person. I couldn't believe my ears. The winner's prize was £150, the same price as my 75-minute shuttle ride from the airport.

"Young Tom [Morris] was like Arnold Palmer and Tiger Woods in one," Jim said, referring to Palmer's alluring sophistication and Woods' unmatched talent, which somehow earned him even *more* fans. There's no way for Rait to actually know Young Tom firsthand, but he had seen plenty of Palmer and Woods and had lived in Fife his entire life. Of all the counties in the world, this was the one in which golf eras can be properly compared. Morris family descendants are still present in town.

Our conversation continued this way for about 45 minutes—Jim and Ronald cluing me in to St. Andrews secrets. If you sneak into the cemetery, they said, look for the pearly white gravestone up against the wall. That's where both Young and Old Tom Morris are buried. If you want to find caddies, go drink at the Keys Bar. That's where Arnold Palmer's late caddie Tip Anderson frequented. They told me to research the Links Act of 1974, a landmark parliament ruling that granted control of the courses to the St. Andrews Links Trust. The bedrock of basically everything I'd see all summer.

As I finished my latte, Jim and Ronald morphed into overeager writing assistants, name-dropping everyone in town I needed to speak with. There's David Hamilton and Roger McStravick, both local golf historians. There's David Joy, an artist honored with illustrating every Open Champion's face for the Parade of Champions wall in the Old Course hotel. On occasion he doubles as an actor playing the role of Old Tom Morris in a local show about golf history. It seems everyone in this town plays the role of historian at some point of the work week, Jim and Ronald included.

I feverishly scribbled down names, occupations and email addresses. It was all one big journalism reminder to just…ask questions. I had half a column sketched out in my head and planned to say one or two things when I met them. But you can't say just one or two things in Scotland. It's always four or five and sometimes 45 minutes. Their openness to sit with a stranger was so freshening to my mood. I had not yet aced the test of *playing* Scottish golf but had somehow earned a cheat sheet for understanding it.

Conversations like this one don't happen much in America. The middle America equivalent of the Cottage Kitchen is great and welcoming in its own right, but no one there is asking a foreigner to sit down for 45 minutes and chat about…everything. They made me feel like I had made their day, completely unaware they had very much made mine. We exchanged email addresses and I promised to reach out later in the summer.

The one thing I didn't admit to Jim and Ronald was that I overheard the juiciest part of their conversation just before joining them. Ronald had been telling a story about a recent interaction he had with Martin Slumbers, CEO of the R&A and one of the most powerful brokers in all of golf. Sandford had run into Slumbers at the Old Course and asked for his thoughts on LIV golfers and if they would be allowed to play in The Open.

"I told him, 'I see [Bryson] DeChambeau is playing,'" Sandford recalled.

Slumbers smiled and, according to the story, said, "He'll be playing *this* year."

The implication was obvious. LIV golfers had upset the status quo, driven purely by guaranteed money from Saudi Arabia, and Slumbers wasn't a fan. He made it clear in a press conference three weeks later, saying, "Looking ahead to The Open next year, we have been asked quite frequently about banning players. Let me be very clear. That's not on our agenda. But what is on our agenda is that we will review our exemptions and qualifications criteria for The Open.

"And whilst we do that every year, we absolutely reserve the right to make changes as our Open Championships Committee deems appropriate. Players have to earn their place in The Open, and that is fundamental to its ethos and its unique global appeal."

Did Slumbers have something up his sleeve for 2023, 2024, and future Opens in this new, brazen golf world? If what he told Sandford was true, I thought, it would easily become international news. Changing criteria in the face of an upstart golf tour would lead to lawsuits and press conferences and drive yet another unnecessary wedge between figures in the sport. Just as eavesdropping can give you some gold, it also delivers things you're not quite sure what to do with.

The people of St. Andrews were charming me so much it felt purposeful. There was that impromptu breakfast with Jim and Ronald, where they paid for my latte. Then in the span of three days during the U.S. Open I was two for two in getting my beers paid for by strangers in the

Dunvegan. Sky Sports broadcaster Jamie Weir bought me a pint at the Central Bar on his way through town and guided me through what to expect in the upcoming football transfer period. I was in the market for a special sweatshirt—the one Tiger Woods wore at The Open back in 1995, with the town crest and motto—and before long I received an excited email about it from shop owner Karina MacKinnon.

Subject line: SWEATSHIRTS!!!!
Come on in and visit.

I wasn't used to this abundance of kindness. The seven years I lived in New York City had sucked the Nice Stranger out of me. St. Andrews was like the small town where I grew up in the northeast corner of Wisconsin, where everyone knew everyone, and even if you didn't, they treated you as if you did.

I crossed the threshold of "officially smitten" that week thanks to a five-minute chat with a second-year student named Dylan. I found him resting on the steps behind the 1st tee after a Sunday stroll with his grandmother and her cocker spaniel. Dylan insisted that if I really wanted to see St. Andrews, I must go on a specific run. He wanted me to run uphill for two miles, past the hospital to the outskirts of town. "It has the best view. Students go up there and drink as the sun rises." Grandma Isobel laughed. Internally, I scoffed. How could it be better than my runs along the North Sea, carving my way between the dunes?

Usually, I'd be skeptical of a sophomore who had spent his weekend DJing at graduation parties, but I decided to give DJ Dylan a chance. Around 8:40 PM on a sunny evening I huffed and puffed my way past the St. Andrews Community Hospital. The slope only increased from there. The flatness of Chicago's running paths had not prepared me. The road quickly shrunk to one lane, the end of which seemed to disappear off into farmland. The one-lane road then turned into a one-lane path, part paved and part gravel with grass peeking up between the tire marks. I was precisely on the boundary where town becomes country, where the plots of land are neatly marked by rows of perfectly aligned trees. Only a couple people lived out here. The potholes I darted to avoid would be potholes for years to come. My legs begged for a break from the incline, but Dylan's favorite view couldn't be more than another half mile. About 10 minutes into the climb, the path narrowed to the width of a golf cart. And shortly after that to shoulder-width. After that, even tighter. People had clearly walked this way before— the dirt was hard-packed—but the weeds hung over the path and ripped at my calves.

This is exactly what your mother would *not* want you to do, Sean. Go jogging at 9 PM, come face to face with the rusting metal carcass of a derelict water testing plant, and…keep going? Trudge around the rock walls overgrown with ivy and on the now uneven path that wound straight into a wooded area and…keep going? One wrong step and you'd be rolling yourself down the hill to that hospital. I broke out of the woods and held my gaze *up* the hill, knowing the view could only be improving behind me.

When this mountain finally crested, I ripped my earbuds off and turned around to see that DJ Dylan was right. Really, really right. *Maybe part of turning 30 is learning when to listen to the 20-year-olds.* I could see every step of the roundabout path I took up here, and beyond it the entire town, the 800-year-old St. Andrews Cathedral, the Hamilton Grand hotel, the world-famous golf land extending outward on its peninsula, and finally the calm, retreating tide of the North Sea. All of it was drizzled in amber, as though reality had swiped to the most sepia filter imaginable. How many jogging routes offer a pot of gold like this? A mile of country land, a mile of neighborhoods, miles of golf courses, and then boundless open water. I sat down on the path and was consumed by the sheaves of wheat that stretched out for miles. The only thing I could hear was wind. No seagulls, no car horns, no bagpipes, no calls of "FORE!" Just wind. Wheat sheaves gently smoothing over other wheat sheaves. Pure, unadulterated nature. All unlocked via one strenuous hike and a tip from a stranger. If this was the kind of detox one could have on the regular, I thought, why would you ever leave? I could sit there all night, and no one would find me. The perfect place for adult hide-and-seek. It would be another 10 weeks before any suds-sippin' college kids would climb this hill again.

I took my time getting down from that perch, enjoying the walk. It had been a weird summer to this point. I covered the most bizarre golf tournament of my life. A friend had passed away suddenly. All my coworkers seemed to have the best week of their careers at the U.S. Open. And I was…here. Doing…*me*. I was lucky to pick a place so welcoming. People don't share enough secrets with strangers.

Chapter 9

Roller Coaster

My family has goofy traditions just like yours does, but maybe yours have nothing to do with puking.

The Zaks are from Wisconsin and of Polish and German descent, and all that really means is imbibing is part of life. During Christmas we gather around wet bars in the basement. On Easter Sunday we'll toss dice, loser takes a shot. High school graduation parties often end with flip cup and the occasional keg stand. If we're going to drink, we had might as well make it fun. And when that goes too far, we might as well *make fun*.

Whenever the pursuit of a good time ends with someone setting their stomach straight in the bathroom, it's a major infraction. It doesn't matter where it happened; the Zak Family deems you to be… on probation. The rules apply across state lines and the penalty is in place for a full year. Every time you grab a drink at a family function, everyone reminds you—*be careful, you're on* probation. Three hundred and sixty-five days' worth of reminders to *Handle your liquor!* If it happens again, probation is extended. Simple rules, really.

Luckily, probation doesn't often concern me. I learned enough lessons in college. Plus, here in Scotland the drinking is good. Guinness is great. Tennent's goes down easy. Whisky is sipped, not slugged. And when it comes to golf, the drinking normally takes place *after* the round. Golf in the U.K. is played on foot with your clubs on your back or on a trolly—almost never strapped to the back of a golf cart. No cart, no cupholders. No cupholders, not much drinking. At least that's what I thought before the Royal Burgess Member-Guest.

"It's a fairly boozy day, FYI," Jamie Kennedy texted ominously. He's a fellow thirtysomething in golf media. "Jacket and tie. Lots of beers. Alternate shot.... Drinks after. Dinner late."

What's not to like? I competed in a member-guest just once before and it ended horribly. Too few birdies and an allergic reaction to shellfish for one member of our team. (Probation? It's hard to say.) I had heard about Royal Burgess, too. Its full name is the Royal Burgess Golfing Society of Edinburgh, and it isn't just the oldest club in Scotland or in the U.K.—it claims to be the oldest golf club in the *world*. Nearly 300 years ago golfers would congregate at the Bruntsfield Links in Edinburgh, decades before the American Revolution. The RBGS held meetings and voted on club affairs at local taverns. One of them still serves beer under the guise of four words: Ye Olde Golf Tavern. Golf and boozing, forever linked.

The RBGS shared Bruntsfield with other golfing societies—society sounds so much cooler than "club"—but when Bruntsfield became too populated, they moved to Musselburgh Links along the Firth of Forth. For about a hundred years, it would share Musselburgh too. The idea of competing clubs *sharing* the same golf course seems absurd on paper—like rival high schools sharing a basketball gymnasium. But the demand of golfers outstripped the supply of golfing land. Eventually, those economics settled into place when RBGS found its own space on the west side of Scotland's capital, near EDI airport, a parkland course that doesn't look too different than what you find in middle America. Trees and shrubs lining the fairways, which were soft and green rather than hard and tan. Those hundreds of years of genteel history now rest in a white clubhouse with dark trim that ultimately looks like a ski chalet.

As welcome as Jamie had made me feel, it was an intimidating façade when I arrived on June 25. The front entrance was locked, and I had been warned to dress my best. Without the proper attire, you can only enter certain rooms at the club, for this is the "Burgess Experience." The best I brought to Scotland would have to do: a turquoise dress shirt with a navy paisley tie, the blue blazer I had been steaming creases out of all week, and the pecan-colored loafers I purchased one day earlier. Shoes so new my half-mile sprint to the bus station earned me blisters on both heels.

Jamie was my teammate, a fun bit of irony since he was also a very talented video producer for GOLF.com's biggest rival, Golf Digest. He's too kind to let silly conflicts mar our connection, but he was certainly wary of my choice in football club. Jamie was a Liverpool man, and I supported Everton, the Chicago Bears to my Green Bay Packers. He was a fading scratch golfer, once good enough to play on scholarship at Jacksonville University, where he surrendered most of his Scottish accent and roomed with Tour pro Russell Knox. He wasn't contributing many handicap strokes to our team's total, but he was a great anchor. His long, fluid swing hit these low, penetrating shots that rose softly through the wind and rolled forever. I was envious of that ball flight. It looked like it had been drawn up via computer. Jamie took me out to Panmure for a practice round and learned that my spinny cuts tended to turn into embarrassing banana slices in the wind. It's not a matter of finding those misses. Rather, it's how far into the adjacent farmland they'll travel. I had lived in Scotland for three weeks, but my game was not adapting at all. Jamie's tip for hitting the low stinger: "Tee it up a half-inch and swing *really* down into it." At Royal Burgess, he would play the odd-numbered tee shots and I'd handle the evens. We'd alternate from there until the ball found the hole. No gimmes. Tournament golf demands it.

Jamie was nowhere to be found when the bus dropped me off just before noon, but name-dropping him went a long way. When I eventually found the pro shop, a staffer hopped out from behind the desk and grabbed my clubs. "Ahh, farr tha Sixsomes?" he went, pulling me into the next room. "Today, guests are treated like members. Isthe one day a yare the club lets its hair down."

I was increasingly concerned about what that meant. Sixsomes bent the typical rules in the way you'd expect, with groups of six players instead of four. But with alternate shot, there would be only three balls in play. In theory, we should play much quicker than a fourball group. The rest of our party was filled with Jamie's mates, a bunch of Scots who had grown up together. This wasn't their first rodeo. The scoring was Stableford, another format to which I was a rookie. Instead of counting stroke totals from hole to hole, you tally up four points for making an eagle, three for a birdie, two for pars, and one for bogeys. Anything worse was worth zero. There's no backward movement in Stableford. My golf friends back home have seen many a 78 spoiled into an 83 by one or two bad Sean holes. In Stableford, you pick up and move on. Plus, pace of play is more of an order than a goal in Scotland. It's spelled out on the sign facing the 1st tee at Panmure:

PLAY WELL

PLAY QUICKLY

PLAYING BADLY

PLAY QUICKER

Stableford helps that. After Jamie arrived, the first drinks were meet-and-greet pints in the clubhouse. Then, during lunch, everyone else at the table said yes to white wine, so I had to say yes to white wine. The looming, unwritten obligation of this event, was that each competitor was to arrive armed with six of *something*. Six beers, six mixed drinks, six of whatever elixir you fancy. I was under the impression that we would simply consume *our* own six bevvies—over a four-hour round, no big deal—but I was proven wrong in the 1st fairway when Jamie started passing out my White Claws to the entire group. Every golfer in the group is entitled to one of everyone else's bevvy, and we'll see who's still standing in a few hours. I was thankful for the sturdy base of beef and potatoes.

Jamie bought the variety pack of Claws on my behalf, saying, "Only fitting these be your contribution," by which he meant, "This is what you silly Americans drink, eh?" He wasn't wrong. I loved seltzers. They hadn't caught on in Scotland quite like in the States, but perhaps today would help. Jamie found the rough, but I found the corner of the green. "So, is this thing just wohtah?" one of Jamie's friends asked. I explained that seltzers had basically commandeered the Saturday American golf scene via days like this one, where drinking came easy.

The sun was out, the boys wore shorts, the rain stayed away. It didn't feel right to be blaring tunes from the boy band Westlife over fairways of the Oldest Golf Club in the World, but we were letting our hair down, too. By the time my first two tee shots pushed Jamie in the right rough, I was being pushed to finish drink no. 4. Jamie's pals had secured the most diverse assortment of potions. Piña colada in a can. A whisky–ginger beer concoction, also in a can. "David Beckham is part-owner of the company," Jamie said, as if that would make it taste better. (It didn't.) But I couldn't shrink in this moment. I was the one who had just turned 30. Everyone in the group was older than me and most of them fathers. It was Dad's Day Out, and I had to hold my own. Up next, martini in a can and a smooth lager after that.

Self-assured amateurs will promise you that they play better after downing a few, but I never believe them. There has always been an inverse relationship between the *feel* of one's golf swing—that sensation of total control—and their increase in blood alcohol content. When the latter goes up, the other disappears. Your arms are no longer the sturdy, memory-bound muscle-bumpers that guide your swing on a repeatable path. They become pool noodles after six Whatever-in-a-Cans. Just loosely hinged limbs connected to a rubber grip, incapable of responding to the delayed synapses in your brain. After drink no. 7, 8, or 9, you lose all perception of where the clubface is atop your backswing. It might as well be perfectly on plane, because I wouldn't know otherwise. I'd said goodbye to feeling my swing at least an hour ago, missing greens left and right. Sending the driver up, up, and away. Fatting the hybrid and thinning wedges. But when I made a tipsy 10-footer for par, I felt on top of the world. *Let's see Tiger do THAT.*

Royal Burgess does not have a halfway house but rather a two-thirds house, tucked behind the 13th tee, and when we found it, we also found a two-group backup. We were decidedly not the only drinkers. Almost the entire afternoon wave was doing exactly as we were. The club had pulled a bartender out to the two-thirds house for these exact reasons. "Don't order just one," I was told. "You'll be here awhile."

"Two of whatever they're having, I guess," I said with a tired exhale. I was in too deep, but Jamie was steadying everything. We were only two over par and moving forward with a gin and tonic in each hand. It's an underrated golfer instinct, the ability to lash at a ball on the ground and immediately pick up its trajectory after impact, but that too goes out the window after drink no. 9. I slapped my driving iron in the direction of the 13th green and was thrilled to hear it advanced to the greenside bunker. Jamie splashed close and I missed the putt. Bogey.

No golf nerd was going to confuse Burgess for one of the best courses in Scotland, but I couldn't help but notice "letting its hair down" was delivering a day with so many...*smiles*. The camaraderie with your partner. The irrelevance of the match. But then the dire competitiveness of the group. You didn't want to finish last and be the ones buying drinks in the clubhouse. We played hero ball, as if the alcohol were more superpower than inhibitor. Putts were read from some sort of yoga position, our bellies scraping the green. Because bad shots didn't really matter. Good shots automatically became great shots. Scary shots became *f—k-it* shots. This was the goofiest golf I had played in years.

Our prize for surviving the 13th hole and the two-thirds house was another gin and tonic—in a can, of course. By the time we reached 18, the earth was swaying beneath my feet. I had been thinking about this dicey tee shot since the moment I set foot on the property, when Jamie so graciously chose the odd-hole tee shots. It was a par-3 set up at 220 yards, playing into a slight wind. If I was serious about putting on a show for my new foreign friends, it would have to be 3-wood. I just wasn't sure I wanted to put on a show. The 18th green butts up next to the clubhouse, maybe 50 feet from that pro shop where I was so kindly greeted six hours ago. Beside it sat a parking lot full of cars. *Cars owned by country club members*, I thought. They would be nice cars. One of those banana slices I had unfortunately been practicing all afternoon could cost a pretty penny, not to mention dent Jamie's reputation with the club.

He wasn't worried. He was bouncing around the tee box with joy. Jamie punched up the volume on his speaker as loud as it could go. Dozens of fellow competitors lined the right edge of the green. *Did they realize they were in firing range?* As our DJ, Jamie had been holding on to a particular song for me, the only American in the group. Perhaps the only American in the field. The guitar solo of AC/DC's "Thunderstruck" revealed itself. A bit of a dizzying tune, I'll admit, with the anxious moaning that builds to a crescendo. *Ahhhhh, THUN-DER. Ahhhhh, THUN-DER.*

I guess I did have to perform.

The blood rushed to my head when I bent over to stick a tee in the ground. The bass drum kept pumping. When I stood up the tee box was off its normal axis. Surely it had tilted five degrees in the direction of the parking lot. *Whatever you do, Sean, this ball is not going to the right.* The only feeling in my body was latent hope. The lyrics were oddly spot on.

AND I WAS SHAKIN' AT THE KNEES....

It was go time. I yanked the club back on cue.

YOU'VE BEEN

Then launched down into contact.

THUN–DER–STRUCK.

If anyone was capturing this swing on camera, they would have seen a wry little smile, right in that moment. Absolutely surrendering my bank account to the whims of the golf gods.

The audience on the tee groaned and they groaned by the green, too. I snap-hooked my 3-wood on an abrupt arc into the collection of trees left of the green. Nowhere close to the hole, but absolutely nowhere near those Beamers, Benzes, and Bentleys. We made double bogey for 79 strokes, 33 Stableford points, and decidedly not last place.

Astute readers can probably tell I'm on a one-way trip toward probation. Isn't that how these days of drunken jubilance play out when your liver turns 30? About six hours of hazy drinking followed my Thunderstruck moment, too. The handful of videos saved on my phone run far too long. When I'm overserved, I tend to act like a documentarian. About 50 of us continued the party into the evening, treating the 1st tee like it was the start of a Ryder Cup, whipping into chants as junior members headed out for an evening round. Glasses were broken and suit coats were grass-stained. One member of the party was convinced he could find the fairway while wearing the jacket he showed up in. Unsurprisingly, he failed to succeed. It took him 60 seconds and a less drunk friend just to balance his ball on a tee. The night ended with red wine and maybe the best steak of my life at Kyloe in the Edinburgh city center. There's a photo of me, back in my finest threads, snapping a picture of Edinburgh Castle. Jamie's words—"That castle is older than your country"—were seared into my memory.

My slumber ended with the slow, constant thumping of steps from above. Human alarm clocks. Jamie's two young boys, Harry and Rory, had overpowered their dad's best efforts for peace. I was sprawled out on an air mattress Jamie's lovely wife Katy had outfitted in their living room. The room was fully lit by the sunshine of a new morning, and it was also spinning. Harry and Rory peeked in to see the disheveled stranger Dad let spend the night. "That's Mr. Sean," Jamie said. *Ahhh, parenting.*

My eyes were bloodshot, my hair in tatters, and my gut roiling. We had discriminated against only vodka. All others were accounted for:

One pint in the clubhouse
Two glasses of white wine at lunch
One black cherry white claw
Piña colada in a can
Haig whisky + ginger ale in a can
Martini in a can
Schiehallion lager
Two gin and tonics at the turn
Gin and tonic in a can
Another unnamed lager
Two pints behind the 18th green
Two gin and tonics on the clubhouse veranda
Multiple glasses of red wine for dinner

Hey, doofus! You deserve to be spinning. You deserve to have rambunctious children disrupting your sleep. You're not 21 anymore.

Jamie graciously filled me up with coffee and a bacon roll from the clubhouse at RBGS after we scooped my sticks. It was stunning how well the debauchery had been cleaned up from the night before. The club's hair was no longer down. It was back to civility.

It felt like the morning after a wedding, when everyone has to go back to their prior lives. Jamie left to wage his own hangover battle as a doting father while I had to battle mine on a bus full of strangers. A bus making only local stops, too; the express wasn't running on the day

I needed it most, lengthening this herky-jerky trip by 45 minutes. Just what I needed. I slumped into a window seat and wedged my clubs tightly into the seat next to me. Wake me up at the last stop.

I was about halfway home when the first signs of trouble arrived. Each pit stop on the local route included wide turns through roundabouts and then squeaky brakes to a halt. The prize after surviving those churning moments was 60 seconds of peace before the coach lurched into acceleration again. I couldn't tell if it was better to go at this slower pace with occasional stops for deep breathing or just speed ahead and get on with it. The driver seemed to combine the two: racing in and out of many stops. To keep from overheating I leaned my forehead against the cool window glass. I strongly considered treating my bus fare as a sunk cost and hopping off to relieve myself in Kirkaldy. But the cab fare from there would run me $100 or more. Was this a $100 problem I couldn't fix with some free meditation and deep breathing?

Stops in Glenrothes and Ladybank came and went. The St. Andrews bus station was our final checkpoint. If I could just get there, I'd be released from this pressure cooker. A stunning brunette boarded the bus in Cupar and seemed to be staying on through St. A. She sat across the aisle and two seats back, and as a means of distraction I forced myself into the thought that if she debarked in St. Andrews, I would ask her out on the spot. Think about *that*, Sean. I was wearing my jacket from the night before, my hair tousled enough to look casual. I did look good, even if my insides were in turmoil.

One more lurchy stop later, unfortunately, there was no question of *if* I would burst my bacon roll, but where and when. Who knows how much longer I had. My mind raced through the options of least-obnoxious place to spray: 1. The back of the seat in front of me. 2. Into my swanky LIV Golf duffel bag. (That might be most fitting.) 3. I could cause a scene and sprint to the front of the bus and dispose in a trash bin, destroying my chances of asking out the brunette. The cost-benefit analysis lasts just a few seconds when you feel like an active volcano. I chose the duffel and was pleasantly surprised at what I found inside: my shoe bag.

Those tiny little totes with just enough room for a pair of kicks are the ultimate sign of golfer luxury. It feels oddly proper to carry your shoes in a bag as you walk up to the clubhouse, rather than pinched between your fingers. You don't need these bags, but they sure look nice. They keep your dirty shoes from everything else. Or your dirty *other stuff* from everything else. I ripped pearly FootJoys out of the tiny carryall and deposited in it as quickly and quietly as possible, praying the hum of the bus would mask the sound of my heaves. The towel attached to my golf bag reached just long enough to clean my lips. I shot a quick glance to the brunette who was across the aisle and one seat behind. She hadn't seen anything. I think.

Exhale.

After a blissful, stinky 10 minutes, the bus pulled in to St. Andrews and I tossed the shoe bag in the first receptacle I could find. I was officially on probation. Thankfully, by the time my family reads this, a year will have passed.

Within 24 hours I was back on Scottish public transit. GOLF.com's resident Gen Zer James Colgan arrived with energy that could rival Jamie's young boys. James had been on a press trip boondoggle with his girlfriend Jamie—yes, James and Jamie—and couldn't stop smiling. This was his first time in Scotland, and my first chance to show off my new home. The bacon rolls and the bookstores and coastal hiking path and, obviously, the golf. I had selfishly arranged a round at the North Berwick West Links, a course only 15 miles from St. Andrews as the crow flies, but more like 85 miles as the car drives. We took trains instead, connecting in Edinburgh.

North Berwick felt too good to be true, partly because the 1ˢᵗ tee is a five-minute walk from the train station, delightful news for the traveling golfer. But also because everyone loved North Berwick. *Everyone.* It was the rare course that received universal acclaim, but I had never heard anyone explain *why.* Why was it "soooo good," as I had heard so many people in the golf industry say? Was it because it wasn't trying to be Muirfield or the Old Course or Carnoustie, and didn't host Open Championships? What makes *this* course better than *that* course is such an esoteric, subjective debate. But somehow North Berwick rose above all of that. I wanted to know why, and also why no one had spelled it out in simple terms.

Our host at NB was Simon Holt, who cackled when I explained how my weekend finished. The Royal Burgess Sixsomes apparently had a nickname outside of the club: the Royal Burgess Shiteshow. Holt has a nickname, too: Sholty—or Professor Sholty to us—as he is as good a source as any for what constitutes a great golf course. He grew up down the street in North Berwick the town, studied economics in St. Andrews, and in his thirties sought greater fulfillment. (Sound familiar?) So he grabbed the latest edition of *GOLF Magazine*'s Top 100 Courses in the World (a lovely choice) and started picking them off one by one. Two and a half years later his insane quest was complete. Only he didn't stop there. He has since turned the pursuit of golf's greatest places into business ventures as a travel consultant. James and I were in good hands. Simon treated us to a chicken sandwich in the clubhouse and we headed straight to the 1st tee. Warming up, I was learning, is a distinctly Americanized golf habit. Most clubs in Scotland don't have a driving range near the 1st tee. If anything, it's tucked hundreds of yards away on a plot of land that became available long after the original course was designed. North Berwick has two felt mats and a pair of nets positioned next to the starter building. There's your warm-up.

Our game for the day was a leisurely one nicknamed The Chair, and a new one for James and me. Everyone plays their own ball using net scoring with handicaps. If you beat the other two players in the group on a single hole, you ascend onto the imaginary chair. It's comfy up there. As long as you tie or win the next hole, you'll stay on the chair, and for every hole you win from your lofty perch, you earn a point. Most points wins. Three or four points is a pretty good day.

It was the perfect game for our round that day because James and I were visitors to this museum. Sholty was our tour guide. We didn't want to be grinding over every single putt, distracted from the surroundings by the difference between par and bogey. Holt explained that everything east of that jagged rock wall on the 3rd hole is called "common land." The original golf course stopped right there at those grey stones, looping back to the clubhouse on the edge of town. It wasn't much, back in 1832, but it was six holes, and it was good enough. The game hadn't decided that 18 was the universal standard. When we squeezed through a gap in the wall, headed to the 4th hole, Sholty pointed out the Wee Course off to our left. "There's a sign, go take a look," he said. "Adults can play, but they must be accompanied by a junior." He wasn't joking. It is maintained exclusively for junior play. It originally served as the North Berwick Ladies' Links, back in 1888, one of the first ladies-only golf clubs in the world.

Our seminar on North Berwick continued with tales of the jealous battle between two brothers, James and Robert Craig, during the settlement of town. The sibling nature of one-upping each other produced two of the most gargantuan homes one could imagine existing in all of Scotland. They were named Carlekemp and Bunkershill, and they both loom over the front nine to this day. Sholty pointed out the four rocky islands off the coast, each distinct from the others. To the left was Fidra, which he used to walk to as a youth when the tide was out. In the middle were Lamb and Craigleith, both an earthy mixture of brown and green.

"But do you see that white one? That's Bass Rock," Simon said, pointing out over the far east side of the course. "Why do you think it's white?"

"Is it limestone?" I guessed. I had taken Geology 100 in college.

"No, bird shit."

Ahhhhh. I could see it better now. Bass Rock is the greatest per capita collection of gannets, a sea-diving species of bird that shit where they eat and shit where they sleep.

In between all these factoids, I was quietly compiling one helluva round. Birdie on 6, then a tap-in birdie on 9. A two-putt birdie on the par-5 11th. Perhaps more importantly: zero crippling double bogeys. Because Royal Burgess sits inland from the coast, and because half of my rounds in June were played at the Deeyooks, as Nigel would say, another inland track, and because the Old Course's greens are bigger than a basketball court and more confusing than tarot cards, North Berwick was my first chance to play a round of true links golf that I was proud of.

I remember thinking while walking the back nine that it makes sense when people describe links golf as more intimate than its American alternatives. In order to succeed on it, you must *use* the turf beneath your feet rather than soar over it. You have to get comfortable sizing up the grass 40, 50, 60 feet away from the hole—or maybe even as much as 70 yards short of the green—accounting for how your ball will interact with mounds and humps you would otherwise ignore at courses back home. This golf can be exhausting, too, but in an engaging way. Your brain needs to be switched ON. It's easy back home to commit to memory how far the 7-iron flies. We've been conditioned to think that's the only number that matters. Links golf wants to know how far it flies, how high it soars, and how far it will roll out once gravity does its thing. Parkland golf is algebra and links golf is calculus, only intoxicating instead of intimidating. When the figures add up and a clear path develops, and then you execute your way down it, there is rarely a greater satisfaction in the game. It ends with a lot of 6-footers for par and 12-footers for birdie. That's a good place to be. That's where I was at North Berwick, and they all seemed to go in. I remember joking to James, "I couldn't miss if I tried," and he knows me too well to think anything of it. But inside, I actually felt it. If it came off the face of my putter, it was going in. I got comfy atop the chair and didn't let up, winning 3–1–1 with a long two-putt for par on 17. With a par on 18, I'd break 80 for the first time in Scotland.

After nervously nudging a 3-wood out into the second-widest fairway in the world—the 1ˢᵗ and 18ᵗʰ run parallel here just like at the Old Course—I finally put my ego aside and played a true links golf shot. I pulled putter from the fairway, maybe 40 yards from the hole.

In America, on that green, green grass, you could never hit it hard enough with the flat stick. So you pull out the soup-ladle 60-degree wedge and try to get cute with the spin. Here, where golf course agronomy isn't nearly as complicated—*It hasn't rained for weeks? Okay, must be firm*—I had learned to just hit the damn putter. Hit it from everywhere. Hit it from 100 yards if you have to. Just get the ball *moving*.

I took the putter back further than I had in, uh, years? Down a valley the ball went, then up the other side, turned by the slope, rolling and rolling in the direction of the clubhouse. I feared I had hit it too hard, which would bear its own special price of humiliation. With North Berwick members pausing their meals on the porch to watch, playing ping pong from one side of the green to the other with putter in hand is the most direct way of saying "Sorry! I'm not from here." Thankfully, I played it mostly perfect, rolling out to eight feet right of the flag. When the hole grabbed my birdie putt and pulled it down, my competitors scoffed. "That was the *only* way today was going to end," James said. "Go buy a lottery ticket, why dontcha." There's the joy of beating your older brother, followed by the joy of beating your father, or even your grandfather, but shortly after those is the unique joy of beating coworkers.

James couldn't be too mad; he shot 82 on his own ball. But it was no 4-birdie 78. Who knows what Simon shot. He didn't care, and we weren't supposed to care. When he bought us beers in the Tantallon Club—which shares the golf course with North Berwick

Golf Club—two members joined us and asked the question you often hear in Scotland:

"So, hod'ya git on?"

We took it like most Americans do, as an invitation to talk about our scores. But they don't give a damn about the scores. "They" being the Scots, Irish, English, etc. "Hod'ya git on?" is always about the match. Who won, who lost, and how many holes did it last for. In which case, James could just sit there, listen, and roll his eyes as I fluffed my ego one final time.

Our train rides home were mostly silent, for no particular reason except I was stuck in thought, working my memory from the 1st tee through the rock wall to the far extent of the front nine and back again, trying to solve the riddle that had stumped me earlier that morning. What makes North Berwick great? And why hadn't anyone simplified the explanation? By the time we made it back to St. Andrews, I settled on this theory: the greatness of the North Berwick West Links makes most sense when compared to a roller coaster—at least for first-timers. After standing in line, you've got only a slight idea of what's to come. There are ups and downs, herks and jerks, many of which you don't expect until you're right on top of them. It lulls you into a sense of comfort and then torques you in an awkward direction. It may seem difficult to explain because there's too much to explain, just like a roller coaster, which hits you in so many different ways in just 90 seconds and then spits you out on the other side. How do you describe a roller coaster? *That one turn, man. I never saw it coming. Wait, how about that epic drop? I could barely catch my breath. How about when it kicked us upside down? My knees nearly smoked my chin. The start! Zero to 60 in three-point-five?* It's hard to think of a four-hour walking experience as anything similar to the Zippin Pippin, but when you spell it out on paper it starts to feel a bit exhilarating.

- Keep driver in the bag on 1. It's a 4-iron off the tee but then a blind wedge up over a colossal wave of turf.

- Rip driver out of the bag on 2 and cut off as much of the dogleg as you'd like. If you miss out to the right, you're playing from a public beach. Literally. Leave it to the left, you're bouncing around on these things called hummocks. They're golf's version of ski moguls. Fun to look at, less fun for your golf ball.

- Keep driver out on 3; it's the hardest of the bunch. Just make sure you lift that second shot off the ground because an ancient rock wall cuts across the fairway, and so does a public walking path. This course has you thinking.

- The 4th is a partially blind par-3. Hit and hope. Zero comfort there.

- The rollercoaster slows on the 5th and 6th holes. It's climbing. *Click, click, click.* Catch your breath, make a couple pars. Find the wrong bunker and *yikes.*

- If you're not careful on 7 your ball will dive into the earth. The ground shaves away just before the green into a hidden burn. It's not safe to stand close to the edge. Use this 20-foot ball retriever to scoop it out.

- What follows next is a four-hole stretch with three par-5s. One plays into the wind, one into a crosswind, and another downwind. Want some birdies? Get 'em now. Are we having fun yet?

- Another ancient wall cuts across the 13th hole, only this time right in front of the green. Hit it too close to the wall? Time to play backward or get as cute as you can with a wedge. Up to you. You put yourself there.

- The 15th is a redan. I want you to purposefully play *away* from the hole and let gravity and grass bend it toward the hole.

- The 16th is a biarritz, where the putting surface has been split into two platforms. In between is a turf crater. Golf's version of a loopty-loop. Don't get stuck in there. Phil Mickelson nearly drove the green once. Then he five-putted.

- Those ski moguls come back into play on the 17th, and that green you can't see? It's shaped like a bowl; just toss it up there and see what awaits.
- No. 18 is the most tantalizing finisher. There are a dozen street cars parked out to the right; a boxy, stone clubhouse behind the green; another ball-sucking basin in front of the hole; and the pro shop dug into the ground on the left. You can drive this green and end your day with a smile, pulling back in right where you started.

"So…what did you think?"

Please, sir. Let me go 'round again.

On the way to dinner that night, James reiterated what coworker Claire Rogers had mentioned a few days earlier:

"Sean, you just seem really *happy* over here."

Chapter 10

Looping

I was equal parts shook and relieved when Joel Dahmen, the 108th-ranked player in the world, finally texted me on June 29. I had spent the last week or so just casually checking in, hopefully staying top of mind for him, sharing details on the upcoming Scottish Open—where I was staying, my arrival plans, what it's like driving on the left side of the road. All the logistics he'd think about when he landed in the U.K. I had spent that afternoon re-reading our text messages over and over. Upon the sixth or seventh re-read, it was becoming clear he hadn't emphatically said those six important words: *Yes, Sean. The job is yours.*

"You're high on the list?" Joel wrote to me on June 20, which was just enough to pique my excitement and send me spiraling with questions. *Why did he use a question mark? That was just an accident, right?* Making me wait—*was he testing me? Was this an auction where cheapest caddie wins the job?* I had told my parents, my family, all my golf buddies and my coworkers. I told my landlord and fellow media members. *Your boy is looping for Dahmen at Renaissance Club. Tune in!* But only now, after nine days of internal angst and just one week before the event, did

Joel finally make it clear: "I am officially registering you as my caddie. What is your best email?"

Apparently he had been waiting on word from his cousin, who was trying to orchestrate a week off from his day job for the trek to East Lothian. It would have been awkward to rescind my backchannel bragging to friends and family, some of whom had already placed wagers on Dahmen to win the Scottish. "Booyah," Joel said when I sent along my email. If this was any indication of our ability to communicate, it was either going to be a horrific week of indecision or a blissful week of The Boys Makin' Birdies. *Booyah.*

We were starting in a good place, though, because Joel is as blissful as Tour players get. The Netflix series *Full Swing* devoted an entire episode to him, the thesis of which can be whittled down to a single quote: "Someone's got to be the 70th-best golfer in the world. It might as well be me."

That's Joel. Raw, unfiltered, and mostly just a realist. In his previous five seasons, his average finish in the FedEx Cup was 68th. Instead of confusing himself with delusional self-belief, he'd rather humble himself with blunt realities. He stands 5'11" with an average build and is probably the only Tour pro who regularly wears a bucket hat. Underneath is a brown, moppy combover. He isn't a world-beater, like Scottie Scheffler, who rattles off wins in bunches. Joel's only Tour win came in the Dominican Republic during the same week a World Golf Championship was hosted in Texas. In other words, he won when a lot of the best players weren't around. And he'd be the first to tell you. But a win is a win, damnit. His name was on top of the only leaderboard in town. On any given day, Joel can do that. And over the course of a great week, he'll push the very best in the world. But he's not one of them, and he's okay with that.

Joel grew up in Clarkston, Washington, on the rugged, less glorious eastern half of the state, across which his doting mother drove their minivan from event to event on the regional junior golf schedule.

He was one of the most talented kids in the country, so each year their travel radius stretched further and further across the Pacific Northwest. As Joel detailed beautifully in an article for The Players' Tribune, his mom, Jolyn, followed along on every hole he played, tracking the number of greens and putts he hit so they could debrief with his dad in the evening. His passion was made possible by his mother's presence—which made it all the more throttling when she was diagnosed with cancer during Joel's junior year of high school and told she had six months to live. He called her his superhero.

Joel navigated that same minivan around the Pacific Northwest that year, this time by himself. At times, he would see his mom on the course, along the fairway he was playing, or up at the green waiting for his approach. She'd be taking notes. Those fleeting moments comforted him, he says, but they didn't solve the fact that she was no longer there for a hug after the round. Joel earned a scholarship to play at the University of Washington, five hours from home, but he didn't care much for books. He played golf and partied, and frankly did too much of the latter, dropping out of school. He could golf his ball around any course better than anyone you knew, but he had given up on the typical route to pro golf.

He wound up working at a local course, squandering any money he made in trips to the liquor store. The work ethic wasn't there, but his talent carried him. He won the Washington State Amateur by an absurd *six* shots in 2007, and in the process met a man named Bob Yosaitis, who fronted Joel $15,000 when he turned professional in 2010. It was an incredible break for a kid who needed it. But within a year, cancer re-entered his life. Joel was diagnosed with testicular cancer. He was 23.

When we met in the parking lot at Renaissance (Re-nay-sanse) Club, Joel was 34 and a cancer survivor. On the front of those bucket hats is the word CANCER with a thick red line running through it. Proceeds from hat sales help fund charities focused on ending the disease. He believes he never would have made it to where he is without those life-altering moments he and his family went through. His mom's last gift was her fight through those loneliest of days, battling chemotherapy in the hospital. You're free to put this book down for five minutes to read his Players' Tribune column. It helps contextualize that guy you see on Netflix, a fan-favorite for lifting his shirt off and helicoptering it during the final round of the frat party that is the Phoenix Open. He knows he's been blessed, and you can see it when he talks about his mom and family. Whether it's on the internet or over a Scottish beer in the pub, when he talks about his mom is when he's most eloquent and filled with gratitude. It makes you think about your own mom. Once again, Scotland felt a long way from Wisconsin for me. It was also a lot windier, so Joel had tucked the bucket hat away. It was ballcaps only in Caledonia.

For these reasons and more, Joel is on a very short list of pros who would dare to consider inviting a media member to caddie for them. Pros mostly keep the media at arm's length, hoping to keep some duality between their private and public selves. Those public selves have elevated monetary value—they're tied to millions in corporate sponsorship dollars—and letting the media in brings you one vulnerable step closer to maybe screwing it all up. But Joel? He loves to chat. He loves the hang. He loves *the craic*, as they say in Ireland. Joel's duality isn't as apparent, and I'd argue that's a good thing. He has no desires to be or act like someone he isn't. He'll be blunt with his thoughts but also listen to yours, which is one of my favorite signs of a player's character. Most Tour pros love to talk—a major part of their job is chatting through things—but very few return the favor and listen. You have no choice but to believe Joel when he says he lives on the PG-B Tour, the ring of elite pros who exist *around* the superstar golfers. The Schefflers, Rory McIlroys, and Jordan Spieths—they live on the PG-A Tour, Joel says, and the only things they really share with Joel are practice ranges, tee times, and occasionally TV time.

(And now, Netflix!) Joel explained this dichotomy to me years ago, and I never forgot it. The closer you get, the truer it feels.

Joel had cut me a nice deal for the week—$2,000 and 10 percent of his earnings—which of course sends the mind racing. *What if... he makes the cut? That's just extra money for the both of us. What if...he finishes 30th? How about 10th?!*

Wait...what if he wins?

It's such an irresponsible thought—and ignorant of everything I had learned in 10 years on the golf beat. But I suddenly had a dog in the fight. My bank account *seriously* had a dog in the fight. There was a $1,200 camera lens in St. Andrews I had mysteriously broken. It needed replacing, so GOLF.com had a dog in the fight, too. The purse for the Scottish Open was $8 million, so if we made the cut, there's a new camera lens right there. Finish in the top 10, and I'm buying a used car. I've needed one back in Chicago. Win and...well, Joel would be on his way to play in the 150th Open at St. Andrews.

The only reason I allowed myself to think this way was that Joel had just balled out at Brookline. A couple weeks earlier he'd found himself in the final pairing on Saturday at the U.S. Open, alongside Collin Morikawa, one of those guys certifiably on the PG-A Tour. The final 36 holes didn't go as well as the first 36, but Joel finished tied for 10th and cleared $400,000. It was one of the first things I asked him about Monday afternoon when we escaped for a practice round.

So, uh, what worked so well in Boston?

"I hit a lot of fairways, I hit a lot of greens, and I didn't make any doubles," Joel said.

Yeah, I get it.

I didn't need him to explain it. Brookline's firm conditions were the main reason he shot up the leaderboard. Soft conditions, by contrast, turn pro golf into target practice. *Hit it here and the ball will stay.* But firm turf makes the ball *go, go, go.* Once it's on the ground, it's out of your hands. I had been learning that in Scotland. The longest players in the world would uncork some 400-yard tee shots that get everybody buzzing on Twitter, but that impressive length just means they'll run out of space a lot quicker on rock-hard fairways. When the grass turns yellowish and plays like concrete, shorter-than-average hitters like Joel can thrive. He plays driver everywhere and he hits it purposefully low, shrinking the distance gap to, at times, nothing. He loves his chances in a competition from 150 yards. We agreed that Brookline was 3,000 miles away, but the setup we'd find at Renaissance could be very similar.

This was the second of three tournaments in the middle of the summer where all of pro golf visits Ireland and the U.K. It starts with the Irish Open, continues with the Scottish, and then to The Open, which is played in Scotland, England, or on rare occasion up in Northern Ireland. The courses these tournaments visit are mostly historic, mostly beloved, and run mostly along the coast. The wind whips, the turf is firm, the ball rolls. Try as it may, Renaissance doesn't check these boxes. It was created in 2008, for starters. It was made for wealthy elites—with six-figure initiation fees—which ultimately helped it land hosting rights for the Scottish Open. An adored links this was not, but it *was* built on precious, sandy soil. It would play fast and tricky. That would be good for us.

My second question was one I had been thinking about for weeks: *Why isn't Geno here?*

Joel's longtime caddie, Geno Bonnalie, needed a break. Not a full-time break, but they had been on the road five of the last six weeks. Geno has a wife and two kids back in Lewiston, Idaho, about a 20-hour travel day from where we were. Joel assured me that even with a missed cut, he "would have made Geno whole." It helped that the Tour was offering each member who played a $7,500 stipend to put toward travel. But that goes quickly. Two last-minute plane tickets and a weeklong stay at the bougie players' hotel would cruise through $6,000 in an instant. "There will be expensive caddie weeks and cheap caddie weeks," fellow pro Ryan Armour told me. "You're either in or out for all of them." Armour was shocked Geno didn't make the trip. But this one felt particularly hasty. Joel was not qualified for The Open at St. Andrews (unless we finished top 3) and headed to Italy with his missus for a vacation in Lake Como. Maybe a break would be good. Plus, I was over here waving my arms like Tom Hanks in *Cast Away*. *Pick me!*

For everyone involved, Mondays on Tour are one big, comfy exhale. They're travel days for most, and this was reiterated by the fact that golf bags were not arriving on time at EDI airport. Keith Mitchell's Mizuno bag had taken a little vacation of its own from Boston to Amsterdam to Edinburgh, two flights that Mitchell himself was never on. A Titleist rep sympathized with him but said they'd been placing AirTags in every piece of luggage they checked. No excuses. Clubs are the most precious cargo.

Joel warmed up next to Keegan Bradley, chief among the players who are *much bigger* than TV cameras would have you believe. Bradley was fresh off a nice finish at Brookline, too, feeling good and waxing on about Patriots QB Mac Jones: "He's looking skinny. I think they're gonna surprise some people this year."

"He says that every year," our Titleist rep shot back.

"And for 20 years I was right!"

Pros always get the last word. Bradley was once one of the biggest names in the game, a top 10 player in 2013 and a major champion, but a ban on anchored putting forced him to completely alter his form. He had since settled comfortably in the 40th to 70th section of the world ranking. In other words, just ahead of Joel. The true biggest names in the game were not here, at least not yet. The PG-A Tour was one island over, in central Ireland, playing a 36-hole charity event called the J.P. McManus Pro-am. No pro-am in the entire world pulls stars like the McManus hit-and-giggle. Both LIV and Tour stars showed up, from Ian Poulter to Ian Woosnam to…Tiger Woods and Rory McIlroy. An exclusive meeting for the Tour's biggest stars—including both Woods and McIlroy—took place that Sunday night while LIV players flew over from their second event in Portland. The topic: *What are we going to do about this LIV stuff?*

Meanwhile, the PG-B Tour gossiped on the Renaissance range. Mitchell had been texting with Justin Thomas, "who is pretty pissed off about all this stuff." DP World Tour commissioner Keith Kelley had just issued sweeping suspensions to its members who competed in LIV events. Players like Poulter, Lee Westwood, or Sergio García who intended to continue playing on the formerly known European Tour would be suspended for three co-sanctioned tournaments (including this week's Scottish Open) and would be fined £100,000 for every LIV event they played in without permission. But that Monday, an arbitrator ruled that the suspensions and fines would be stayed for now. Four players would be allowed to compete in the Scottish Open, ballooning the field size from 156 to 160. It was clear that a lawsuit was brewing between LIV golfers and the PGA Tour, too.

"So you're going to sue the PGA Tour," Mitchell reasoned aloud. "Essentially suing Tiger Woods. Because you're not making enough money? Are you *crazy?*"

This really was the weirdest of times. Joel and Mitchell swapped info they had gleaned over the last month, like the details of Pat Perez' LIV contract: four years, $30 million. Then Mitchell did a funny thing. He turned in my direction and asked, "So, what do you think of all this stuff?"

There was no one behind me. "Oh, I, uh, I'm actually a golf writ—"

"Yeah, I know who you are," he said.

Oh. Our relationships are rarely two-way streets. A Tour pro had never asked for my opinion before.

"Well, I, uh, don't really have a huge problem with people taking money, but I, uh, don't really think they should be able to play both tours."

Way to go, Sean. Very original, walking the party line.

My own duality was being tested, but I really, really liked it. Carrying clubs had pushed me inside the circle of trust, and that mattered. Because the PGA Tour is just a bunch of intersecting circles of trust. There are the players at the center, whose circles intersect with their caddies, coaches, and family. There are managers, agents, and even sports psychs who all have their own circle. If you can enter the string of circles on the agent end, maybe they'll introduce you to the coach, who might get you close to the caddie. Get comfy with the caddie, and soon you'll be chatting up the pro. I had jumped the line because Joel responded graciously to a DM. You make your own luck.

My caddying experience to date amounted to a couple dozen rounds at the club I grew up working at, a couple Wisconsin State Opens, a couple U.S. Open local qualifiers, and the 2020 3M Open, where I looped for Martin Trainer when his full-time caddie Monday-qualified into the event. (Nothing screams lack of commitment to the job than trying to qualify into the same tournament on your own.) But Martin wasn't exactly the most lucrative bag, and I got a taste for that when we shot 76–76. I needed to be reminded, now two years removed, of all the caddie commandments.

Where to place the bag on the tee: almost always to the right.

Where to place the bag around the green: almost always toward the next hole.

Where to look for the prevailing wind: nowhere! Write it into each page of the yardage book before the round.

How to rake bunkers: *push* the sand at first, leveling things out, then pull it delicately to finish.

Most importantly, how to deliver the distance from your player's ball to the hole. That's your Yardage, capital Y, and nothing is more sacred. Finding it is a constant test of second-grade addition and subtraction. In the odd chance your pro hits it far off-line, you might graduate to Pythagorean Theorem. When you check in as a caddie, you are handed a yardage book, which has cute little pictures and an aerial view of all the landmarks on every hole. Each page is filled with dozens of black, yellow, and red symbols you use to pace off how far your ball is from the hole, from the front of the green, to go through the fairway, or to stay out of that death bunker you promised they would avoid. Every pro can do this math themselves, but not every pro wants to. Their job is hard enough. I was by no means a math major but aced my way through calculus in high school. And yet, it's not uncommon in the heat of competition that my brain skips like an old Walkman and the response to *What is 14 less than 173?* is…169. Or 149. Ten yards high or 10 yards low is massive. This was extra important with Joel, who was used to Geno tabulating every number.

My first real test came Tuesday afternoon in a money game match against Team Canada: Mackenzie Hughes and Corey Conners, who played their college golf together at Kent State. Rounding out the foursome was our teammate and fellow Canuck Nick Taylor, Joel's roommate at UW. They all agreed: "Joel is an honorary Canadian. Washington is close enough." The stakes were light—a couple hundred dollars a man—and the game was simple: two-man fourball, all birdies count. Everyone plays their own ball and your team's best individual score is what counts. When your team makes a birdie and a bogey, it's one under. But when your team makes two birdies, it's two under. "Usually it's a pillow fight," Joel said. "Or someone goes so low it's not even a match." The worst result he's ever seen was a ridiculous 17 under over 18 holes, Dahmen on the losing end.

On this day, it was mostly a pillow fight. I delivered 17 good numbers and one bad number, though Joel caught me as I did the math out loud. These practice round days are the real grind of a career in caddying. There's mostly nothing on the line, and yet you're still asked to do your job with a similar intensity for no additional pay. It's part of the gig. Players are allowed to go through the motions, but caddies aren't. In fact, you probably do more work than normal, marking the likely hole locations and keeping track of multiple balls as the pros chip and putt from all directions.

Mostly, practice rounds are a fantastic time to just…talk. I quickly mended any awkwardness with Hughes about that one time stats guru Mark Broadie and I defined him as the most average player on the Tour. (Average among the greats is very good!) Conners is a soft-spoken gent and is more locked in during practice rounds than most. Taylor's voice might be soft, but he's as approachable as they come. He slaved through college just like I did, spending more time memorizing the shortcuts on Mario Kart than he did in the library. The main difference between our college years was that he also became the No. 1 amateur golfer on the planet. His Mario Kart reputation was so significant that the groomsmen in his wedding forced him to play golf in a full-body Yoshi costume during his bachelor party, and then gifted him a customized headcover with a racing Mario on it. It's extremely worn out, but he still uses it. Golfers be superstitious.

Taylor was like Hughes, who was like Connors, who was like Mitchell and every other pro and caddie that week. They were all so confused and all very curious about the battle with LIV Golf. Everyone knew a little bit, but nobody knew everything, and everyone wanted to know more. "Sean, what do you know that we don't know?" Hughes said when we reached the back nine. They wanted our round to stay off the record, and I figured it was best for my caddie privilege to grant it. No one really understood how a judge was able to grant four players sudden access to the tournament at the last minute, but that just fit the theme of the summer. Every day brought another LIV story. Players whispered about LIV invites like it was high school cafeteria gossip. There was plenty of suspicion about players beating their chest publicly for the PGA Tour but then considering LIV offers in private. One caddie shared a tale about how quickly things were changing. He had planned on driving from Brookline to the Travelers Championship with Brooks Koepka's caddie, Ricky Elliot, but those plans changed on a dime when Ricky returned to the caddie house after play Sunday night. They weren't driving to Travelers anymore because Brooks wasn't playing Travelers anymore. He was headed to LIV.

No conversation could be had without invoking that three-letter bugaboo on everyone's mind. Billy Horschel sashayed down the practice range like a self-assured gunslinger in an old Western film, ready to unload his pistol. He was headed to his press conference. "Just wait," Horschel said aloud, raising his eyebrows. "I've got something for ya." An hour later the transcript included an 893-word dispatch that started with "They made their bed," continued with, "Leave us alone, honestly," doubled down with, "It's ridiculous to hear some of the comments these guys make," and ended with, "We can keep going. I have time. My practice is done today." Golf writers don't need much, and that was plenty.

Joel fist-pumped Tuesday afternoon when he was informed he was not needed for the Wednesday pro-am. I thought he was just excited to avoid another round of golf with strangers, but mostly it was because he had been invited to play Muirfield, the course next door, widely regarded as one of the 10 or 15 best tracks on the planet. Joel was set to have the typical Muirfield day—18 holes of alternate shot in the morning, a boozy lunch, and 18 more holes after that—which really just feels like the perfect Joel Dahmen Day. A little spirits and a lot of golf on one of the best courses in the world. I was extremely jealous, but maybe just as happy. After two days of caddying, I needed a break. Staff bags are not light.

I sat in on press conferences instead, got humbled by Scottie Scheffler when he admitted he didn't read the cover story I wrote about him, and then took a 90-minute lap of the back nine that afternoon. Just me and my notes, visualizing where Joel's bullet drivers would roll out to, like I imagined good caddies did. My fortune cookie message from Tuesday night had lit a tiny fire in me. "Prepare yourself for the future," it read. "Tomorrow will become the future." Now was the time to do the work. I stepped off pretend yardages and pictured the tiny arcs Joel's ball would follow into greens. I sat on a dune left of the 13th green for about a half hour just watching waves pummel the Isle of Fidra off in the distance. (It allegedly inspired the story of *Treasure Island*.) Renaissance might not be the best links course in the world, and it might be a manufactured, money-fueled attempt at recreating golf history, but this little corner of the property was gorgeous. And a life in golf couldn't be such a bad one if it somehow delivered me here.

Leaving the course Wednesday evening, I bumped into Xander Schauffele as he chatted with Viktor Hovland's caddie, Shay Knight. Shay didn't seem interested in making it a three-way conversation, but what did I care? I wanted to chat with Xander, who had won the Traveler's Championship 10 days earlier and then won the McManus Pro-am on Tuesday. "Are you the hottest golfer in the world right now?" I asked.

"Oh man, I don't know," he said, giving me the classic media treatment. "I'm good right now but I think Scottie still has the title."

Xander is much cockier when he's not in front of the media, and he proved it when I told him I was looping this week.

"Wait, so I am I talking to you as media or as a caddie?" he asked.

Fair question. In other words, could he trust me with the gossip? He knew things were brewing. And he knew his name kept coming up in LIV rumors. I told him I was both, pointing to the credential around my neck, which was the only one on property with access to both media dining *and* caddie dining. (Caddie dining is much better—it's hot and made to order rather than buffet style, cooked for the masses, scrambled eggs in a bag.) I played the caddie card for now, asking him and Shay for their best advice. Xander's was simple but alarming: "Keep Joel on time." Shay's was annoyingly predictable: "You know the three rules: show up, keep up, and shut up." *Thanks, Shay.*

It's funny how our jumbled brains can be so aloof and content before bed, but then slide into order ahead of an early wake-up call. But the second that alarm went off at 5 AM I knew something was wrong. I had laid my outfit of the day neatly on the hotel desk Wednesday night.

On top of it I placed my credential, room key, backpack, and wallet, but when I woke on Thursday one important thing was missing: my yardage book. *Our* yardage book.

I stored it in my back left pocket all week, and spent Wednesday afternoon stepping off those make-believe yardages and dialing in my workflow. Those things I convinced myself good caddies do. But in an effort to sit comfortably on the 45-minute shuttle bus back to Edinburgh, I had pulled the book from my back pocket and set it down on the seat next to me, leaving it there when I blissfully debarked for dinner. All that work I did, all those little dots I charted—the fact that there's a funnel in the back right of the 5th green, or that the entire 11th green falls off to the right, or that we went driver-driver on 16 and that feels like the obvious play—things I would love to reference for Joel during competition to remind him I was a serious looper…they were gone. I rode in a cab out to the course that morning, absolutely sweating. *Which iron did he play into the 6th hole Monday afternoon? And what did he tell me to write down about the club choice on 13?* My brain was mush. I couldn't confess to it, either. That would put bad juju into the air. Instead, I lied to the folks in caddie registration. You're not supposed to receive more than one book per caddie, or more than two books per player-caddie duo, but I pleaded ignorance—*first-time caddie! I don't know what I'm doing!* Luckily, they took the bait.

The intensity ramps up on Thursday mornings and I had not exactly eased into it with Yardage Book Stress. The scores start to count and the decibels shrink. Conversations with fellow caddies are short. No one lingers on the range. It's cordial, sure, but the movement is purposeful. Point A to Point B. My pro seemed to be battling a case of the tugs with his driving iron, but clearly wasn't too bothered. Cam Smith had just left the hitting bay next to us.

"That guy's going to LIV," Joel said between swings, once Smith was out of earshot. "After the playoffs, though."

Hovland walked by in the other direction. "He might be, too."

We were due on the tee soon, an 8:15 AM start alongside Sepp Straka, a burly 29-year-old Austrian who grew up in Georgia (the state), and Mikko Korhonen, a 41-year-old Finnish father of four. Straka had won The Honda Classic earlier this year. He was ascending. But Korhonen hadn't won a tournament since 2019. The only PGA Tour events he competed in were three major championships (two missed cuts, one T63). He was the definition of what the industry calls *journeymen*. Journeymen spend decades writhing in this stupid, stupid game, following the winding path in and out of relevancy. They're really, really good—never great. They don't have closets full of untouched golf shoes from sponsors. They probably travel with one white pair and one black pair. Maybe a blue pair that needs washing. They fly coach and almost never pass up an opportunity to play because they know the essence of pro golf is repeatedly knocking on the door. You never know when it's going to swing open and your best golf is going to show up. That mindset was why Joel was playing this week.

In the minutes before 8:15, my pro flipped a plastic tee on the ground in between us. The sharp end pointed between my legs. "Ah, you lose," Joel said, handing me Korhonen's scorecard. I stuffed it away in the caddie pouch alongside a banana, a rules sheet, and my incredibly dumb, new, untouched yardage book. Joel didn't seem to notice. *Here goes nothing.*

Earlier that week we agreed on using 2-iron off the 1st. It was a new club to Joel's bag, but he liked it for the firm turf. It would go straight, it would land around 230 yards, and as long as nothing got in its way, it might roll out past 260 or so. But perhaps Brandon Wu had screwed with Joel's mind a bit during their round at Muirfield. Wu said the obvious play was to just rip driver up the left side and hope for a good lie in the wispy fescue. Whatever ounce of indecision that Wu injected into Joel's mind showed up in that first swing—a big block out to the right. Suddenly, your favorite caddie was hard at work, finding the ball in the trees, running over to a marker, stepping off the lateral yardage—A-squared plus B-squared equals C-squared—imagining the landing zone and trying to keep the heart rate reasonably low. Joel punched out, pitched on, and two-putted for 5. Bogey, *real* quick.

Another lesson arrived on the 3rd hole. Walking off the tee, Joel resigned himself to the idea that his perfectly struck 3-wood had kicked straight and into the one pot bunker we were hoping to avoid. The only place you can't make birdie from. Miss it and you have a great look at making a 4 on the short par-5. Find the bunker and it's pitch-out time. My eyes weren't special, but I knew that ball wasn't in the trap. *One of a caddie's best traits is understanding when to speak up,* I told myself. I didn't need my man walking 200 yards with misinformation stewing in his brain, bringing down the vibes even more. "I'm positive it stopped short," I said. "And that's kinda a fantastic angle from over there."

No lies were told, your honor! The ball was not in the bunker, veering short of it at the last instant, just one yard off the fairway and very playable. It had settled on a slight downslope that leads into the sand. Joel would have to lean forward in his stance and swing with a descending blow. He's done it thousands of times.

What I didn't know was how much Joel wanted me to speak. We hadn't really talked through what *kind* of caddie he wanted me to be. He could probably beat me playing left-handed. Who was I to tell him that 2-iron he wanted to play seemed like it might catch the lip of the bunker? So I shut up and let his club do the talking. The *thwack-thud* that followed was a perfect answer. The 2-iron didn't have enough loft and Joel's ball clipped the mound of turf atop the bunker, bounding forward just 100 yards.

"I didn't see *that* happening, Sean," Joel said immediately after impact. There was some aggravation in his voice. He wasn't happy with the result, but he also wasn't happy with the sequence of events that got us there.

"Don't tell me what the lie is gonna be from 250 yards away," he said. "It's a weird thing, but I'd rather be surprised by a good lie than find one that was worse than we expected."

This was an old caddie trick. In the pursuit of optimism, I had never once thought about it. Webb Simpson's caddie, Paul Tesori, had taught Geno years ago to either say nothing at all or dream up the worst lie possible. *Sorry, Joel. Not only is it plugged, it's also in the face of the bunker. I don't know how that happened, but you're going to have to hit backward just to keep playing in this tournament.* Lesson learned! Joel made a good par from the fairway, but it was a birdie opportunity wasted. You don't get many.

My third lesson came on the back nine. After looping the front in two-over 37, Joel made birdie on 10 and roasted a cut-stinger drive up the 11th fairway. With the wind at our back and just 176 yards to the hole, it was an obvious 8-iron. The entire hole sloped from left to right, so the lie was a touch below his feet. Joel didn't want to end up short right of the green, so he overcompensated.

"Oh, fuck you," he shouted.

The club choice was spot on. His ball started left and stayed left, flying 176 yards, the perfect distance… right into the hairy, nasty, grabby grass the Tour likes to call "native area." Or rather, the area they don't trim, allowing nature to decide your fate. We didn't see it bounce, which is always concerning. The self-berating continued. "Instead of leaving it out to the right where you'd be fucked," Joel said, "you hit it to the one place you'd be double-fucked." *Double-fucked* was a new one for me.

What should have been an easy 4, maybe a 3, became an automatic 5 in an instant. Joel left his approach on 12 out to the right and then hit it 20 yards past the flag on 13. (Bad yardage? Who knows!) On 14, his approach fell one yard short of what it needed to carry and landed in a trap. This was an exhibition of the golf you don't see on TV. It was Goldilocks golf—one left, one right, one long, one short—none of it *just right.* Add it all up and in just 45 minutes we carded one nervy par and three silly bogeys.

I had gone mostly mute, the worst possible way to be when your player's scorecard is bleeding. But what do you say? Did Joel want jokes after bogeys? A pep talk? Or maybe nothing at all from an 8-handicap. I had brought up hoops on the front nine, and Joel told me all about his high school career as a pass-first point guard. That felt good. But should I roll out *another* conversation about Gonzaga basketball? I didn't have the right words, so I went with no words at all, and that was when I knew I had underestimated Geno Bonnalie.

My proudest, snidest, most confident self had wondered just how important the bond between player and caddie really could be. Why couldn't I do the same job for Joel that Geno did? Because Geno has known Joel for decades. He knows his wife and his family and his secrets and the dumb things to say when dumb things need to be said. He knows the right ways to distract his man when he needs to be distracted. They can speak without speaking. Just the lift of an eyebrow or a simple "hmm" says it all sometimes. Joel once called Geno "a monkey" during a tense moment in Korn Ferry Tour Finals, where struggling PGA Tour players go to re-earn their Tour membership. Geno grabbed him by the shirt, pointed in Joel's face, and called him a motherfucker. Joel apologized, they tied for sixth, qualified for another season on Tour, bawled in each other's arms that night, and never looked back. They're brothers. Joel and I were just buddies.

On our final hole of the day, Joel played a knuckling low-ball into the wind and then a ropey 2-iron that hung out short and to the right. I had been so locked in on our own trials that I was clueless on where our playing partners stood. Straka started solid but was limping his way in. Probably two over, but at least he was being talkative. Korhonen barely said a thing, mostly grunting whenever I offered to pull the pin for him.

"I feel like he could be anywhere from one under to five over," I said to Joel.

"That's interesting," he replied. "He's at two under, maybe three."

Suddenly, it dawned on both of us. "You've been filling out his scorecard, right?" Joel asked ominously.

Uh, no. I had not. That scorecard he handed me on the 1ˢᵗ tee had 21 empty squares on it. *Oh, boy.* He snatched the card from my hands and pressed rewind.

Short on 2 for bogey.

Birdies on 3 and 4.

Hooped that 20-footer on 5.

But then he gave it back on 6.

On 7, par; 8, par; 9, par. Three putts on 10, par.

Joel rattled off every score Korhonen made in about 30 seconds, maybe the most impressive thing he did on the course that day. Korhonen was indeed three under and nowhere near what I thought. Joel didn't bother handing the card back—I had proven an incapable keeper—stuffing it away in his pocket and walking away with his 60-degree wedge. He bumped a hasty chip through the green and then shorted the chip coming back. He had left 12 feet for bogey in the kind of sequence of events where a good caddie steps in and verbally presses pause. *Slow down. Go through your process. Let's make this one.* When Joel tapped in for double, I couldn't help but feel guilty. Facing a dicey up-and-down for 74 is not the time to go mentally wandering back to the 10ᵗʰ to figure out if Mikko had two- or three-putted from 60 feet. It was a 76 for us, six over.

Joel is too nice to have been upset, but he had every right to be. Maybe his mind was already in Italy. When I asked what I could have done better, he was charitable: "Honestly? Nothing." It must take a lot to get him mad. Or just one hooked 8-iron. I ditched his clubs in the storage facility and plopped down at my desk in the media center. I was exhausted, and what did we get out of it? To make matters worse, my other boss wanted me to get back to my day job. The main takeaway became the title: "Caddying on the PGA Tour is WAY harder than it looks." Golf, at that level, is way harder than it looks. The good news was Thursday afternoon turned into what locals call a "proper links day." On the TV, it was perfectly sunny, with temps in the mid to upper

60s, but in person there was a constant wind of 15 mph and gusts pushing 25 mph. In America, it would keep people from submitting scores to their handicap. In the U.K., they call it "fun."

Torrid winds whipping over the course would not normally be a big deal, but tournament officials had set up the 16th and 18th to play as long as possible. No. 16 was 575 yards on the scorecard but now played dead into the fan. No. 18 was a 483-yard par-4, also straight into the wind. Each required about a 220-yard carry to the fairway.

Players stormed in off the course. Patrick Cantlay was livid, coming up short on 18 after hitting driver, 3-wood. Tommy Fleetwood's caddie, Ian Finnis, was flabbergasted. "Ridiculass. Ridiculass," he said. The 6'6", towering looper from Liverpool speaks so fast with that Scouse accent he seems to skip some consonants. Maybe that's why he repeats himself. "Tohmee could'n reach. Tohmee could'n reach. Justin Thoma could'n reach. If Justin Thoma can't reach the fairway, is-somethin' wrong."

I wasn't about to argue with him. Not far from us, Mackenzie Hughes was tearing into a Tour staffer near the scoring tent. I eavesdropped with one ear and chatted with his caddie, Jace Walker, with the other.

"My guy is one of the longest guys out here," Jace said. "If he can't reach [the fairway] on a good drive, you've got a problem."

Hughes is not one of the longest guys out here—remember, he was Mr. Average 2019—but it didn't matter. He usually hits it about 300 yards off the tee. A short hitter he is not. If he was straining to reach the fairway, you *do* have a problem.

"We better not change the tees up tomorrow," Hughes said to the tour official. It's a great setup debate, and one that happens at times. If the afternoon half of the field had to play in a particularly unfair setup, given the conditions, shouldn't the morning half deal with the same setup when they swap starting times on Friday? Or, if you're a tournament official, do you learn from the mistake and not make it a second time?

I played it cool on the outside, but the duality of Sean Zak bounced around my insides. Tormented players and caddies—this was all great fodder for articles on GOLF.com. But also, that leaderboard was coming back to us. And much quicker than I imagined. When we finished, it looked like Joel would need a 65 on Friday just to make the weekend. Now, a smooth 67 would do the trick. Joel was *plenty* capable of that. We could even make a couple mistakes and survive.

Late that night, Joel sent me a picture of the hole locations for the second round with five words: "Have a pint and study."

"Strokes Gained: Believe," I told him.

"How about the fact that your pro doesn't hit it great all the time or where it's supposed to go?"

Yes, there's that, too. Whatever mopishness he was feeling quickly burned off within an hour, because shortly after 11 local time, Joel texted again. This time it was a screenshot of an unsent tweet that read: "You want 1 a side tomorrow @IanJamesPoulter? #livmas"

Along with it, a two-word message: "Career suicide?"

I could just see Joel chuckling away at the Marine and Lawn hotel, drafting up silly tweets while lying in bed. He was the perfect player to be looping for this week, one of the most awkward weeks in recent Tour memory. He was always going to cut through the B.S. with a one-liner or two. As his caddie, I knew it was not in his best interest to draw unneeded attention to himself, especially after a below-average day. Poulter has an outsized number of Twitter followers, too. They'd roast Joel. The media member in me felt differently, of course. Drama is good for business. "Hahahahaha that's so good," I said, hopeful he'd press send anyway. Sadly, he did not.

The beauty of an early-late tee time draw is also its curse. Play bad enough on Thursday and Friday's round is nothing but a cruel formality. Proof of existence. He's not injured; he's just missing putts. But if there's a chance at making the cut, it's beneficial to tee off late on

Friday. You'll know roughly what you need to do to make the weekend. We needed that 67. Three under. I received many critiques from my friends back in America, but dampened them by promising, "We're starting on 10. If we make birdie there, we're in business."

So when Joel's 15-footer on 10 settled at the bottom of the jar, I could feel the texts streaming in. *Dahmen might do it today.* His approach on 11 landed short of the hole and rolled 15 feet by. That's a great shot in this country. Easy par. He played his shot on 13 out to the right of the flag, using the slope to nestle at 23 feet. Another easy par. We were into the wind on 14 and Joel clubbed down, sending the ball on a lower arc and using the slope again to urge his ball closer to the hole. This was Scottish golf, folks. All it took was 18 dumb holes and we were finally doing it.

His tee ball on 15 made me giddy. I had passed him the driver and waited up the fairway as he walked back to the tee on his own. By the time he handed it back to me, he was wearing a big smile. "I got that one good," he said. It ran and ran and ended up 365 yards down the fairway, the second-longest ball of his entire season. This was the side of the golf course that Joel said "actually has some character," and it made sense. There were shot shapes forming in his eyes. When he pitched to kick-in range for a birdie on 16, I recounted the last two hours in my head. He had hit five drivers, one of them off the deck, one 3-wood off the tee, and a driving iron out of the rough. He was sniping greens and just barely missing his putts. The clean-ups were comfy. We. Were. *Livin'.*

This must be what Scottie Scheffler had meant during his Wednesday press conference when he said golf in this part of the world is just more fun. He and Sam Burns had just ripped through Ballybunion and Lahinch—two Irish favorites—on a quick little boondoggle and Scottie couldn't stop using that word: *fun.* Golf over here forces you into creativity, Scheffler said. The ball doesn't sit where it lands. It moves. It's way more chess than checkers. Players who lack imagination can win just about anywhere in America, but you need a golfer's *mind* to win in Scotland. Scheffler has a golfer's mind. Joel has a golfer's mind. And yet somehow, they were both in danger of missing the cut.

Our good vibes skidded to a halt with one bad swing on 17. Joel had been a bit aggressive, going right at the hole, drawing it too long and through the green, which dropped off into a cove of uneven, matted-down rough. This was where spectators had been lubricating.

"I'll buy you a beer, Joel!" a courageous one said while we assessed his chances. These lines always make me laugh as a writer. They even make their way into stories sometimes. But I can see how they only serve to annoy the player and caddie who are holding onto a thread of hope that they'll actually make some money this weekend. Ultimately, the chip shot was too difficult. The ball was sitting down and had to be clipped perfectly. When we made bogey, it felt like we gave three shots away instead of just one. Momentum exists in your mind.

Our final nine holes needed to be played in one under at the worst, maybe two under. And since the typical golf broadcast does not vitalize what could ultimately be some of the most impassioned play—the kind played on Friday afternoons within a shot or two of the cut line—the world will never know how good Joel's par on 1 was. (Up and down from 143 yards.) Or how delicate his short-sided chip was on 2. Or how convinced we were that his approach on 4 was going to rattle the flagstick. (It bounded through the green.) Or how the apex of his drive on 5 never eclipsed 20 feet, peeling off the perfect amount and cruising up the fairway. (The ball flight made me shiver.) Like the pancake blocks on plays that end in pass interference or the back-door passes that result in missed layups, these are the beautiful things in sport that constantly go unappreciated. They exist purely for the hardos and hopefully in Joel's memory as much as they do in mine. When we made a sloppy bogey on the cute, 114-yard 6th, it was now or never.

"I will not give up until it's absolutely over," Joel said as we walked to 7th tee. I told him we needed three straight birdies.

"Alrighty then," he said, shoving his tee in the ground. "That gives us nine shots from here to the house."

Thwack!

"That's one, Sean! We've got eight left."

It's good to give writers deadlines. Joel's tee ball tumbled and tumbled until it came to rest 404 yards from where he hit it. That is not a misprint. It was the longest tee shot of his Tour career. It was ages before we caught up with it.

After Joel hit a wedge to the back edge of the green, 18 feet from the hole, he changed tune again.

"What do you see?" he asked. He hadn't asked me for a single read all week. Maybe that's what golf is like in the now-or-never state. *Alright, media caddie, prove your worth.* I walked to the other side of the flag, bent down, and signaled a line about one cup outside the left edge. He mostly agreed—it was certainly breaking to the right, and was just a matter of how much—but we'll call it my read because this is my book.

When it dropped into the hole, I finally felt it. Satisfaction. I may have been mostly carrying the clubs and tracking the balls and raking bunkers and doing simple math—no mistakes there, I might add—but this was the first instance of shared responsibility for a result.

"Heyyy nowww," Joel said as he walked to the hole to claim his prize. Step 1 was complete.

It would be natural for me to dive into detail of Step 2 and then hopefully Step 3, but ultimately this chase resulted in my final caddying lesson of the week. It was our 17th hole of the day, our 35th of the tournament, and the 8th hole on the property. Like Nos. 16 and 18, it played straight into the wind, uphill to a crowned green. Undoubtedly among the toughest holes on the course. So when Joel nuked another punch driver, once again we were in business. But as we reached the fairway area where it was expected to be, there was nothing waiting for us. Whatever angst amateur golfers feel in our gut when we can't find a perfect tee ball, multiply it tenfold when you're searching for a pro's tee shot in a now-or-never sprint at the cut line.

The truth was his bullet ball had run through the fairway into a section of fescue surrounding cross-bunkers. The lie was…fine, but it was also avoidable. Joel turned around and squinted back at where we had come from. Then he uttered seven words that I'll never forget: "Sean…did we move up a tee?"

Despite the ruckus surrounding the 16th and 18th holes Thursday afternoon, it never occurred to me that tournament officials might change the setup on 8 as well. They had moved the tee markers up one teeing ground, which amounted to a 34-yard boost exactly when you didn't need it. *No wonder Sepp Straka hit a smooth 5-wood.*

My tail was tucked firmly between my legs now, bailed out only by the fact that the lie wasn't too bad. "Geno has never screwed that up," Joel would playfully tell me later. This mistake was the cousin of giving a bad yardage into the green. I had unknowingly given Joel a bad yardage to the end of the fairway. Caddying at the Tour level is filled with those little moments where the sharpest competitors and keenest caddies answer the questions right 18 times outta 18. Seventeen right answers might be 94 percent, but that isn't a passing grade. Joel played what looked like the perfect shot up to the green, but it got caught in the wind and rejected by the false front. He would be chipping up a turtle's back for his third. It was never gonna happen.

If I properly made note of the tee box change, maybe Joel plays that 3-wood instead and maybe he gets a lie in the fairway and as a result maybe he catches it extra clean instead of just pretty clean. Maybe then his shot cruises through the wind and one hops to a stop 12 feet away and we make another magical dual-read. On to the 9th hole we'd go—Step 3—and now the TV cameras would be watching us. *Maybe, maybe, maybe.* Instead, our hopes ended on a double bogey, and for the second straight day we found ourselves talking about Mikko Korhonen. He was sizing up a 3-foot, 7-inch putt from every possible angle.

"This is the throw-up zone," Joel whispered to me. I was confused. "It's so close, you should make it. But you're so nervous you might throw up. The throw-up zone."

I wanted to throw up now that Joel had mentioned it. Korhonen needed to *not* throw up, then make that par putt, and then make a par 3 on 9 to play on the weekend. I felt an odd sense of pride when he did exactly that. At least *one* person from this group was playing tomorrow. Straka finished with a rather listless 76 and Mr. Dahmen with 71. (He also kept track of the scorecard all day.) The golfer's mind in Scottie Scheffler sputtered with five bogeys on Day 2. His silver lining was an expedited trip up to St. Andrews. Darn.

"I'm sorry we didn't get you that made cut," Joel told me outside the scoring tent. "We'll have to try again some other time." Between him, Martin Trainer, and my four attempts to get coworker Dylan Dethier through local qualifying, I was now oh-fer-six in caddie cuts. As my other coworkers like to say, "Show me the numbers, Sean!" I had a feeling Joel wasn't serious about that "some other time" where I'd caddie for him, but it didn't matter. That second-round rally was a lesson unto itself. We were golfing that ball.

Chapter 11

Utopia

The banners were brief, as banners tend to be, but they did their job at the Scottish Open. WELCOME TO GOLF COUNTRY, they said in size 10,000 font, draped across buildings and walkways at Renaissance Club. It wasn't clear if "Golf Country" meant Scotland, the entire U.K., or just this little half peninsula called East Lothian, but I wasn't going to argue with the banners.

If you aimed directly west of Renaissance Club, a well-struck 3-wood could land on Muirfield, one of the best in the world. The three courses at Gullane—one of them a former Scottish Open host—are less than two miles west of that. Littered about the coastline is an endless list of one-name tracks: Luffness, Archerfield, Craigielaw, all the way over to Dunbar, which locals swear is most underrated of all. In the middle is the town of North Berwick and its charming West Links. The roller coaster of golf fun.

As a matter of reputation, the West Links is more Girl Next Door than Prom Queen, underappreciated but sneakily desired, and never more apparent than this week. A majority of players in the Scottish Open field (Joel Dahmen included) were staying at the Marine and

Lawn Hotel, their bedroom windows facing the 16th hole. Some pros couldn't help themselves. Max Homa made the cut on Friday and then played all 18 holes at North Berwick in the afternoon. "I never play 36 holes a day during a tournament week but for North Berwick, I had to," Homa said. "I saw it on a video back in the day and I've been wanting to go for years." I think he's the only Tour pro who has ever played an emergency 18 between his second and third rounds.

By the time pros came home from work, the West Links was draped in soft, golden sunlight. If they wanted to pick up food in town, the shortest route was the gravel path that runs along its final three holes. The 18th is shaped much like the finisher in St. Andrews, measuring just 277 yards with a deep, sudden valley between the fairway and green. You could sit there for hours and craft a dissertation on lag-putting and chip shots.

It was behind that 18th green on Saturday afternoon that I ran into my television screen. Turning the corner around the North Berwick clubhouse was the voice of the sport, Jim Nantz, with coffee in hand. He was staying at the Marine and Lawn, too, and was headed back for two reasons: 1. He had spilled coffee on his polo and 2. It was a work day. His voice would commence the third-round broadcast in about three hours.

"Mr. Nantz, how we doin'?" I asked, not expecting much of an answer.

"Hello, how are you?" he replied as we crossed paths. We had never met before and if it weren't for Joel Dahmen this would be the extent of our interaction. But right then smiley Joel popped out of the clubhouse and Nantz halted.

"Do you know Sean?" Joel said, pulling me in. "He works at GOLF dot com." We shook hands; I was in the circle of trust again, thanks to Joel.

"Ahhh, yes. Sean. Sean Zack?" Nantz said. "I've been reading your stuff over here. It's all been really good."

Your first order of business, whenever you get to St. Andrews, is to visit this intersection. Golf Place and The Links, where the Golf Gods exist.

Timestamp: 5:28 AM. Unlike most sought-after experiences, a tee time on the Old can actually be acquired by simply sleeping on the sidewalk.

The best days in St. Andrews might be Sundays, when the Old Course is closed for golf but open for everything else: picnics, walks, runs and definitely fetch.

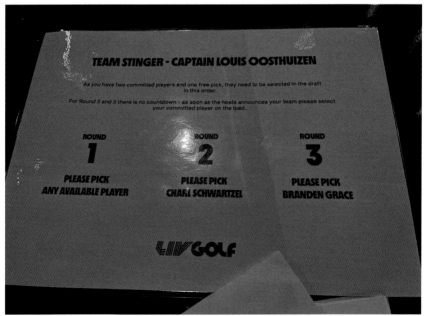

A reminder for captain Louis Oosthuizen—and everyone else—that LIV Golf was absolutely figuring things out as they went.

An image that will stick with me forever. Phil Mickelson launching his LIV Golf career with two logos on his person: his own and that of Augusta National.

A sunny afternoon on the Himalayas Putting Course has it all: jeans, loafers, button-downs, sundresses, bare feet, sunglasses, purses—even doggos.

What happens when you're six beers deep, just threw away the course record, and are presented with a lie on the pavement? Ask Luke List.

Moments after Woods made his ceremonial walk up the 18th fairway, he hushed this jam-packed room with the idea that it may have been his last Open at the Old Course.

It's easy to get romantic about golf when The Open champion is being crowned later that day, just down the street from the grave of the game's godfather.

You could see it in their faces. Rory McIlroy is teeing off on the final hole of The Open, but most spectators had resigned themselves to the fact that he wouldn't be lifting the trophy.

Why pose with Xander Schauffele's name plate? McIlroy's was up on the leaderboard. Woods' had been snatched by a couple of college students.

It takes four tries, 91-year-old Tom Kenmack told me. Hence the four golf balls.
Aye, aye.

Timestamp: 10:28 PM. A few minutes after disbanding Rich Halliday, here I am with Pete Couhig, just halfway done with the 18th hole. This is why they call them Dark Times.

If there was one scene I wanted to slow down and enjoy for a few more hours, it was Clara Young's qualifier in front of family and friends at North Berwick.

David Buhai, on the left in the white hat, numerous beers deep, actively part of #HusbandCam while his wife wins the Women's Open.

St. Andrews is built to look the same, over time, no matter if it's 1890, 1990, or 2090. But I think my drone captured a good one here that will always say "summer 2022."

Eight years on the golf beat had prepared me to not act like a giddy teenager, but I couldn't help it. Jim Nantz simply glancing at my work was an honor. Appreciating it? That was a massive boost to the ego, and a reminder that you just never know who's reading.

Luke List appeared from the opposite direction, walking out of his way to shake Nantz' hand. There's a short list of universally revered people in golf and it starts with Nicklaus, Woods, and Palmer, but not long after them you'd find Nantz. Everyone wants him to broadcast their crowning achievements, which he had done for List's first career victory at Torrey Pines in January.

After a quick chat, we let Jim go tend to his wardrobe and headed to the West Links starter shack. Luke and Joel were about to peg it with Luke's caddie, Jeff Willett (nickname: Skillet) and Tom Hoge's caddie, Henry Diana. The pros looked out of place with their massive staff bags, but North Berwick had zero caddies available. Some had been pulled to loop at Renaissance, and many had been working extra hours all week. I watched as three teenage loopers with the tee time ahead of Luke and Joel were asked if they wanted to put their clubs aside and caddie for a couple Tour pros. "What's they'uh names?" one said. You'd think the chance to rub elbows with pro golfers and get paid handsomely would be a no-brainer, but they declined! I watched them shrug their shoulders and race off on their own round. I couldn't bring myself to tell Joel or Luke their name recognition didn't travel very well overseas. They'd have to wheel their bags around on pull carts.

Instead of playing myself, I was just here to enjoy the walk. I wanted to know how the pros would tear apart this 6,500-yard course, the 13th oldest in the world. Would my sterling 78 two weeks ago look like chump change? Probably. List is one of the longest players on the Tour, averaging 315 yards off the tee. But how would that jive with the *quirk* of the West Links? Remember, North Berwick has you carry tee shots over the corner of a public beach. Leave it out to the right and you're expected to play from the sand, so long as the tide isn't up. Would these guys make the redan par-3 look like a simple pitch and putt? Where would their game run smack into the trickiness of golf antiquity? I was intrigued. A member named Neil had answered the call and biked over to forecaddie for the group.

You didn't miss much through the first 90 minutes. Perhaps the weather, which was 72 degrees and cloud-free. Or the black Labs that chased after each other in the rough. (Dogs are extremely welcome at North Berwick, another reason why it may be Golf Heaven. Leashes are so optional they seem frowned upon.) Joel made birdie on the 1st, but List's scorecard was circle-free through the first six holes. I recognized a couple familiar figures off in the distance. It was a good thing Joel didn't send that tweet Thursday night.

Ian Poulter was five holes ahead of us, but only a gap wedge away when we reached the 7th tee. He was out walking with his son, Luke, who was practicing ahead of the English Amateur. Poulter's sherpa around the West Links, of course, was none other than Simon Holt. Sholty! One week you're steering Sean Zak and James Colgan around the old links, the next it's Poulter and Co. I bounced over to say hello and ended up walking the one and a half holes with them. The last time I was near Poulter I stuck a recorder in his face at LIV London as he insisted he would appeal his PGA Tour suspension. He was living up to that promise, too, but didn't seem to recognize me.

"All the stars are out today," I told Simon when I reached them. "We've got Joel Dahmen and Luke List playing up 7 right now. Ian Poult–"

"Joel who?" Poulter said. "I know Luke, but who else did yeh say?"

Wait. Was he really so pretentious to not recognize Joel? Did his Rolodex of contemporaries only extend to the PG-A Tour?

"Wait, you don't know Joel?" I asked, completely dumbfounded. "He won that Punta Cana event a couple years ago."

"Nah, never heard of him," Poulter said, pursing his lips and shaking his head, not an ounce of emotion in his face. He turned away to coach up his son, who left his lag putt woefully short. I didn't think it possible that anyone in pro golf didn't know Joel.

"That's stunning," I whispered to Simon, who was equally confused. This wasn't the time to ask for clarification, as Poulter's coaching had gotten animated. "You're not going to be able to do that…" were the last words I could make out before Ian lowered his voice. Luke was headed to play at the University of Florida in the fall. Halfway up the 12th hole, I readied my goodbyes for the group. Simon mentioned aloud that I was working on a book, I think as a warning to Poulter to watch what he says.

"Ah, what's it about?" Poulter asked.

I gave him the full pitch: "Well, it's mostly my experiences over here as an American. Three months in St. Andrews, covering the first LIV event, the women's event at Muirfield, playing with gentlemen like Simon here."

"Very interesting," Poulter said. "I look forward to reading it."

If you'd like to know exactly what to say when talking to an aspiring author, copy those last six words from Poults. When I caught back up to Dahmen and List on the 10th tee I learned Luke had overpowered the 8th and 9th for consecutive birdies. He nearly holed out on the par-3 10th before hitting about a 400-yard tee shot on 11—driver-pitching wedge for another offensively easy bird—and then pitched it close for yet another on 12. The only word to describe this style of golf was *provocative.* The kind that makes golf purists shake their fists. It's not supposed to be this easy. But no one in our group wanted it to stop. Luke's barrage continued on 13 when he hit another ridiculous drive—maybe 380 yards this time—finishing hole-high on a mound of fescue on the wrong side of the rock wall that crosses in front of the green. He flopped over it and canned a 20-footer for a sixth straight circle on the scorecard. He was probably on his sixth beer, too.

List and Dahmen had emptied a case of Tennent's pint cans into their bags and were progressing through them about as well as you'd expect for a sunny day off from work. This was the tipsy golf that Saturday morning amateurs aspire to. (For the record, Joel was making birdies too—just not six in a row.) When Luke pulled driver on the 14th, Trevor Immelman's course record of eight-under 63 was officially in danger. The hole earned its nickname, Perfection, because playing it well was supposed to require two perfect shots. One that would travel about 230 yards into an angled fairway and then a second, touchy wedge shot up and over a hill before trundling onto the green. Luke opted for one perfect swing, smashing driver on a rope, up over the dune and just right of the tall, candy-striped pole that signaled the green. Forecaddie Neil nodded approvingly.

"I *thought* it might have been 3-wood," Luke said when we reached the hole. He was too long for this golf course when it played downwind. His ball ended up *past* the green, again around 380 yards from the tee, nearly on the beach. He chipped to four feet from the fescue and everyone in the group mentally moved on to the next. Seven in a row.

There's something funny about four-footers, though. The Tour average from three feet is a virtual certainty: 99.5 percent. Missing one out of 200. But once 12 inches of grass is added to the end of that 99 percenter, the Tour average suddenly drops to 92 percent. From there, the best golfers on the planet miss one out of 12. It's a bewildering drop in success rate. The kind that unravels confidence and swims around in your head. The ball doesn't get any bigger and the hole doesn't shrink, but it *feels* like that.

During the 2022 season, 193 Tour pros registered the minimum number of rounds for their stats to be counted. From exactly four feet in 2022, Luke List was Mr. 193, missing one out of every four. Xander Schauffele, who was busy contending at Renaissance, made 123 out of 124 in 2022. Luke made 97 out of 128. Does he know his 4-footer stats? He has to. You already know what's coming. Yes, of course, Luke's conquest of North Berwick and attempt for a seventh straight birdie grazed the right shoulder of the hole and did not go in. I groaned loud enough for him to hear me 30 feet away. Skillet, Luke's caddie, couldn't have been too surprised. I hoped wherever Trevor Immelman was at that exact moment he felt a random burst of energy. North Berwick is one of his favorite courses in the world.

Bless Luke's heart and his sobriety in this moment, but the miss didn't bother him much. Thirty minutes later he was crouched down on both knees, driving iron in hand, hands planted on the pavement of Pointgarry Road, the street that runs parallel to North Berwick's 18th. These are the odd, golf-yoga positions you find yourself in when six straight birdies isn't enough to close out the match.

Needing an eagle 2 to tie Immelman or a birdie to tie Dahmen and Diana, Luke heel-cut his tee ball and the wavy mounds of the fairway and deposited it under the back left wheel well of a silver Ford hatchback. Name another sport where that sentence would apply. But because Tour players think they are magicians, and because Luke had slugged a number of tall boys, he analyzed the angle of approach *beneath* the car, rather than punching back to the fairway. No one was going to tell him he was already standing out of bounds. This was a 1 in 100 shot. Maybe 0 in 100. The result was his ball playing Plinko on the car's underbelly, emerging on the opposite side, between vehicles now. Everyone giggled. Without changing clubs, Luke took an abbreviated backswing and punched at the ball again. This time it kicked upward off the cobblestone, bounced off the hood of the second car and trickled back inside the fence line.

"Anddd we're back in play," he said with a squirrely, I-really-shouldn't-have-done-that grin.

It felt like we were in grade school, lucky the adults weren't around. Goofy golf, brought to you by the people normally who take it super seriously. He two-putted for a double bogey and 67. No asterisks were needed. Luke's creativity was appreciated from the dozen or so people lunching on the clubhouse patio. Poulter's group was among them. When I said hello once more, he admitted he was "just taking the piss" out of Dahmen earlier. Some joke, huh!

Keith Mitchell was sitting on the patio as well.

"You missed Luke tryi—"

Keith cut me off.

"Oh, believe me. I saw *that*," he said with a laugh.

Mitchell was content as can be, a pint in hand, still wearing his spikes after a 73 in the third round at Renaissance. He had company, too. Ted Scott, Scottie Scheffler's caddie, had finished a couple groups ahead of us, along with Brian Vranesh, a former Tour pro and current caddie for Si Woo Kim. This was his *third* loop around North Berwick that week. Couldn't get enough. Joel ordered a dozen beers for the group.

NB assistant pro Scott Young grabbed one of them. He was wearing the widest smile I had seen all week. Some of the best golfers on the planet were suddenly in his Scottish backyard, right where he had grown up playing, like they had crawled out of the tiny television in the pro shop. I couldn't help but smile pretty wide, too. A number of side conversations had kicked off, and somehow I was shifted to the center of the circle. I kicked my feet out and slumped back in the sunshine. All I wanted to do was listen. There was no discussion about LIV. It was all about hole design and scores and ancient walls and funky lies. Or the conditions up the coast at Renaissance Club. Or how the hell Homa shot 66 on Saturday after playing 36 holes on Friday. What it's really like at Muirfield? What it's really like during a Si Woo Kim temper tantrum? (Mr. Vranesh has some bewildering stories. We'll leave it at that.)

One beer turned into two and two into three. Chris Kirk arrived carrying one of his three sons on his shoulders en route to dinner in town. Russell Knox and his wife followed in his wake 10 minutes later. After about 90 minutes Joel tapped me on the shoulder. He could see it happening. "We had better leave now before we stay here all night," Joel said. We were getting sucked into the vortex of a perfect Joel Dahmen Day and our tardiness was nagging his wife, Lona, who had been waiting for well over an hour back at the hotel. Her leash is longer than most, but she was hungry and growing impatient. It was time to get moving.

I carried Joel's bag one final time, those thousand steps or so back up the gravel path. We examined Catriona Mathew's house and dreamed about owning one of the lucky sea-and-course-facing cottages in town. "Don't give my wife any ideas," Joel said. We crossed paths with Adrian Meronk, the best golfer in the history of Poland, a smiley, 6'6" 29-year-old who had just won the Irish Open. He shot 9-over at Renaissance, a minor victory for the duo of Zak and Dahmen!

"He's *way* taller than I imagined," Joel said. My mind was still at the clubhouse.

"Yeah…so, how often on Tour do you have a scene like the one we just had?" I asked.

"Never," he said. "Luke obviously isn't playing the local country club after a missed cut at the John Deere."

If you want an idea of the difference between Golf in Scotland and Golf in Illinois, there's a start. Making the cut with Joel would have been a blast, but maybe it was okay that we missed. Our bank accounts would have been fuller, but not our golfing souls. When we reached the hotel restaurant, we found Mitchell had beaten us there and was seated with his sister and brother-in-law. Keith promised multiple times that the fish 'n' chips were the best he's ever had. From any other Tour pro, this recommendation might ring hollow, but Keith has spent his fair share of time in the old country. His sister graduated from the University of St. Andrews, and she endorsed the No. 1 entree as well. She would know what good fish 'n' chips looks like. Three orders, please!

Two more Guinnesses later, dinner had bled into cards in the lounge, which bled into drinks from the hotel bar. Joel and Lona introduced me to gin rummy, the card game of choice at PGA Tour hotel bars. Joel claimed that Charley Hoffman's greatest skill may not be his ball-striking but rather his ability to form runs and sequences and take your money in a game of gin. Player-turned-broadcaster Colt Knost confirmed this fact when he plopped down next to us. Twenty minutes later, his colleague Amanda Renner joined, along with Jim Nantz's wife, Courtney Richards. Our group hang grew and grew. Twenty minutes after that Luke List sat in. And then Dottie Pepper and her husband David Normoyle, a golf historian. We all tried coaxing Frank Nobilo into *just one drink*, but he passed. Nantz himself escaped out the balcony door at 9 PM, keeping a promise he made to his six-year-old son. They had a putter and wedge in hand, headed for a lap around the Wee Course, that bite-size par-3 track.

Back in our circle, Dottie and Joel engaged in a lively debate about, what else, *What are pros supposed to do with the crazy foreign money being injected into the game?* Dottie was vehemently against the matter. Joel was playing devil's advocate. "What are we *supposed* to do if more big names go?" he asked. It was the question every Tour pro was asking themselves. If LIV becomes the new norm, better to be on the inside than the outside, right? I was a bit surprised to hear Joel talk this way, but it was good I did. My Scottish Open week had been about one thing: leveling up with pros like never before. That meant understanding their lives, wants, and needs better than ever. A lot of my job can involve treating pros like zoo animals. We watch from the rope line as they go about their business in the fairway. Their 50-hour work week is often reduced to a handful of shots or 30 seconds' worth of highlights. Fans shout at them regardless of the outcome and then go back to their less visible lives. But what are those animals really trying to do out there by playing golf? Most are just trying to make a living the only way they've understood how "make a living" is supposed to look. They're trying to provide for their family—Joel and Lona had just announced they were expecting—and enjoy the pursuit of mastering their craft. They're trying to *not* have to apply for a desk job somewhere. Or at least postpone the day when they have to do that. And so the threat of LIV Golf to most of them is not such an affront to their moral code like the majority of golf fans would like. It's much more an affront to the way they see 2024 and 2025 and 2026 playing out. It makes the waters choppy when they would otherwise be calm. It impacts income projections and alters mortgages. The PG-A Tour knows how good they've got it, but I'd argue it's players on the PG-B Tour that really know they've got it good because they know it's very possible they'll lose it. Joel would be irresponsible to not consider LIV's existence for a much longer runway than Dottie, Renner, or I would. That doesn't mean he was interested; all it means is his job requires him to be inquisitive. And to read and react differently with every piece of new information. That's what made the Scottish Open so fascinating. It was the peak of uncertainty about which side was winning the war.

Joel and Dottie weren't the only ones deep in convo. Knost and Normoyle went back and forth, too. Amanda and I mostly watched and listened. The former was unsurprisingly pro-player, but the latter was as researched as anyone I had heard talk about LIV, players and managers included. Normoyle knew about media rights, endorsement deals, tournament sponsor contracts, you name it. He spoke as though he was in the room in 1994 when Arnold Palmer dunked on Greg Norman's first attempt at a breakaway golf league. He spoke as though he was in the room in Ireland this week, with Tiger and Rory and the power-broking agents. I was so impressed that I chased him down when he and Dottie headed to their room. It was around 1 AM. I needed Normoyle's cell. Or maybe I just wanted him to have mine. I still had half a summer to live in St. Andrews and I figured he'd be a fantastic pen pal. His advice for this book was intriguing. "Don't put everything in there," he said. "Once you share something in the book, it's no longer yours." I was going to have to chew on that at a more sober time.

I really hoped chasing Normoyle down would be my final move of the night. I had been quiet quitting on the drinking for at least an hour. I reached double-digit beers on the day and was grappling with the idea that I was the only one in this group whose hotel room was 24 miles away, in another county. We had lost Luke List and we had lost Courtney Richards. Lona had long retired, too, but her husband was just getting started. When I sat back down, I found Joel had replaced my empty Guinness with a full one. Earlier in the night I told him there would be trains running back to Edinburgh at all hours but apparently that was a lie. The Trainline app had gone blank, and so had my face.

Thlack, thlack, thlack.

This night won't end. Three more knocks on the balcony doors. Bartenders had locked them around midnight, but Jay Danzi was on the other side of the windowpane now, to my surprise. For a split second I considered being cheeky and asking him for the special password to enter. Danzi is Jordan Spieth's agent and notoriously stingy toward journalists. He doesn't need us for anything, but in this moment he needed to be let indoors. Perhaps some early AM beers in Scotland would be the perfect opportunity for us to break bread. He had been out to dinner and rather than struggle with the spotty cab service this late in a sleepy town, he hoofed it home instead. He was out of breath, ready for a beer, and keen to keep much of the next few hours off the record. I was happy to oblige.

Danzi had a busy week, having demanded a retraction from *Golf Monthly*, a European magazine that reported Spieth was headed to LIV Golf. Danzi shook his head, annoyed, when I brought it up. Word spread quickily Friday afternoon, just as golf fans were waking up in the States. Was it shocking? It was *stunning*. But was it how the entire summer had been going? Absolutely. Knost himself paced down the range to confirm with Danzi what he already knew to be true, that this was literal fake news. There was no way Jordan was going to LIV. Spieth tweeted out a statement later that night calling it categorically untrue and ending with, "Those who truly know me, know what is most important to me." The report may have been complete hogwash, but it was important for Spieth to respond. These were weird days.

At the bar Saturday night Danzi admitted that, yes, modern journalism isn't easy. Writers get things wrong now more than ever before. The truth can be blurry. But a mistake of that magnitude simply cannot be made. He never received a single request for confirmation or comment. "All it takes is one writer to ruin relationships for the rest of us," I said, hoping my sympathy might earn some respect. In any other summer, Danzi might not be here right now. But in the summer of LIV Golf and its never-ending rumor mill, Danzi needed to be extremely present. Days like Friday proved it. His main client is really his only client, and he may be the most valuable client not named Tiger Woods. So Danzi was there in the bar, keeping awake until 3 AM Scotland time because that would be 9 PM Dallas time. He stole away to FaceTime with his son about a youth baseball game back home.

The jig was up around then. Uber drivers weren't going to venture this far from Edinburgh. Lyft didn't even exist in Scotland. Local taxi drivers weren't answering their phones because they were rightfully asleep. I needed to be rightfully asleep. I also needed to pick up laundry from Renaissance Club. Free wash, dry, and fold for all caddies and players, courtesy of the PGA Tour, was still cheaper than Landlady Lorraine. When the front desk clerk couldn't find me a ride, I briefly considered sleeping in the dunes on the beach. They always look so comfy. The sun would be up soon.

"Well, do you have anything available here?" Joel asked. I scoffed, knowing he'd be stubborn enough to buy me a room. One player who had missed the cut had departed early, leaving a corner suite wide open and prompting our first player-caddie argument. After six days together, finally, something we could disagree on. Joel won the fight and flashed his plastic at precisely 3:04 AM. We both wobbled into the elevator and made very loose plans for breakfast in the morning.

It didn't take long for me to pass out once my head hit the pillow, but I do remember thinking about how fascinating life was like on the inside of the Tour bubble. You never know who will be sitting at the hotel bar. (Thanks to Knost for the drinks.) But that evening and that afternoon and really everything happening in North Berwick reaffirmed for me the importance of golf writing. Of golf storytelling. There's a reason the Tour is often called a traveling circus. There are livelihoods at stake, downtime, drunk times, tense times, and frivolous times. And then a new city to do it all in again next week. If golf and pro golf seem like a Rubik's Cube to those of us on the outside, it's comforting that life is sometimes just as hectic and confusing inside the bubble. I knew my window peeking in probably wouldn't be this open ever again. In that, it was a stunning success. I woke the next morning with a crippling hangover that put whatever happened after Royal Burgess to shame. I had learned nothing about mixing in water(s) before bed. Normoyle had texted me a quote from C.S. Lewis:

"Even in social life, you will never make a good impression on other people until you stop thinking about what sort of impression you are making. Even in literature and art, no man who bothers about originality will ever be original: whereas if you simply try to tell the truth (without caring twopence how often it has been told before) you will, nine times out of 10, become original without ever having noticed it. The principle runs through all life from top to bottom."

Now there's some sound writing advice. Whatever I was doing seemed to be working, because Nantz gave me and North Berwick a shoutout on the CBS broadcast while Homa contended at Renaissance.

"He played over at North Berwick after his round here. I saw Luke List do that. Joel Dahmen and his caddie, Sean Zack the writer. They were having a fun time. Many of the players, they were so *inspired* by it."

Welcome to Golf Country. Or Golf Utopia, as I like to call it. Xander Schauffele, our hottest golfer in the world, won again. I'm sure he felt it now.

Chapter 12

The Open

I t was the summer of 2018 when I first vowed to cover the 2022 Open. I was 26 years old and bleary, fresh off a redeye and driving on the left side of the road for the first time.

I drove in from the west, along Road A91—the way many foreigners do—which is ultimately a rather conspicuous entrance to town. From the east or the south, you enter St. Andrews from atop a hill with a view of the entire town, church spires sticking into the sky. But from the west, you drive a flatter route *along* the Old Course, and at any given point there is something between it and your vehicle—hotels, 100-year-old stone buildings, even a rugby pitch. Only when Siri said, "Turn left on Golf Road" did I know I must be close to Mecca. Taxi and shuttle drivers will actually veer off their route and down Golf Road to give visiting golfers their first peek. They know how crucial the ancient course is to their business. And they know once the traveling golfer sees the Holy Grail, the gratuity spikes.

I cruised through the roundabout and hung a left at the Dunvegan, every golfer's favorite St. Andrews pub. "One of the best hangouts in the world of golf," says the sign on its window. On the left of Golf

Road is the Auchterlonies shops, a golf retailer more than a century old. On the right is a three-bedroom shack nicknamed "Golf House," which University of St. Andrews students rent for £2,300 a month. One hundred yards ahead sits the old greystone clubhouse of the Royal and Ancient Golf Club of St. Andrews, purveyors and governors of the game for hundreds of years. The clubhouse grabs your attention, sitting out on its own with no neighbors attached, a rarity in town. But about halfway between my rental car and the R&A, my eyes diverted to the left. Walking by himself at the golfiest intersection on the planet, just outside the boyhood home of Old Tom Morris, was... Hall of Famer Ernie Els.

The Big Easy! A four-time major winner and two-time Open Champion sauntered by himself, smiling his way up the sidewalk. It was just 18 years earlier that his score of 11-under beat 154 other players and lost to just one, that being Tiger Woods, who won by eight. *My god—is this what life is really like here?*, I thought. *Golf royalty milling about with the plebes?* Like if you turned on to 161st Street in the Bronx and ran into Derek Jeter, out for a stroll. Yes, that's what St. Andrews is like when an Open of any kind visits Fife, East Lothian, or Angus, three golf-rich counties of Scotland's eastern seaboard. An Open in "Golf Country" is a gathering. It cannot be missed.

I had barely stepped off the train from Edinburgh when I recognized my first golfer in the wild: Mito Pereira, the 26-year-old Chilean who led the entire weekend of the PGA Championship before making the worst swing of his life on the 72nd hole. A better swing and his life changes forever. Pro golf is cruel like that. A better swing and he's not lugging his own suitcases off the train at Leuchars Station. But here he was. His girlfriend smiled when I wished him good luck. Maybe in a few days I'd be asking him how he was contending in his first Open Championship.

The second familiar face I saw in St. Andrews was a lot more interested in talking to me. It was writer Michael Bamberger. In some ways, he was responsible for the excursion I was on. Thirty-one years prior, during the summer before I was born, Michael and his wife, Christine, set out on an extended honeymoon. Michael had landed a gig carrying the clubs of Peter Teravainen across the varied summer stops of the European Tour, starting on the southeastern tip of France. The original golf study abroad trip. He took a one-year stay from his job at the *Philadelphia Inquirer* and Christine quit her gig at an advertising agency in New York City. The goal was to experience Europe while Michael caddied among a circus of characters, visiting Spain, Italy, Monaco, Scotland, England. Scenes like I had just witnessed at 2 AM in North Berwick.

When I asked Christine how they did it, now three decades removed, she said, "We weren't afraid." They wanted adventure and knew life in America was always waiting on the other side. Michael wrote a book about it titled *To the Linksland*. Coincidentally, the final tournament Michael caddied in was the Scottish Open, too. He and Teravainen also missed the cut.

Michael showed off his Scottish depth when he texted me that afternoon, "Wee nine-holes tonight?" and after an important nap my North Berwick hangover finally relented. I found him on South Street, not far from where he and his missus lived when they stayed in St. Andrews in 1991. "I remember it was above a hair salon," he said, but St. Andrews had changed just enough in 30 years. There weren't any hair salons on South Street anymore. The good news was we were headed to Anstruther, a fishing village 20 minutes south of town.

I had heard the tales about Anstruther, but wasn't sure a 9-hole, par-31 course that maxed out at 2,500 yards was worth the effort, especially on the eve of Open week. But Michael is one of the best golf writers who ever lived. We met in 2014 when I was the lucky young journo on *Sports Illustrated*'s golf team. He'd write unique, meaningful stories and I'd help with background research, tracking down names and phone numbers. I was exhausted from my week down the coast but Michael was a bit of a golf writing guidance counselor. There was no better person to start Open week with, even if our taxi driver ripped through the winding country roads, nearly extending my probation.

Golf with Bamberger can include so many things—he's as inquisitive as they come—but it is one thing above all else: rapid. He's the fastest golfer I've ever played with, partly because he never seems confused by the movement of his golf ball, like you and I often become. Michael knows his game intimately—it's low shots that run, built perfectly for Scotland. A lot of 4-irons off the tee and 4-iron again from the fairway. Who knows if he ever slips the club back in his bag between shots. He reads putts in a few seconds, never plumb-bobbing, and makes his stroke. If it goes in, great. If not, on to the next. The kind of indifference one can only achieve after a bout with the putting yips, as Michael would admit to. His swing is impressively smooth for a man in his sixties. He thinks it's more of a lunge, but it's not. I expect to see that move long into his eighties, because Michael is a runner and not much for the drink. He stays in incredible shape.

When we crested the tidal wave of a hill on Anstruther's 1st hole, we were both pleasantly surprised. Anstruther was the kind of golf you grew up creating in your backyard. Where one hole begins just steps from where the last one ends. Where you hole out and analyze the 360 degrees of space around you and design a new hole on the spot. A half-shot par-3 followed by a long par-4. Why not? You play toward a WWI memorial at Anstruther and then tee off at an ancient naval lookout post. How about three par-3s in a row, one of them eroding off the rocky shoreline? It's no surprise that most of the holes trace back and forth across the property. Go there and come back. That's backyard golf. It's fun and it's cheap and reminded me of summer afternoons with my grandpa in the churchyard next door, crafting new holes as we went. Grandpa Mack would have loved Anstruther. When you play down that massive hill on the 9th hole, Anstruther can end, or your second trip around can begin. It was dreamy Scottish summer weather for Michael and me, the sky clear enough to see across the firth to North Berwick Law, near the hotel where my hangover began that morning. We whipped around the course a second time.

Michael and I talked about plenty that evening—namely, the potential for this book and if we thought Phil Mickelson was in financial trouble—but it served as a great introduction to what an Open in St. Andrews really means for American golf writers. It's less a work trip with a bit of golf and more a golf trip with a bit of work. On Tuesday evening, my coworkers Alan Bastable, Josh Berhow, and Dylan Dethier ventured with me to Elie, where we found another quartet of golf media: Bamberger, Alan Shipnuck, Mark Cannizzaro, and Bob Harig. Dethier finished with a birdie under a glint of sun at 10:05 PM. *Zak and Bastable, 2 and 1.* The next night we gamed the Balcomie Course at Crail Golfing Society, the seventh oldest in the world. We played the 18th at 10:07. *Zak and Bastable, 3 and 2.* Other groups of writers played Elie when we were at Crail and played Crail when we were at Elie, but everyone was watching the same sunsets. A mushroom cloud of yellow erupted on the horizon. It made me happy that Scotland was showing off.

Back in St. Andrews, there was a looming sense that history would soon be made, and in particular for one of the people milling about. I spotted Joaquin Niemann racing by us Monday afternoon, late to dinner. A couple minutes later, there went Sepp Straka with his brother carrying ice cream cups from Jannettas. Maybe this was Sepp's week, now that he didn't have me and Dahmen in his group, unaware which tee box we were playing from. The Strakas crossed paths with Thomas Bjørn, who was chatting with reporter Jamie Weir at Central Bar, and Catriona Mathew, who was on a direct path for that ice cream shop herself. If you visited town and *didn't* run into a golf legend, you were probably unlucky. Dine out at the right places and you'll see Scottie Scheffler and his wife pop in to grab take out. You'll see Pete

Cowen, Brooks Koepka's swing coach, and Ricky Elliot, Koepka's caddie, diving into some fish and chips at Tailend. Koepka himself? Who knows, but after missing the cut he was spotted at The Vic, St. Andrews' only club-like establishment, which stays open until 4 AM. The perfect (and only?) spot in town for a guy who enjoys his nights in South Beach and Vegas. On Wednesday evening, anyone lingering around the course would have seen Ian Finnis, Tommy Fleetwood's caddie, sneaking in some final prep. While polishing off a pint around 10 PM, an email pinged Finnis' phone. First-round hole locations. He got up from the pub and walked all 18 holes that evening, counting his steps in the darkness to the spot on each green where the hole would be cut at dawn. To that I say, why the hell not? Just don't lose your yardage book.

This is all part of the allure of a modern Open. The event has become one of the biggest in all of sport, but it has somehow not outgrown the tiny towns of its upbringing. Portrush, in Northern Ireland, is home to about 7,000. Hoylake, in the west of England? About 6,000. Troon, on the opposite coast of Scotland, houses about 15,000. There are only so many beds, restaurants, pubs, or grocery stores. Remember my first night, back in June? Surrey the waitress had informed me that, before long, people would be selling access to their barstools for £20.

My barber was all excited that he ran into Dustin Johnson in the convenience store. Everyone who's anyone has flown in, set up shop, and is rubbing elbows with everyone else. After midnight, when rowdy drinkers spilled out of the Dunvegan onto North Street, that quite literally could have been a nuisance for Corey Conners, who was sleeping across the street. You don't get that at major championships in the States. When the PGA Championship visits St. Louis, pros rent out mansions in gated communities. When Tiger Woods plays the Masters, he doesn't even stay in Augusta, Georgia. He's often across the Savannah River in South Carolina.

This week, Woods was in the Old Course Hotel, like many fellow pros. Technically, the hotel was considered inside the ropes and rooms were held exclusively for players, agents, caddies, and power brokers. One can only imagine the impromptu meetings in hallways and elevators between pro-LIV and pro-Tour figures. This was the final major of the year and after it both sides of golf's civil war would go their separate ways for eight months. Sergio García played his practice rounds with fellow LIVers Abe Ancer and Patrick Reed. Ian Poulter, Richard Bland, and Sam Horsfield did the same.

The LIV rumor mill swirled around Aussie Cam Smith, unsurprisingly, but Adam Scott, too. Scott seemed keen to keep the door to the rival tour ajar. LIV was dangling Wade Ormsby, one of his best mates, as a potential teammate. I watched Henrik Stenson, Europe's Ryder Cup captain, chirp down from his balcony to Kevin Kisner, one of the player directors on the PGA Tour's policy board. There was serious concern that Stenson would ditch his post as RC captain in favor of the LIV money. Truth is, he had already been negotiating with LIV for 10 months. Like many things in the summer of 2022, a deal was essentially complete in private. All that was left was making it public. And waiting for the reaction.

Kisner didn't seem bothered. He was the head honcho of a practice round group that included Sam Burns, Scottie Scheffler, and Sepp Straka. When one of their caddies placed a Trackman device on the 18th tee, Kisner scoffed loud enough for everyone to hear: "Man, what are people trying to learn carrying around those boxes on every shot?" At 39 years old, this was Kisner's old-head way of schooling the youths. *You reach, I teach.* There was a heavy tailwind. What would the Trackman and its high-def sensors tell us? It's *this* club or it's *that* club. Also, it's *Wednesday.* If you're measuring spin rate in a tailwind on the 18th tee on Wednesday afternoon, it's not gonna be your week.

Even if he wasn't playing well, it wasn't hard to imagine Kisner winning at St. Andrews. He's a feel player and whoever was going to win would have to *feel* their way up and down the wavy terrain. Visualized with the mind and enacted by the hands. Rory McIlroy called the conditions the "fiddliest" he'd ever seen at an Open. The fiddliest! An adjective that meant "requiring an attention to detail."

"Fiddly hasn't really been my forte over the years," McIlroy said, "but I'm hopefully going to make it my forte this week."

At 5'10", 165 pounds—and that's generous—Kisner might be similar in dimension to McIlroy, but they do not play the same game. McIlroy can overpower courses, while Kisner *has* to hit it straight, hit it solid, then chip and putt like a mad man. He's not taking St. Andrews to its knees. But neither did Zach Johnson when he won here in 2015. Slow and steady *can* win the race. Kisner smoothly popped his drive into the air and out to the center of the widest fairway in the world. "Okay guys, go have fun in the Valley of Sin," he said, referencing the famous gulch at the beginning of the green. Scheffler and Burns both gave the Trackman zero worthy information by thinning 3-woods up the runway. They still had no problem reaching the drivable green. St. Andrews was playing firm as ever. "Oh come on," Kisner shouted at Burns. "Tell the world you almost topped it." Wednesdays at majors are so meaningless. Players go through the motions of a practice round just to pass the time until Thursday, when the shots finally get real.

Cameron Young did mean things to the Old Course Thursday morning. Fresh off completely bombing out of the Scottish Open at 13 over, Young flirted with the course record and set the early pace with an 8-birdie 64. Early in the week, R&A CEO Martin Slumbers had scoffed at the idea of a player shooting 59, promising that he would be the first person there to shake their hand if they could pull it off. I applauded Slumbers' candor but started to worry about him when the first wave of players was already making us think about it. McIlroy played eight groups behind Young and reminded the world that we're contesting this tournament on ancient property. His tee shot on the par-5 5th was one of those perfect, pummeled McIlroy drives. A baby draw, it hopped once, twice, then crashed into a plastic box. *What?* McIlroy's ball had collided with the hard, green shell of what locals know as the March Stones. Centuries earlier, white gravelike stones the size of a basketball were carefully placed across the property to mark where the course acreage ended and "common ground" began, similar to the land on the east side of the rock wall in North Berwick. On one side of the stone, a "G" was engraved, and if you could see it, you were standing on the golf course. Only in Scotland. Jamie Kennedy's comment about Edinburgh Castle reentered my mind. *Is that stone older than America?*

If you think a perfect golf shot clanging off a green, felted box in the middle of the fairway is dumb, you wouldn't be alone. Just know that McIlroy shrugged it off, made birdie, and cruised to an opening 66. Perhaps even dumber fate found Tiger Woods. He wore a tight, white mock turtleneck long sleeve under a navy blue sweater vest. The grandstands reverberated when he was announced in "Game Number 45." Woods hit a smooth stinger into the wind and didn't bother to watch it. For those of us who did, it looked great for 14 long seconds before it trickled into the center of an unfilled divot. He did not shrug it off and make birdie. Rather, he leaned on a wedge and spanked through the dirt, much of which ended up in his face. He cleared his eyes in time to see his ball one-hop into the Swilcan Burn. When Woods missed a shortie for bogey, it was official—no one's Open started worse. And it didn't get any better.

Woods added bogeys at 3 and 4 and then hooked his tee ball on 7 so far that he nearly pegged Scheffler, who was playing up the 12th. Woods' ball rolled into Admiral's Bunker, a sandy grave so far offline it's barely indicated in the yardage books. That bunker is only supposed to be in play when the course is played in reverse, like it was in the 1800s. (Admiral's earned its nickname when an old admiral was distracted by a lady nearby and fell into the trap. There are levels of irony for Woods there.) The three birdies he made were offset by three bogeys coming home, in what was a depressingly slow afternoon. I shivered from the bleachers behind 18 as Woods' group played our way at 9 PM, which meant they wouldn't finish in under six hours. It might have been the slowest non-delayed round of golf he'd played in a decade. And still the grandstand heaved beyond capacity, waiting to watch him finish. One spectator ignored the orders of a marshal and climbed up the side of the grandstand entrance, clinging to the metal guardrails for a view of any kind. He tightly gripped a bag of merchandise in his other hand, an obvious Open first-timer and maybe only-timer. It's absolute lunacy to risk injury to watch a pro golfer try and two-putt for birdie, and yet that's what Woods does to people. He sends them up the side of temporary bleachers at 9:06 PM, even when he's finishing with a par for 78. When the next group of Jon Rahm, Jordan Spieth, and Harold Varner III reached the green, more than half of the crowd had emptied out.

Part of the struggle with Tiger Woods' current state is that The End—capital T, capital E—could be 10 years from now or it could be 10 months from now, and he gives us nothing but mixed signals. The End nearly arrived in that car crash in February 2021. And because of that, The End hangs over his every appearance, including that second round at the Old Course. I set an early alarm just to watch him tee off in the morning mist. Everything was much colder than it needed to be in the middle of July, but that's Scotland. More than 60 people and dozens of cameras created a semicircle around Woods on the far end of the driving range, where he prefers to warm up. I cringed watching his putting session. It was filled with constant back stretches, linking his fingers behind his back, pushing his gut outward, then bending over at the hip, turning left and right with his feet locked into the turf. Old man stuff.

Thanks to his brutish first round, the hushed discussion was not about whether he'd make the cut or not, but rather about that big *R* word. Who knows when Woods might retire, but if it was anytime soon, this could be his final spin around the Old Course in an Open. Was he thinking about that? Had he thought about pausing atop the Swilcan Bridge to wave to all of St. Andrews like golfing greats did before him? Everything Woods had done this year was leading to this moment. He decided to game it at the Masters and limped off the property. He showed he was equally magnificent and frail at the PGA Championship, making the cut and then withdrawing. He sat out the U.S. Open just to prep for St. Andrews, taking a quick buddies' trip through Ireland with Rory McIlroy in the lead-up, apparently risking it all when he and McIlroy developed Covid symptoms after their trip.

Everything about the week had led to this moment, too. There was no robotic, unapproachable Woods. We saw playful Woods instead, chirping Lee Trevino throughout the Celebration of Champions, a cute exhibition on Monday afternoon. We saw forceful Woods, putting his stamp of disapproval on LIV Golf in his pre-tournament presser. "What these players are doing for guaranteed money, what is the incentive to practice?" he asked the room of reporters. "What is the incentive to go out there and earn it in the dirt?" That clause hits harder in the linksland, where each strike on the baked-out turf kicks up a cloud of dust.

On the Saturday evening before The Open, Woods was restless after checking in at the Old Course Hotel. There are only so many places a golfer's mind can go when staying in a hotel named after your favorite course in the world. So after dinner, Woods texted Justin Thomas, who had just missed the cut at the Scottish Open, that they should go walk the course. It was boyish Woods—three clubs and a putter was all they needed—playing until the sun went down. We've all done that, but I wondered how many times he had. Golf's purest version—chipping and putting under the stars—was not afforded to him often, so he basked in it.

Thomas told me Woods didn't think anyone would notice. About a hundred people did, and did so respectfully, not rushing in for selfies or autographs. They gave these golf buddies space, trailing behind in the fairway. There's a highlight reel of the evening on The Open's YouTube channel. It's three minutes and forty-nine seconds long, with no music and very little audio. Fill in the sounds for yourself. A calm breeze, clubs thumping turf. Woods hit nippy wedges that didn't move a blade of grass, and others where he dug the clubhead in, pinching maximum spin out of the ball. Class was in session, and everyone there was lucky. Little girls in pigtails. Event volunteers on break. Even one local who was out walking her pug. I wasn't there; I was too busy drinking Guinness with Joel Dahmen (which is the only acceptable alternative). Right around the time Joel and I pivoted to beer No. 8, say 10:30 or so, Woods finished out under the gloomy city lights on 18. Thomas called it "one of the coolest evenings ever." Woods was a bit more concise, calling it "neat," labeling Thomas his "little brother," and saying, "We just went out there and just had a great time."

It was both surprising and predictable to see the normally stoic Woods be so emotional. *Everything Has Led to This* meant something for him it didn't mean for the rest of the field. He had been looking forward to this week for years, even before his car accident. But we had never seen him this wholesome at a PGA Tour event, let alone a major championship. It was so much more relatable than the Woods we saw for so many years. He didn't want to be relatable in the 2000s. He wanted to be a rigid *force majeure* that arrived out of nowhere and left the game changed forever. I think that's a tiny reason why his infidelity scandal was met with such public dismay. He had forever stiff-armed relatability and shunned the outside world from getting in close. When the golfing mortals asked for detail on how he mastered the game, Woods was short. Curt, even. And then when his private life thrust him into public vulnerability, he had virtually no sympathizers. But this 46-year-old version of Woods was showing his truest desires by showing up to The Open. And I think it continued right up onto that bridge.

After playing their final tee shots Friday, Woods forged ahead of Max Homa and Matt Fitzpatrick, who admitted they planned to hang back and let him have this moment if he wanted it. But he didn't. Woods took his hat in his right hand and made 13 strong paces up and down the bridge, without pause.

"He did not stop," Nick Faldo said with a chuckle on the American broadcast. "So what does that mean?"

Faldo made that walk himself in 2015 and paused to wave goodbye to St. Andrews and his Open Championship career. It was one day before his 58th birthday, and he even pulled out a special sweater for the occasion. Understandably, he was thinking about it way more than Woods.

In a perfect world, I would have been inside the ropes, maybe up behind the green, feeling the sound waves wash down over both me and Tiger. But I was rushing back from the 14th hole, where I had lunch with Izzy DeHerrera, one of the executive producers of that documentary that inspired me to come here. That was some full-circle salmon we ate.

I caught up to the action near the practice green, along the 1st tee. Will Zalatoris paused his warm-up to watch. Tony Finau whipped out his phone to capture the scene. McIlroy tipped his cap as he began down the 1st fairway. Thomas did, too. Homa and Fitzpatrick hovered behind about 30 yards now, and Woods could feel that honorary loneliness. Each step seemed to crank the volume dial a little further. About two minutes in, after again waving his cap left and right, he yanked it down snug and wiped his eyes. The most emotive week of his entire career.

My best attempt at lip-reading was a series of *Come on now, come on now* as Woods stood over his ball in the fairway. The tension in his face finally broke when Fitzpatrick caught up to him and made a joke. Woods played a long-iron chip through the Valley of Sin—more old man stuff you don't see much anymore—missed a five-footer for birdie, and tapped in for par. He shook hands with his group but saved hugs for his caddie Joe LaCava and Fitzpatrick's caddie, Billy Foster, who filled in to loop for Woods in the 2005 Presidents Cup. It might be the only time in his career Wood has hugged someone else's caddie during an event.

A few minutes later, Woods arrived at the press tent to find more than 50 reporters crammed in, shoulder to shoulder. I couldn't get within 30 feet of him, let alone dream of asking a question. He stood tall on the elevated podium, hands on his hips, but when he spoke it came with a sense of doubt. "To me it felt like this might have been my last British Open here at St. Andrews," Woods said. Our man does not like to make declaratives on hypotheticals, so this was some out-of-character honesty. It might not be his last Open at the Old, but it might be. Woods was being a realist, and he said three important words with newfound comfort: *Life moves on.* Tiger's life would move on from competitive golf at some point, and he was aware of it. "I think the next one comes around in what, 2030?" he said. The R&A had not made any announcements on the matter, but Woods is rarely wrong about these things. Everyone in the room did some quick mental math. Tiger would have aged eight more years by then, so he'd be making that walk over the bridge again at 54. "I don't know if I will be physically able to play by then," he said before adding, "the ovation and the warmth, it was an unbelievable feeling." We all felt it.

The next few hours showed how narrowly focused sports writers can be. And this is no critique as much as an observation. It is well understood that Tiger Woods is a story every day he competes. And on this day, *the* story. But there was another, similar one brewing. About two miles away—as far away as you can be on the Old Course—Phil Mickelson was hovering around the cutline. Unlike at Augusta National, where the course sits in a valley and rabid applause from any hole pulsates throughout the property, St. Andrews is routed outward and back, and very flat. The wind grabs your words and whisks them away. So Mickelson couldn't have heard the ovation Woods received. Perhaps he felt it, since spectators speak with their feet, too.

On paper, Mickelson's trudge toward the finish could be just as compelling. Here was one of the game's greatest champions, one birdie from playing the weekend. He might not receive the same ovation as the greatest golfer who ever lived, but he deserved recognition. And Mickelson was six years Woods' elder. He would be 60 in 2030, which is one year north of when past champions are exempt into the event. The way things were going, it wasn't a certainty that Mickelson would ever play St. Andrews in an Open again. He had declined to play in the Celebration of Champions that week and was politely asked by the R&A to not show up for the former champions dinner. He was being treated as a pariah, no different than Greg Norman, who was also asked to not be in St. Andrews. The R&A had made its stance on LIV Golf particularly clear when Slumbers labeled it a "free lunch" and said it "undermines the merit-based culture and the spirit of open competition that makes golf so special."

Naturally, most of the press did not notice as Mickelson made bogey on 12 and then double bogey from a bunker on 13, stifling his hopes of making the weekend. Fortunate to not be on the Woods beat, I hustled to the far right side of the 18th for the best view of Mickelson's finish. From there I'd see how populated the grandstands were and could hear conversations from fans lining the fence. Would they actually boo Phil? Would the applause rival Tiger's? Or be so muted that it wouldn't feel like applause at all?

Just as I got into position, I spotted David Normoyle, Dottie Pepper's husband. He was watching along with Tyler Dennis, a PGA Tour executive vice president. Dennis joked that Mickelson might get treated the way high school student sections treat opposing basketball lineups—with the crowd opening newspapers nice and wide to distract themselves as the visiting team makes its grand entrance. You couldn't blame Dennis for feeling this way. Mickelson had caused him and the rest of the Tour's C-suite plenty of grief in the last few months. They *love* the status quo at PGA Tour HQ, often to a fault, and Phil had flipped the status quo on its side and lit it on fire.

When Mickelson took the tee, it was around 5:45 PM. Fans would be forgiven if they had gone seeking their supper. But the difference in setting was so stark it felt orchestrated. When Woods' adoring fans filled the bleachers, they created a vibrant collage of golf-shirt pointillism. Mickelson's finish was dominated by the navy blue tone of empty seats. Only a couple hundred fans sat in the stands, perhaps 20 percent of what Woods found. The street viewing looked more like a hallway, with people coming and going—no one leaning against the fence to watch a golf legend maybe cross the bridge one final time.

Instead of taking the bridge on his own, Mickelson hopped in tightly behind Lucas Herbert. Instead of pausing to wave a hand, he didn't break step. Instead of removing his hat and gazing at all that surrounded him, he kept this hat on and his head down, on and off the bridge in just a few seconds. Only a few fans shouted out his name. Mickelson played a pitch to a couple feet and brushed in his birdie to finish at five over for the week. He earned the obligatory amount of applause offered to anyone who finished with a three. Phil tipped his cap, shook hands with his group, and moved out of the way. It was all so routine.

I was uninspired, and I was halfway across the bridge to the media center when it hit me. There wasn't a single person trying to ask Mickelson about his future. The reception was bleak, which didn't make for a great story, but it was a story nonetheless. And thus it became one of those moments where sports journalism can feel like kicking people when they're down. Asking Mickelson for his thoughts after a second-round 77 felt a bit cruel. But there are figures in each industry that rise above the standard treatment—for whom the questions must be asked, and even expected. Part of the act of prioritizing their career, gushing over their brilliance, and keeping a record of their peaks is also being there to ask about the valleys. This was one of those times.

Like we'd done so many times in their joint careers, I wanted to ask Phil the same question we asked Tiger: *Did you think at all to pause on the bridge, that this could be your final time playing a St. Andrews Open?* It was simple enough. I found just two other reporters in the flash zone. When I made the request to speak with Phil, the R&A media staffer shot me a glance like, *Are you really going to make me do this?* She didn't want to deal with the valleys either, but the other journos agreed with me, perhaps out of boredom. One was from a German outlet—he shrugged his hands out of his pockets. "Okay, I'll go ask," she said.

Almost as quickly as she left, she had reappeared: "Guys, that was a firm 'No.'"

The issue for Phil is…that's a story too. He had dug himself a hole in public perception and his golf wasn't pulling him out of it. Another spin around with reporters wasn't high on his list. He wanted a ride to the private airstrip in Leuchars and to move on as quickly as possible. That is absolutely his right, but on a day where the golf world basically bowed down at the altar of Mickelson's greatest rival, it was a reminder of how differently they've handled those peaks and valleys. You can count on one hand the number of times Woods has declined to talk with media after one of his rounds. Good, bad, ugly, or otherwise, he is always answering.

The only ovation within 20 decibels of Woods' on Friday came after 8 PM when McIlroy strolled up the 18th. Martin Slumbers exited his office onto the top-floor balcony of the R&A clubhouse to watch. McIlroy was 10 under—three shots behind Cam Smith and one behind Cam Young—bounding ahead of everyone in his group in that cocksure way he gets when he knows his game is on. It takes a while for McIlroy to get there, to that elevated sense of comfort during a major championship, but he was showing it Friday evening. I was enjoying the watch.

He may have missed his birdie putt, but McIlroy had properly grabbed hold of everyone's attention and maybe their desires too. After he finished, Slumbers didn't bother waiting to watch Collin Morikawa finish out. (You know, the reigning Open Champion.) He was off to more important business. Six hours later, in the middle of the night at The Vic, a European football–style chant broke out for the Northern Irishman.

Ro-ry,
Ro-ry–Ro-ry,
Ro-ry–Ro-ry,
Ro-ry–RO-RY–RO-RY!

There's a certain wretchedness in the erratic schedule of a golf tournament. There are the few manic hours of scoring time and many more crawling hours of waiting time. Viktor Hovland, scheduled to play in the penultimate twosome with McIlroy, eased into his Saturday by bingeing episodes of Showtime's *Billions*. McIlroy tuned in for a couple international rugby matches. For me and the GOLF.com lads, Saturday began with a sprint around Anstruther, where we found even more golf writers getting their links fix.

On the way back through town, I spotted Max Homa eating lunch at Mitchell, a trendy, Americanized restaurant on Market Street. I found it funny that Homa was hanging around after a missed cut. He could afford a plane ticket anywhere in the world but decided to relish all St. Andrews could offer. Hours later he was in the Whey Pat, a beloved local pub, enjoying a pint among the locals and watching golf on the telly. I remembered that just a week ago, Homa played more golf than anyone on Tour when he squeezed in that extra 18 holes at North Berwick. He's a golf junkie who hadn't reached his fill.

The same went for Brian Zeigler, whom I found roaming about the front nine Saturday afternoon in search of ice cream. Zeigler caddies for Bryson DeChambeau, who teed off at 10:30 AM, made five birdies and an eagle, and ultimately shot an apparently disappointing 67. That's what Zeigler portrayed anyway. He dropped the bag off in storage and was now getting more steps in with a high school buddy. The sun was up, the weather was good, the golf was getting *really good*. Zeigler was in the middle of a nine-week stretch on the road and could use a break. But he and his pal were taking their dads north from St. Andrews to Inverness in the Scottish Highlands, then down for a peek at Troon and Prestwick. Seven rounds in five days is the kind of break from caddying that only a golf sicko could envision. But that's what Scotland does to American golfers.

We chatted for 15 minutes as I walked in the direction of McIlroy's group, which was making the turn. As I pried for info about DeChambeau's move to LIV, Zeigler raved about everything—how LIV was finally treating the caddies like humans, paying for their hotel accommodations and flights to and from events. His flight from Scotland to D.C. for the upcoming event was not cheap, but it was fully funded by golf's newest tour. How could he possibly see it as anything but great? "That, and the players are *finally* getting paid," Zeigler said. *Money, money, money.* That was the line that did it for me, exposing just how far on one side of the debate he was. There's thinking LIV should exist for anti-monopolistic purposes. Or, for older veterans, there's the belief that you'd be silly to pass on the $30 million check that someone—anyone!—is offering. But the belief that Tour players were not being paid their market value is an especially hardened stance. And Zeigler is a smart dude. We've talked at length about artificial intelligence, physical boundaries of the human body, and advanced poker strategy. He's an analytical thinker. He knows that this new pro golf "market" is not the rational kind taught in economics books. But Bryson's circle of trust rarely disagrees with him.

It was time to pursue some real work, so I left Zeigler and Co. and flicked on my over-ear headset that streams BBC radio. It makes covering a golf tournament on a 92-acre property much easier. I found

Scottie Scheffler and Dustin Johnson on the 11th tee, laughing about something with their caddies. Clearly there had been no love lost when DJ committed his future to another tour. Scottie is too simple to hold a grudge. They stood in the shadow of a grandstand filled with McIlroy fans and were holding up their play because McIlroy himself stood in a bunker about 50 yards away, one shot back of Hovland. My inside-the-ropes badge was mostly useless because McIlroy supporters had slowly inched their way under the ropes, too.

Prior to this day, there were two moments in my decade of golf coverage that resulted in goosebumps. They both came via Jordan Spieth shots at Augusta National, with the perfect recipe of stakes, anticipation, superstardom, and shot-making. From the center of the fairway bunker 20 yards short of the 10th green, McIlroy played a full swing, attacking down at the ball and striking into the soft sand. It carried the hill on the front of the green, landed softly, and bounced twice forward until the flagstick got in its way. Down it went.

McIlroy threw both hands in the air and then punched his right one forward as he spun around. His caddie, Harry Diamond, didn't move an inch. He just turned his head with an *Are you kidding me* smile. Just once, I'd love to caddie for a shot like that. Scheffler and Johnson had no choice but to continue laughing. The stands along the 11th tee erupted to the point where they might have been unsafe. They're built to handle weather, but when everyone lurches up out of their seats, who knows what could happen. Those not in seats heaved forward against the ropes. Others who had been watching the 12th hole came sprinting over, joining in the chants for a shot they didn't even witness. The radio reporter in my ear lost his freaking mind, too.

"CAN YOU BELIEVE THE SCENES? PEOPLE ARE JUMPING UP AND DOWN! IT'S AN UNBELIEVABLE BUNKER SHOT. RORY FIST-PUMPS TO THE CROWD. OH, I CANNOT BELIEVE WHAT WE'VE JUST SEEN. WHAT A SHOT! RORY MCILROY JUST LEAP FROGS EVERYBODY. MINUS FIVE FOR THE DAY, MINUS FIFTEEN FOR THE

TOURNAMENT. WE'VE GOT A NEW LEADER AT THE OPEN CHAMPIONSHIP, LADIES AND GENTS!"

Goosebumps Moment No. 3. After two days of hovering in its periphery, McIlroy seized the tournament for the first time and kick-started a party. "That was the best shot I've seen in the history of golf," one spectator exclaimed when the crowd began to quiet. Pity the group of Cameron (Smith) and Cameron (Young) who were struggling and had to follow McIlroy inward that evening. The horde was going to move ahead of them, and it was only going to grow. The groups ahead of them would feel it, too. DJ and Scheffler? Check. Patrick Cantlay and Adam Scott? No one seemed to care. Talor Gooch and Tyrrell Hatton? Sorry, boys. This was a one-man show.

The spectators had finally, officially anointed the People's Champ. The distinction isn't always clear on Day 1. Sometimes it switches over the course of a week, which McIlroy knows all too well. He shot an opening 79 at the 2019 Open at Portrush, about 60 miles from his hometown. When he missed the cut that week, they chanted his name and brought him to tears. The next day, Irishman Shane Lowry grabbed the baton and became the most beloved Open Champion of the decade.

After 54 holes in St. Andrews, it felt obvious, but I was curious if other players took stock of those things that non-competitors care so much about. I asked Scheffler, "Does it feel like there's a crowd favorite?"

"Yes," he said, looking puzzled.

"Who is it?"

"Inn'it Rory? I mean, they're chanting his name out there. Yeah, I think he's definitely the crowd favorite. How can you not root for Rory?"

He spoke for a lot of us. McIlroy played the final eight holes in one under, a fine tally, and was matched by Hovland at 16 under, four clear of Smith and Young. Sometime that night, McIlroy looked out through the window of his hotel suite, stared across the 1st and 18th

holes, and saw his surname atop the big golden leaderboard. Not just on it. *Atop* it. Imagine making Tom Brady sleep on a three-point lead after three quarters of the Super Bowl. Only he's sleeping in one of the luxury box suites. And the scoreboard lights pour in through the curtains. Golf tournaments are wicked.

A month earlier, when McIlroy shot an opening 62 at the Travelers Championship, I was overcome with anxiousness. *Go on—have your fun in Connecticut. But I need you to do this in Scotland.* "If Rory wins at the Old Course," I tweeted hastily, "golf is the most romantic sport ever. If he finishes T2 with a double on Sunday, I will walk into the North Sea and never return."

It was fitting that around 11:30 Sunday morning, McIlroy found himself in the final pairing and I found myself wading around in the North Sea. My coworkers and I went for a run that morning along the perimeter of town, from the East Sands beach up the Fife Coastal Path and onto The Scores, a street that cuts through the prettiest section of the university.

As the local in our group, I led us away from the path for a peek at the St. Andrews Cathedral and its surrounding cemetery. Within it lies the grave of both Old Tom Morris and his son, Young Tom, the first great golf prodigy. This somber visit had become mandatory for any traveling golfer who felt compelled to pay their respects to golf's greatest family.

Years ago, the purveyors of the cemetery ruled that the ancient stones were too ancient and decided to keep the cemetery closed to all but family members of the deceased. All summer long I watched golfers walk down North Street only to turn away, dismayed by the notice zip-tied to the iron gate: "Scotland's changing climate since the 1960s is accelerating the decay and increasing the risk of material falling from height." In fairness, Americans cannot fathom how stone decays. To us, wood decays. Trees decay. Love decays. But stone is stone.

The Scots have been building with it much longer than we have. The St. Andrews Cathedral stands 100 feet tall and overlooks the entire graveyard. It was built in 1168.

Much to my surprise, this week the gates had been opened. A staffer stood at the entrance with one of those crowd-control metallic tally counters. How could they not? Remember this Open's tagline: *Everything Has Led to This.*

The Morris family stands out on the far east side of the cemetery. Old Tom's grave is often mistaken for Young Tom's, as the latter is absolutely stunning. Young Tom is depicted in a bronze statue against a pearly white backdrop, wearing a peacoat and a tam cap, addressing a shot. "In memory of 'Tommy,'" it reads. He passed on Christmas Day, 1875, at just 24 years old, four Open Championships to his name.

Steps away from Young Tom's grave is his father's, a plain grey rectangular box laid flat in the ground. It had been colored darker by that morning's rain. On top was the simplest description:

Tom Morris

Born 16 June 1821

Died 24 May 1908

How is Old Tom's grave such a visual afterthought?

The answer stands at the head of his grave. Another pearly white monument stuck out of the ground that marked the death of everyone around Old Tom. Young Tom was the second son. The first, also Thomas, died at four years old. Young Tom's wife, Margaret, died during childbirth just three months prior to his Christmas death. Old Tom's wife, Agnes, passed away in 1876, followed by their youngest son, John, in 1893 and then Jimmy in 1906. Old Tom died in 1908 (of complications from a fall down stairs at the New Club) as one of the most famous golfers on the planet, but there had to be a sense of loneliness in his final years. His only remaining family were two generations younger than him. A dozen golf balls had been laid on the stone.

This is tempting fruit for sportswriters, and the three of us were appropriately geeking out. It's almost impossible to write about a historic open in a historic town with a potentially historic result without mentioning this gravesite and marrying it to the nervous energy that coursed through town Sunday morning. No other sport can really achieve that. The NBA Finals is not played where James Naismith is buried.

Eventually our run concluded with a chilly bath in the North Sea, which was good because Bastable was training for an upcoming triathlon. We spent more time out there than I thought we would, mostly just looking back at it all. We're so accustomed to seeing St. Andrews from one specific direction. Normally it's down the 18th hole, or from the town side. Never from the water. From there you can appreciate the grinding journey of 18 holes. Sometime later today, the leaders would walk out through that crowd ahead of us, then meander two miles out to our right. It will take them at least two hours to get there, and so much will have changed by the time they do. Next they'll spend about an hour out in The Loop—holes 8, 9, 10, and 11—making no physical progress back toward home, but progress on their scorecards nonetheless. Then finally, they'd begin the two-mile march home, the results of which they'll be asked about for days, weeks, and maybe the rest of their lives. Water dripped from our shorts as we passed the media center and a line of giddy ticketholders entering the grounds. In just eight hours, this climax I'd been waiting for all summer would be over.

It pays to be hyper-aware in our profession, always taking note of where things are or where people are looking. It pays to record the melody of bagpipes bouncing through town in the morning. It pays to count the number of golf balls that lay on Old Tom's grave and snap a photo of the chalkboard outside the Dunvegan, which was updated with daily messages. This Sunday, "To all Rory fans, don't throw the confetti yet!" Writers need to memorize the significance, the statistics, the history, the *meaning*. We need to remember quotes and dates and twirl them together into something coherent. Our favorite subjects, most often, are the players who can think on that spectrum, too. That's McIlroy, who began the week doing a Q&A with CBS' Kyle Porter, citing an old Jack Nicklaus quote: "To be remembered in this game, you have to win an Open at St. Andrews."

"Hopefully, if I never do that," McIlroy said, "hopefully I'm still remembered, but it would certainly put me on a different plane, which would be really cool."

McIlroy chatted with Porter about his hyper-awareness and how it helps him. How he notices his surroundings—fans, media, scoreboards, and other players on the course—rather than sinks into tunnel vision. So when he reached the 1st tee, he probably noticed Slumbers and Co. had stepped out onto the R&A balcony behind him. I, on the other hand, noticed former Villanova basketball coach and golf junkie Jay Wright walking alone among the spectators. I also crossed paths with McIlroy's father, Gerry. He's a stout man with thinning white hair who typically watches in a calm manner. He smiled ear to ear that day, shuffling up the right side of the 1st. *Is that how he hides his nerves, with one big Ulster smile?*

Golf tournaments hold such elongated promise for so many. Viktor Hovland believed he could win when he watched more episodes of *Billions* Sunday morning. He likely believed a bit less when he didn't card a single birdie on the Old Course's outward stretch. McIlroy plodded along with good-not-great form. He made a two-putt birdie on the par-5 5th. He two-putted again for birdie on the 10th, earning a two-shot lead with eight holes to play. He had not made a single mistake but cruised along unassertively. This was a style Tiger Woods made famous: no bunkers, no three-putts, birdie the drivable par-4s and the par-5s. That's how you close out a 54-hole lead at St. Andrews. It must have felt foolproof when Hovland was sputtering, but it becomes less reliable to plow along in 4th gear when a mulleted

Australian banshee shifts into 6th. Cam Smith played the first nine holes in 34 strokes and halved the gap between McIlroy and himself after birdies on 10 and 11. When he added a third straight circle to his card on 12, he trailed by just one. A fourth straight birdie followed on 13. Smith's putter was ablaze. I chased out of the media center just in time to watch him tap in for a fifth straight on 14. Nineteen under and in the lead. "Put another shrimp on the bahbee, Cam!" one fan shouted. McIlroy fans had to be nervous.

Nearly every major championship gets to a point like this, where the plot crystalizes. Only a handful of holes remain, and you know which ones are gettable. You know which players are in control and which are up against it. There may only be two with a chance. The pace of play stays the same, but every bounce seems more significant than the last. Like when McIlroy's approach into the par-5 14th landed in the face of a mound, killing its energy, and nestled in a gully short of the green. A lost opportunity. When Smith's slicing drive on 15 kicked through the rough and settled in some downtrodden hay, it was, *Phew…that was close. Wipe the brow.* They each made par and felt wildly different about it.

On the 16th tee, I did a double take as Filippo Celli raced by. The 22-year-old amateur from Rome had a dream week. He met his favorite golfer, McIlroy, during an impromptu practice round on Monday. He then made the cut and spent Sunday morning shooting 71 to take the honor of low amateur in the field. That earns you a spot in the trophy ceremony next to the winner. "Going out for the presentation with Rory McIlroy, it will be a dream," Celli said afterward, unafraid of jinxing Rory. He set out with his father, inside the ropes, and stormed right past one of the greatest rounds in Open history on a beeline to watch his hero.

After another underwhelming McIlroy par on 15, I spotted Gerry McIlroy again. He was pressed up against the wire fence, blending in among the masses. He was no longer smiling. If anything, he looked scared. A helpless parent, unable to communicate with his son. Being a golf parent is wrenching, I figured. He's seen Rory compete in so many golf tournaments, but it's hard to imagine him wanting one more than this. McIlroy had gone eight years without a major championship and had been building all season long. He holed out from a bunker to finish solo second at Augusta National. He held the 18-hole lead at the PGA Championship and finished eighth. He hovered on the leaderboard all week at the U.S. Open, but a Saturday 73 felled him into a T5 finish. This was it for majors in 2022, and it was slipping away. Another two-putt par on 16.

Then there's the 17th. There isn't another hole in the world quite like it. From the tee, the line of play is not out to the open field or at the spires of buildings in town. It's along the northern façade of the hotel, over a shed that once housed a railroad station back in the 1960s. Thus, it is nicknamed "Road." Caddies urge players to play over the space between "Old Course" and "Hotel" on the sign in front of them. Past the shed, the fairway angles hard to the right, leading to a green that angles back to the left. A deep bunker is wedged into the center-left of the green and a paved road lines the other side. Approaches here—like on the 12th at Augusta National—are the ultimate hit-and-hope.

With his back now firmly against the wall, McIlroy roasted a drive on 17, maybe his best swing of the day. Smith had inexplicably left his approach short of the greenside bunker but held tightly to his magic wand. What remained was as close as real golf gets to mini golf: Smith needed to make a pretty full swing with his putter, ride the ramp of earth, skirt the edge of the pit, and hold the green to give himself a look at par. If he shorted it, he would probably surrender The Open. If he went long, he might end up playing from cobblestone. But a hot putter is golf's ultimate cheat code. It doesn't care what your wedges are saying. All it wants is a look at the hole, and Smith gave it that, goading his Titleist up the hill and onto the putting surface. It wasn't sexy, but amateurs were now going to try that same putt for decades to come.

I walked alongside McIlroy, who had suddenly lost that bounding pep in his step. Pinched between him and the hotel, I was a bit too close to the chaos to hear what happened on the other side of the shed. Smith had made his par putt. Center cut, never a doubt. We were still more than 600 yards from the finish line, but McIlroy's chances had been severely squeezed. Just like Dahmen had taught me when we were trying to make the cut, I counted up the shots McIlroy had left. He would have to coax his ball into two different golf holes in five strokes. He must have felt the urgency because he made another fantastic swing, sniping the front half of the green and rolling out to 18 feet. If you asked him to list the most important putts of his life, that 18-footer would surely rank in the top five. If it drops, anything is possible. It might rank No. 1 on that list, too, even after it refused to break into the cup. He turned to his caddie, mystified.

"Left?" McIlroy said with a somewhat defeated look on his face, a reminder that golf's greatest moments are really just a string of binary data. They break left instead of right. They stay short instead of reaching the hole. Putts that drop and putts that don't are just zeros and ones in the hard-wired code of a tournament. Smith made the one he needed. McIlroy did not.

There was nothing he could do but walk to the 18th tee and watch from afar as Smith tapped in for an eighth birdie and 20 under. The last time a player had done what he had—shoot 30 on the back nine in an Open at St. Andrews—was 12 years earlier. It was Rory McIlroy. Cameron Young had given everyone hope, though, when he drove the green and made his putt for eagle. McIlroy needed to do the same.

A week's worth of fretting about a player shooting 59 or LIV Golf's place in the game or how much wind is needed to protect this ancient course had faded into the background. And what a delight that was. The most melodramatic summer in the history of this centuries-old sport was forgotten for an afternoon and substituted with *real* drama.

McIlroy didn't catch his drive perfectly and he knew it, pleading it to GO. *GO!* It landed softer than most and didn't roll out. He would have to chip in.

Earlier this summer I spent an evening watching YouTube highlights of Open finishes at St. Andrews. The ropes that separate patron from player are dropped after the final group tees off 18 and fans pour inward onto the fairway. When they reach the Swilcan Burn, as they did chasing Tiger Woods in 2000, the smart ones don't try and clear the burn in one fell swoop. They splash into the water quickly and burst out on the other side, sprinting up the fairway some more. It was happening once again, this time right in front of me. McIlroy trudged ahead up the center of the fairway, and I flanked the right side, just inside the waist-high white fence. It would need to be reinforced after thousands of people leaned against it all week.

Anxious faces whizzed by in my periphery. "This is what it's like when the home team loses a football game," I heard one say. A secondary fence stood in the center of Links Place to delineate the ticketholders from non-ticketholders, who were climbing up stairwells and hanging off the side of buildings for a better view. A couple dozen had secured the best view of all atop the Hamilton Grand. Oddly enough, I locked eyes with Peyton Manning, who looked out from the private balcony of the Rusack's Hotel. I cannot be certain that Peyton recognized me from the podcast we filmed three months earlier, but when I nodded my head in his direction, he nodded back at me, so believe with me if you'd like. In a private room nearby, the official engraver of the trophy had already started tapping into the Claret Jug.

I soon found Michael Bamberger lounging comfortably on the slope inside the fence. We gave each other that knowing glance of, *Something is about to happen here. And no one really knows what.* If you'd told me a week ago when we teed off at Anstruther that we'd be lying on the turf along the 18th as McIlroy came up with a chance to tie, I would have been aroused all week.

"Sean, look at those flags," Michael said softly as I plopped down next to him.

He didn't have to say anything else. The dozens of flags surrounding the arena, affixed to the top of the bleachers, all hung limp. For the first time all week, the tailwind that helped carry tee shots—even the poorly struck ones—toward, onto, and sometimes even past the green had vanished. It was as if the Golf Gods—remember, they live here—had demanded stillness. Whatever history would take place on the 18th would be up to McIlroy himself.

He didn't waste time. Perhaps he knew how impossible the shot was. McIlroy could have played it 100 times and he'd make eagle maybe once or twice. He was 27 yards short of the hole, the same yardage of his epic eagle on the 10th hole Saturday. If this was a bunker shot, he'd have a much better chance, digging spin right out of the sand. Instead, he was on baked-out fairway. Viktor Hovland played first, to the right of McIlroy, rapping his putter with not nearly enough oomph. It curled along the most famous false front in the world and trickled back into the Valley of Sin. Leaving it short is sinful.

McIlroy had to think about that. No one would forgive him if he left this one short. So he grabbed a wedge, pulled it back waist-high, and struck through the ground. It started left of the flag and nothing was going to turn it back right. It skipped through the hill, bounced a foot left of the flag, and rolled out to 19 feet, issuing in a bunch of things. Firstly, groans and exhales. The engraver could start hammering letters now. Security guards bolstered the surroundings of the 18th green. Photo and speaker equipment would soon be pushed into place. "Now you can hug me," Smith said, about a hundred yards from the action. He was talking to his agent, Bud Martin, who knew his client's value to LIV Golf had just increased by tens of millions of dollars.

It was eight straight irritating pars for McIlroy, who responded with a single wave to the crowd before running his fingers through his hair in an exhale of his own. When he and Smith crossed paths, they were already on different journeys—one headed out for the trophy ceremony; the other headed to the press to explain himself one final time. McIlroy maintained his composure for 10 minutes, saying all the right things. He had stayed level all week, in his "cocoon," as he called it. But when the mic was turned off and he stepped away, the next thing waiting for him was a golf cart and his wife, Erica. He sat down next to her and began to cry. Maybe the most emotive week of his career, too.

Instead of rushing to hear McIlroy speak, I hung out on 18 and just watched. I wondered how different this whole scene would look if McIlroy's name were atop those golden leaderboards. This was extremely unfair to Smith—*what ifs* chasing around my mind after he just played one of the greatest final rounds in Open Championship history. In golf history. Every putt looked like it had been spit out by computer software, struck perfectly on every X-, Y- and Z-axis. It was one of the finest putting performances I've ever witnessed. If *Everything Has Led to This*, then *this* was pretty damn incredible.

Smith was a fantastic champion, brimming with emotion while he accepted the trophy. He joked his way through interviews by saying, "I'm definitely going to find out how many beers fit in this thing." He was also a champion on a beeline for LIV Golf and he was asked about it later that night. "I just won The British Open and you're asking me that?" Smith said. "I think that's pretty not that good." When pressed for an answer, he deflected some more.

"I don't know, mate. My team around me worries about all that stuff. I'm here to win golf tournaments." He was a winner with a weird kind of asterisk.

Smith was the inverse of McIlroy in so many ways, which made the pivot a bit trickier for everyone to maneuver. It didn't sink in for me until our stories had been written and we began the trek back to our team's rental house. For some reason, when Tiger mentioned the next St. Andrews Open would be in 2030, it didn't make me count *my* own years. Only his and Phil Mickelson's. But as we charted our way through the town I had come to know so well, I couldn't help but make my own tallies. I was barely getting used to being 30, and the next time I might do this in this town I would be 37. I would have to get lucky.

I couldn't help but imagine what this walk would have been like if Cam Smith and Cam Young didn't show up on Sunday. This walk home would have included a pit stop at the Dunvegan to soak in the scene. And then maybe another one at Greyfriars down the street. Perhaps we would have found Gerry there. Or even Rory himself. A McIlroy win would have reverberated into the night, like when Tiger won the 2019 Masters. Patrons loitered longer than ever that day at Augusta National, even as thunderstorms approached. No one wanted to leave because that would be acknowledging that it had to end. Had McIlroy won the 150th Open—this Open of all Opens—the singing in the streets would have been louder. The Vic may have never closed that night. The hangovers would have been worse. There would have been more tears and more trash. More photos and more flights missed. More of…everything. Instead, St. Andrews sleepwalked through the motions of another Open come and gone, forced to accept the result.

Chapter 13

The Aftermath

No matter which people rule the golf world, no matter who is on the city council for St. Andrews, this place was never going to be like this again. That was the thought I couldn't shake Monday after The Open.

It wasn't a negative thought. At least not as negative as it may sound. Maybe we call it micro-depression. The biggest reason I was here was over now. Done. And I was already feeling a bit existential about St. Andrews. The version I had in front of me would not last forever. You think it might, when you visit for a week. But not when you stay for a summer.

It's difficult to have this view as you walk through town, where every intersection is defined by buildings made of stone. Where every handrail is crafted from wrought iron. Where the only things that touch the cemetery are rain and wind. Where strict, narrow architecture guidelines determine which new building proposals are adopted or cast aside. Appearing historic, and even unchanged, is a key tenet.

There's a diagonal embedded within the sidewalk on the south side of South Street that marks the very first meridian, laid by James

Gregory in 1748. He taught calculus in the same university buildings that host students today.

The spire of Holy Trinity Church, which looms above the commercial center of St. Andrews, is the same spire that visitors have looked up at for centuries. The humps in the fairway on 18 are the same humps that have deflected golf balls forever. The highlight reels playing on a loop in the R&A museum reveal that the fence rails behind 18 green have *always* been painted green and the fence posts always painted white.

There are signs affixed to houses only accessible by foot that say this house—this greystone house with its clay roofing and moss growing out of the corners of its stone fence (there's always more stone)—was built in 1755. *Older than America.* Mother Nature can throw everything she's got at this fortress, and it isn't going anywhere. St. Andrews is filled with this kind of persistence. How could it ever change?

But over time, all this stuff *does* get manipulated. The world demands change. There were about 350 trailer residences on the far east side of town 20 years ago. Now there are 430. The town population has grown by about 10 percent. The bed-and-breakfasts, all lined up in a row on Murray Park, they don't get the same access to tee times as they used to, completely changing their business structure and making their owners wonder if they want to stay in the lodging business at all. There were six St. Andrews courses 20 years ago. Now there are seven. Even the Old Course—which is lauded for standing the test of time—has added, removed, and moved around bunkers in the last decade. That stone house built in 1755? It has a modern electrical box drilled into its side now. Slyly etched into the sign beneath 1755, it reads, RESTORED 1972 AND 1998. The world demands change.

Maybe it was that these things reveal themselves over the course of a summer, or maybe it was Tiger Woods' insistence the next Open wouldn't visit for eight years, or maybe it was that all my media friends had experienced this place for a single rip-roaring week, and I knew deep down the St. Andrews *they* knew was only a fraction of the real thing. I just couldn't help but take mental snapshots of everything that Monday after The Open.

It was a good thing for my mental health that coworker Dylan Dethier booked his return flight for Tuesday. Delay the separation anxiety for another 24 hours. He wanted the true tour, so I gave him the true tour, starting with a round of golf at the Deeyooks and a ride home from cabbie Nigel. At 31 degrees Celsius, Mother Nature had delivered one of the hottest days on record in the history of St. Andrews. A heat wave consumed the country, setting national records multiple times that week, but Nigel wanted to talk about the Open.

For him and his fellow cabbies, it was an Open "on *stah-roids.*" He made multiple daily trips to the Edinburgh airport, after which he'd experience a nice lull as the golf was played before absolute mayhem in the evening until well after midnight. In the end it was worth it, as they pulled in about £4,000 each in cash. Nigel had been on Team Rory, of course. He's a bit of a romantic. "Ah, yaknow how sometimes some people are just *destined?*" Nigel told us. "He felt like that." It was a shame the wind didn't blow, Nigel figured, or McIlroy would have benefitted. After nine minutes, finally, a comment about the record-setting heat: "Bahh, it's a night fer sinking a few berrs." We couldn't agree more.

So Dylan and I laced up our walking shoes and I guided us through the back alleys of town, past the regal façade of the old *St. Andrews Citizen* newspaper office. We kept on a direct path for the Dunvegan, plopping down in the center of the Dunny around 7 PM. The bar was mostly full, which made their wait staff happy—not because it was mostly full, but because it was not *completely* full. This was the first night in about 10 nights that the bar was below full capacity. They'd been working harder than the golf writers.

For better or worse, Dylan and I have a disappointingly similar palate for two friends who travel a lot together, so when we often order the same thing, I get annoyed. But in this case, I made him order the simplest, best meal the Dunvegan serves, the steak and ale pie. It is as pub-grubby as pub grub gets: beef, onions, and carrots mixed into a brothy stew, covered in flaky pie crust with thick-cut chips on the side for dunking. (At least that's how I preferred them.) I would eat it three nights out of five if three nights out of five at the Dunny weren't a horrible wellness plan. Sunday's final round broadcast was playing on the televisions inside.

We spotted ourselves on TV as Cam Smith's banana slice drifted into the rough on 15. Seeing it from this new angle, the result made even less sense than it did in person. A drive as meager as that one deserved to find some trouble, I think. Instead, Smith played a smooth mid-iron into the green and two-putted for par. If he gets a hairy lie in the rough, he's probably making bogey. Discussions about other *what ifs* circled around us in the bar. We weren't the only ones thinking it. I wondered when McIlroy would allow himself to sit back and digest the highlights just like we were, doing his best to avoid the what-if game. Maybe never. Certainly not anytime soon.

The most innocent version of McIlroy looked down on us from a photo hanging on the ceiling. He wore a black zip-up hoodie over what looked like a grey T-shirt from the Gap. This was at least a decade old, back when he kept his hair long, those black curls bobbing onto his forehead and over his ears. "Kindred Spirits," the caption beneath the photo read. "Scotland and Ireland—Sheena and Rory." McIlroy was pictured with Sheena Willoughby, the owner of the bar, whose face is all over the place, on every wall, on every ceiling, and in every crevice of the Dunny. Alongside her in every photo was a visiting (and often very important) golfer. There's Sheena and Ernie Els. There's Young Sheena—same blonde pixie hairdo—with Arnold Palmer. Then there's Sheena and Tiger Woods next to Sheena and John Daly with his iconic blond mullet. To dine in the center of the Dunvegan is to be watched by golf royalty.

The only *live* pro golfer in the Dunvegan on Monday was Dylan, who intentionally maintains that distinction for reasons he and I (his caddie) have long debated. I was glad Dylan was finally seeing this St. Andrews saloon because it is *the* pub for visiting golfers. (It became *the* pub for students during Covid restrictions, too, staying open later than the others.) It sits on precious real estate, about a pitching wedge from the Old Course's 18th green, and just sucks visitors inward. Part of that is Sheena, always smiling even when there isn't a camera around. Part of it is Luke Fotheringham. He's normally the gent behind the bar, tapping the Tennent's and mixing cocktails. He's the one who will actually tell you a story or two. He's been there when Brooks Koepka jumped behind the bar to pour beers himself. He's been there for some of Ernie Els' rambunctious drinking victories. Shane Lowry's, too. "Those seats back there?" Luke told me in June. "Shane-o was dancing on top of them during last year's Dunhill."

Luke's the one who poses with pros when Sheena isn't around. Both of them had slaved through a busy week. It was Sheena's sixth Open as owner. Fotheringham did his best to make last call around 1 AM every night. And after about nine straight nights of that, he was pouring drinks Monday while Sheena raced around seating guests. The show goes on. They'd get a two-year break before the Women's Open arrived in 2024 and then a six-year break before the next men's Open, if we can trust Tiger. *Would Sheena be around for that one? Without her, can the Dunny be the Dunny?*

On our walk to the Dunvegan, I had pointed out The Golf Shop of St. Andrews, a tiny abode on North Street owned by a lady named Karina MacKinnon. The chalkboard sign out front read, BEST PRICES BY PAR! It was Karina who emailed me earlier this summer with that excited 'SWEATSHIRTS!!!!' subject line. Karina's shop had recently become famous for selling a unique crewneck with the official St. Andrews town crest printed large and centered on the front.

Back in 1995, Karina's shop sold a white sweatshirt to a Titleist employee who sewed the brand name into the crest and then passed it on to the young amateur golfer everyone was paying extra close attention to. His name was Eldrick Woods.

Mr. Woods made a sterling debut that week wearing what Karina's shop now calls its "Gold Crested Sweatshirt." Images of it continue to go viral in golfy social media circles. Karina sells the sweatshirt in eight different colors. The bestselling one is aptly named "Woods White."

What you can see of Karina's humble shop is just a single room that stretches about 15 feet wide. There are the items on the left wall and there are the items on the right wall, and that's it. But tucked in the back corner were those sweatshirts, which it seemed everyone wanted Open week. "Agh, it was mentul," she said. "Absolutely mentul."

With just a single Instagram post sent to her 1.8 million followers, Kathryn Newton, one of our Hugo Boss influencers from early June, changed Karina's business for the rest of the year. (Maybe influencing isn't that bad!) Newton shared eight photos of herself wearing the red crewneck, playing golf down the coast at Crail on July 8, just a few days before hundreds of thousands would be visiting Fife. Karina's store doesn't even have an Instagram page. It has 400 likes on Facebook.

But Newton spent the week at the Old Course Hotel calling in order after order for her friends, which Karina would hand deliver by driving down North Street. Her inventory was depleted so quickly that Karina had to create a new, analog recording system. To that point she had only ever sold orders she could immediately fill, but now she was writing down names, credit card info, addresses, and sizes in an old black binder. If any prospective buyer couldn't find the size or color they wanted, she logged the order manually. She really had no choice. If your name was in Karina's binder, your credit card was, too. You'll get your sweatshirt...eventually. It just might take a month or two.

She worked 14-hour days, bringing her mother in to fold sweatshirts and package them in plastic. She sold just shy of 900 sweatshirts that week, about 12 times the norm. But thus go the spoils of owning an exclusive item that everybody wants. To hear her retell it, she barely survived. But only she knows how important it all was. Her business was closed for most of 2020 and 2021.

"I went for walks with my son," she says, laughing now about how she spent the time during lockdown. "Watched the bank account go down." St. Andrews was a bleak town during the throes of the pandemic. If a city like New York can be thrown out of equilibrium in an instant, towns like St. Andrews don't stand a chance. "We had the Open to look forward to," she said. "Just crossing our fingers that we didn't go into lockdown again, or that Covid spiked, or that there'd be a new variant. Everybody was terrified." It wasn't until I interviewed her that she pointed out the town motto is also embroidered into the crest on her sweatshirts. *Dum Spiro Spero,* it goes. "Whilst I breathe, there's hope."

When Dylan and I finally stumbled out of the Dunny, fat and happy, we trotted downhill toward the course. I wanted to show him that, even though Rory McIlroy's soul had been stolen here just 24 hours ago, the Old Course would still be in a state of limbo. I knew the hidden entrance into those big golden leaderboards would be unlocked, so I pushed Dylan inside and up the wooden stairway tucked within.

Every player's name in the field was in there, printed in all caps on nine-foot sheets of gold plastic, propped up on sturdy, metal shelves. If we weren't careful, someone would hear us, but were we even trespassing? I unfurled the SCHAUFFELE plank nice and wide so Dylan could send a pic to Xander. We were rightly geeking out—horsing around in the belly of the beast by which golf history is first recorded. I'm absolutely struggling to contain my laughter in the picture, but Xander was pretty unimpressed. "You guys play?" Xander asked. Remember, he was the hottest golfer on the planet entering that week. He got the good side of the weather draw and it didn't deliver him a single great nine-hole stretch. A bunch of good ones, no great ones. The only way tying for 15th can be disappointing. So naturally Xander sounded confused when reporters asked him about the course setup. "Almost felt like a USGA event in '15 or '16," Xander said during his exit interview. By that he meant "tricked up and unfair." He's entitled to his opinion, of course. I thought the setup was magnificent and fiddly, just like McIlroy said. But I wasn't hitting the shots.

To our surprise, every player's name plate remained except for one: Woods. A couple college-aged hooligans had already snatched it. The R&A will have to print a new one for 2023. "Imagine owning one of the HOME or AWAY planks that sit in the scoreboard in Fenway's green monster," I said to Dylan. He's a Massachusetts man. I could see his gears churning.

There are planks for every number, zero through nine—blue for above par and red for below—and every letter in the alphabet, which is needed for the final message that hangs on the leaderboards until they're torn down by construction workers:

Well Played

Cameron

See You At

Royal

Liverpool

2023

I rummaged about searching for the three-letter entirety of my last name. Dylan still hadn't said much at all. He hovered just inside one of the name slots, peering out over the seagulls and the golf below.

"Man, this is so cool," he said, and while that may seem like a generic quote, his voice trailed off at the end. He said what he was feeling. My tour was on its way to a 5-star rating.

We weren't completely alone in our grandstand intrigue. A young man named Caleb sat cross-legged in the first row, wearing Birkenstocks and thumbing through a paperback version of *Ulysses* by James Joyce. He had flown in Sunday, completely unaware that *Everything Has Led to This*, but now he had one of the best reading nooks of all time. He had great back support, just enough innocent background noise to keep him focused, and an unbeatable view if his mind ever wandered. It was nearing 9 PM and the sky was a peachy-pink haze, blending into turquoise. Caleb ought to be painting a picture instead.

Dylan and I didn't have books to read, but we did have golf to watch. The R&A blocked off Monday's tee times in case The Open spilled over into a fifth day (like it did in 2015), but since there were no weather disruptions we had 20 handicaps gaming it around the fiddliest Old Course ever. Most of them were playing as part of a Mastercard sponsorship deal, grinding just as seriously as Xander had.

"Why don't you come down here and hit it," one shouted to me. I had groaned a bit too loudly when he left his lag putt 12 feet short. He glared back when his par putt missed, too, scooping his ball on the other side of the hole. It's okay, he's new here.

Another player put on his best Kevin Na impression, lunging to grab his ball at the exact moment it fell into the cup. "There's cocky putts, and then there's *that*," Dylan said.

We could sit there and watch all night. Two golf pals who had spent the summer apart. We were fed. We had drunk. Our energy was spent. Dylan had been filming snippets of my tour for a video he wanted to make, and what better way to end it than with some innocent commentary of golf played by strangers. That's a wrap. But then...

"Fore right."

"FORIGHT."

"FORRR RIIIITTTTTTTTEEE!"

The last one was more of a hair-raising scream. It came from the direction of the 18th tee box, about 400 yards away. The *THUTWACK* that followed a beat later was so obvious—golf ball meeting vehicle. It wasn't clear which part of the car was *THUTWACKED*—the hood, the roof or, worse, a windshield. "We're going to have to go investigate that," I told Dylan. He kept the camera rolling.

When we reached the scene of the incident, to our surprise, we found no errant golf balls rolling around the pavement, but rather a smiley Mark Rolfing, the NBC broadcaster and former player. And just as we shook his hand, major champion and fellow broadcaster Paul Azinger ripped around from behind a white Sprinter van. He had cracked the case. "They're all in the same group," Azinger blurted out, walking right by us, "and one of the guys jacked one and hit their *own* van. He hit his own car!" I've watched a lot of Azinger on television, and never has he been this animated.

Rolfing and Azinger were enjoying their day off just like we were, relishing the American temperature on this endless, Scottish summer night. Their wives were waiting for them in the rooftop restaurant next door, but these two golf junkies were happy to keep them waiting a little while longer.

"How about that yesterday?" Rolfing asked. I answered his question with another one.

"Have you ever seen so many putts fall into the dead center of the cup?"

Before he could reply, Azinger jumped in with another drive-by answer: "*Cammm* Smith. Those putts would have gone into a *thimble.*" A classic Azingerism. Dylan soured Rolfing's mood, if only for a moment, to discuss the news of the day: Rolfing's longtime friend and coworker, David Feherty, was the newest golf icon headed to LIV, joining their broadcast team for who knows how many millions of dollars. The news was fresh, maybe a few hours old. But it clearly troubled Rolfing. "It's sad," he said. "It's just creepy, man."

It certainly was a bit creepy. A day ago, golf history had been made, but today it felt awfully ephemeral. Cam Smith hit putts so well that Azinger was absolutely correct. They might have fallen into a thimble. But the lasting nature of those putts didn't feel very clear just yet. They existed in a bit of a haze, clouded by the questions that Smith faced in his press conference and his stumbling responses. *I think that's pretty not that good.* Reports circulated that, indeed, Henrik Stenson was surrendering his Ryder Cup captaincy. Feherty was moving on from a 25-year PGA Tour broadcasting career. What could the rest of us do about it? The Old Course was moving on, one push-slice at a time. We probably should, too. We weren't invited, but we tailed Rolfing and Azinger up to the rooftop bar to soak in the best view in town.

Two Australian golf writers had already beaten us to it, Evin Priest and Ben Everill. They were eating seafood at the edge of the balcony, toasting to and still beaming from their countryman's win. Don't ever let a golf writer tell you they "don't care who wins." Every single one of us cares on some level about which player's victory will be the most invigorating to our work. Playoff holes are the bane of a deadline's existence, but they often make for a great story. Sudden death is a better story. A Rory win would have carried American golf websites for days, maybe weeks. But we'll save that for another day. Evan and Ben helped Smith find out how many beers fit in the Claret Jug late Sunday night. When you become friendly with a pro golfer, it's admittedly fun to watch them triumph. We watched down on the 18th as the offender who sniped the Sprinter van made what he thought was an innocent par, unaware that his fairway lie came from someone tossing his ball back in bounds.

Out on the horizon, cranes and forklifts were in place, having started the process of breaking down the tented locker room and player training facility. The NBC studio to the right of the 17th fairway had been hastily disbanded. The desk Brandel Chamblee opined from each night was broken into about nine pieces and discarded to the sidewalk like spring cleanup. Maintenance staffers had begun filling in divots on the cratered driving range, which borrowed a hole from the Jubilee Course. In a few hours, the singles queue would begin to form again. As it should.

In 2030, the singles queue as we know it may not exist. The Links Trust has tried brainstorming new systems by which it could fairly dish out those final tee time slots, not ruin the ballot access for local golfers, and also—perhaps most importantly—keep visiting septuagenarians from sleeping outdoors on concrete. They haven't devised the perfect system quite yet, but with another eight years anything could happen.

The Swilcan Bridge is bound to change. That bridge that Tiger Woods walked over on Friday is so old that there is no official record of its age. It's just "at least 700 years old," that's all. In an effort to make the surrounding area of the bridge more tenable to foot traffic, the Links Trust commissioned a stone extension of the walkout areas on both sides. It caused an international uproar so significant that the Links Trust rushed out a public statement and immediately broke ground in reverse, removing the newly laid stone. The intent, rest assured, was genuine. But pleasing millions of people who feel a sense of ownership of that bridge and what it looks like—because they once took a photo on it—might be an impossible gig.

Even the rooftop bar we were standing on was extremely new. You wouldn't know it from the street, where its washed stone facade blends into its century-old surroundings, but it was all part of a massive addition to the Rusacks hotel. The hotel added 44 rooms, but the bar was its cherry on top. It was finished in 2021, just in time for the 150th Open, and used as a prop for hosting media members throughout the week. The goal was obvious: get the word out that this is the new crown jewel hotel for future visitors. It has completely altered the corner of those photos people take on the bridge. Depending on where the sun sets, it casts shadows on the course that were never there before. Does any of this matter? My most selfish ego thinks it does.

St. Andrews had become my secondary college town. My study abroad town. And we always get bothered, deep down, when our college towns change. Every time I return to Madison, Wisconsin, a new luxury apartment building has stretched into a different part of the skyline. Sometimes two of them, depending on how long I've been away. St. Andrews had changed *a ton* in the years since Michael Bamberger and his wife made their journey through Scotland. There's a Subway now. And Starbucks. And Pret A Manger.

When Dylan and I reached Central Bar for our final "Ah, what's one more" beer of the night, we were fed, we had drunk, we had spent even more energy, and we had added two scoops of ice cream from Jannettas. The Central had mostly returned to its normal, sleepy self. A week earlier we were desperate just to get the bartender's attention. So busy they ran out of Guinness on night 1 of Open week.

The Open was so fresh and yet it was hard to imagine all the chatter that filled these streets. No one bumped into us. Barely a car or two drove by. One foursome of buddies jumped out of a taxi with clubs in hand. *Sit where'er you like,* was the order. Only a dozen patrons were there, all spread out on the patio. St. Andrews was exhaling.

Among the folks remaining was a man in his thirties who had flown past his drinking limit and slumped against the front window, blubbering out the words of a FC Celtic sing-song.

Scott Brown won th-league,
Scott Brown won th-league,
Scott Brown won th-league at Rugby Pahhhk.

I thought this was the moment Dylan might finally fall for the romances of European football, but it didn't work. When he shipped off for Edinburgh 10 hours later, it all felt a lot more real. The Open had come and gone, and for the first time since I arrived, I had no clue what was next.

Chapter 14

Kindred Spirits

I had two assignments for the day, both extremely achievable, which was fantastic for my post-Open life. I needed assignments for this closing stretch of the summer now that the main reason for visiting—at least according to my bosses—had passed. Today's mission was to visit Anstruther again and capture drone footage of its 5th hole, nicknamed "Rockies." It once earned the honor of Britain's Hardest Par-3, and it absolutely deserves it.

The other assignment came from Colin, a frequent taxi driver of mine, who advised that when I was done looping around Anstruther, I should head north from the clubhouse and saddle up at The Wee Chippy, a restaurant in Anstruther Harbour. "The best fish 'n' chips in Fife," Colin said. That's an easy sell for me. I had become obsessed with the dish, mostly because I didn't care for the rest of the Scottish food table. It was the closest thing to the Friday Night Fish Fry culture I grew up on.

It was July 23, the first Saturday after The Open, and inconveniently also Club Championship day for Anstruther Golf Club. The members-only competition took priority, naturally, so I had 90 minutes to kill before I was allowed to play. I launched the drone in the sky and buzzed around for maybe 30 minutes, the duration of one drone battery life. I wasn't looking to capture the glamorous, bright green turf that defines so much golf content on YouTube. This was more about the ruggedness of the shoreline, which looked way different from above. The sea had pulled boulders away from the land in chunks, almost in triangles like the jagged back of a stegosaurus. A pair of golden retrievers and their walkers trotted on a curvy dirt path below. I soared up over the tiny fishing village and in a matter of seconds I had passed over all of Anstruther. It's just 240 acres or so, home to about 4,000 people. And thus, its nine-hole golf course was the perfect size. You don't go there looking to get full on golf. It's an appetizer at most. But maybe your favorite appetizer, ordered on repeat.

Unfortunately, it was a gloomy afternoon. The drone footage would reflect that. Rain clouds were forming out over the wheat fields west of the course. With about 45 minutes to burn, I tossed a ball on the putting green and began wearing out a path from hole to hole. A lot of people practice putting with two balls, hitting the same putt twice to see what they can incorporate on their second one that they missed on the first try. I had just watched creaky, 46-year-old Tiger Woods do this two-ball warm-up a week ago, but I prefer just the one. Make it or miss it, just like the real thing. It locks me in to focus mode, makes me actually *read* the practice putts as if they're do or die, which is probably why—especially considering the forecast—I figured I was alone. But while I had been grinding, Tom Kenmack snuck up behind me.

He was so unlike me in every single way, even if our last names rhymed (Blue sock, Sean Zak, Ken-mahhk, etc.). Tom was 91 years old and had ridden his red mobility scooter a couple hundred yards down the hill from a senior living facility. He had no goals of standing completely upright. Old age had bent his back into a hunch years ago, so now he stood about 5'6" with his forehead hanging out over his toes. The top of his head had gone bald, leaving a ring of white hair around the sides and back. He sure was dressed well, though. The collar of a dress shirt peeked out over his teal argyle sweater. He lumbered around gingerly in a pair of black slacks and brown leather dress shoes. The man was dressed for church, and who knows—maybe he was headed to evening mass next. Or maybe *this* was his religion? He pulled a lime green doggy bag out of his pocket and unfurled four beaten-up golf balls onto the green, pivoting toward the first cup, maybe 15 feet away.

"Do you come here often?" I asked.

"Agh, nouu. Jus' started a fortnight ago."

He left his walking cane strapped to the back of his scooter and used the only other instrument he brought to hold his weight: a Ram Zebra putter from the '90s that his nephew had gifted him. He lined up to play his first putt and gave it a wristy slap. The ball swung out to the right about six inches, curling back to the left, crashing into the flag stick, down into the hole. I cackled.

"Aye, aye," he snickered to himself, smiling. Putt No. 2 didn't come close. About four feet short.

"Ack—t'was a fluke!" he said, rushing to set up his third. It curled on the same trajectory as the first, squeezing into the jar. "Ah, no t'wasn't!"

Welp, my practice session was officially over. It was time to learn everything there was to know about Tom Kenmack.

It was true, Tom had only been putting for about two weeks, ever since that nephew visited ahead of The Open. He got swept up in the golf fever that took over Fife in July and wanted to try his hand at the short game. Every few days he would ride that scooter down to the club and pass the time exactly how I was passing the time before my round. Putting practice doesn't cost a dime.

"I do it for amusement," he told me. "It gets me some fresh air. I do it for an hour, and that's enough for me."

Aspirational. Tom tried Big Boy Golf once, decades ago. He worked on his family's farm in Edinburgh, on which students from the local university would visit and play out imaginary golf holes in the field.

He watched from afar, but on occasion during work shifts he'd stumble upon one of the balls they left behind. He always tucked them away. When he'd collected an even 10 bullets, he convinced himself it was time. He was ready for the real thing. He borrowed an old hickory club from his dad's collection and began mimicking the swings he watched for years.

Within an hour, every ball he owned was lost again. "T'was the beginning and end of me golf cahrreer," Tom said with a belly laugh. This was the cutest golfing man in all of Scotland.

Tom didn't make it up the road to St. Andrews for The Open, but he did catch plenty of it on TV. He thought Rory McIlroy would win too. *Join the club*, I told him. His nephew stayed with him that week, a major bonding moment for them.

We spent the next 15 minutes rotating around the putting green, me trying a putt and then him taking four whacks at it. His mechanics weren't perfect, but he tended to make one of the four. He held the putter with a baseball grip and peeked up at the hole right at contact. But in a few short weeks he had learned one valuable thing about putting: at its core, lining up the clubface for straight, flush contact is really just a left-hand or a right-hand feeling. We hold that grip with both hands, but we *feel* the face *meeting* the ball as an extension of our rear palm or the back of our lead hand. For righties, it's a right-palm or back-of-your-left-hand feeling. Tom was very much a right-palm putter. I am too.

Between putts, I lobbed questions his way, but he was like a teenager engrossed with a new video game. He was happy to answer but never looked up from the putt ahead of him. I learned his favorite game was lawn bowling, where competitors roll slightly oblong, hard plastic balls across a patch of dry, firm, perfectly manicured turf, trying to squeeze them as close as possible to a tinier white ball called the jack. It's a European cousin of bocce ball, only lawn bowling balls are not perfectly round, so they don't roll perfectly straight. The best bowlers, like golfers, understand how to manipulate the curving arcs in either direction. Much like golf, bowling is very simple to the viewer, endlessly tricky to those involved. Fiddly, if you will. It made sense why Tom enjoyed the putts that required a bigger arc.

Before long, those rain clouds released a soft drizzle. Tom looked upward and spoke to the sky like it was his neighbor, "You know, I'm not going to stay out here if it's going to rain." Fair enough. There would be drier days for putting practice. He pulled out that lime green bag and plucked his balls up one at a time. Never in my life had I met a golfer like this man. He was the oldest, greenest, most innocent golfer, maybe in the entire world! Golf for him was nothing like the kind being played elsewhere in Fife. It was not about getting better. It was about just *doing something*. He was never going to have one of those ruinous days where he can't seem to close the clubface. He's never going to toil on the driving range into the night, battling an episode of the shanks. I was jealous of that. I asked Tom one final question before he began his return voyage up the hill.

So, what have you learned? It was the same question that had been lingering in my head since The Open left town.

He answered immediately, like it was an absolute truth: "Aye, that it takes four tries to find the road."

It felt almost scripted that I met a golfer like Tom at a place like Anstruther. Like he was some ghost of my golfing past reminding me to chill out and enjoy the ride. Anstruther was the best example I had found in Scotland of the golf I grew up on. The derivative version of the game that was bite-sized. Most of the par-3s are short, but the ones that are long get turned into par-4s for the juniors and the ladies. Each tee box is right next to the previous green. Everyone plays from the same tee boxes, just like we did when my grandpa taught me the game. When I caught the golf bug and became helplessly addicted.

Anstruther is like the basketball hoop in your driveway. Of course there are better, flashier, perfectly maintained hoops out there in the world. You see them on TV. Some are indoors, the rims all measuring *exactly* 10 feet, with fresh nylon, glass backboards, etc. But for a long time as you learned the game, the hoop in the driveway was the only hoop you knew. It didn't matter that the backboard was caked with dirt from the ugly springtime weather, or that the rim clearly leaned in one direction. A hoop is a hoop. Your hoop is *your* hoop. And when you came back from a long time away, there's nothing like getting some shots up on *your* hoop.

Anstruther's putting green was Tom's driveway hoop. The only golf he knew. And like he said, an hour of it was plenty. It took me about two hours to loop twice around Anstruther's nine holes, carving out a middling score of 74 (eight over) with no birdies. I ventured down to the Wee Chippy to finish my second homework assignment. The droning was a B-plus, and the fish was cooked to an A. I just happened to ruin it when I went to douse my filet in salt, but accidentally grabbed the sugar shaker. Colin thought it was funny. My stomach did not.

I came to Scotland to learn something about golf, unsure what it would be. I didn't know who my teachers would be, either. I figured I'd find them naturally. Or they'd find me. But my angst about the game called for something more macro than micro. I still needed to fall deeper in love with the sport.

I learned a lot about the future of pro golf those first two months. It was on a one-way path to money. Money here, money there. Money for playing, money for not playing, sometimes even money for not playing well. If Phil Mickelson wouldn't get the pro game all the way there himself, someone else would grab the baton. Thankfully, Scotland is one big reminder that there is so much more to golf than the people who play it best.

When it came to *my* game, there was so much room for growth. There always has been. It's the golfer's affliction. There is *always* room for growth. Cam Smith could *still* improve his putting. And I needed Scotland for that, too. I needed three months of proper golf absorption—playing, watching, even *hearing* different shots in this different *kind* of golf to round out my arsenal. Two college buddies were visiting at the end of August, both of them better than me. I wanted to close the gap with new skills. To be able to say, "Oh, that short, skiddy 9-iron from 50 yards? You didn't see it coming. I've got that now. I learned it in Fife."

In my eight weeks or so, I had successfully filed for divorce from my 60-degree wedge. Back home, the 60 is all you know. The 60 is comfy. It was invented in the '80s to get the ball in the sky, taking the turf elements out of consideration. It allowed for big swings to short targets. (Unsurprisingly, it was an American who created it— Dave Pelz. He worked for NASA before coaching American golf pros who loved getting the ball in the air. His star pupil: golf's greatest risk-taker, Phil Mickelson.) But in this part of the world, the earth deflects the 60-degree wedge. That little round arc of meaty metal that sits beneath the face of the golf club—which smoothly glides through the wetter, softer turf in America—is called "bounce," and in Scotland that's exactly what the 60 does. It bounces off the hard-packed ground, clips the ball closer to its equator, and sends it scuttering through the green. Professionals literally shove their wedges into a grinding wheel when they visit Scotland, wearing away as much bounce as possible, trying to make their 60s more like a spatula than a soup spoon.

My divorce from the 60 made room for a healthier relationship with my 52-degree wedge and a much healthier relationship with the Ground Game. Because of how links courses are designed—with clear landing areas in front of the green that allow for the ball to roll up onto the putting surface—and how the climate keeps these green entrances so rigid, the proper links pitch shot considers…everything. It is *not* about flying the ball to the hole. Rather, you fly the ball somewhere very short of the hole, maybe on the front of the green, maybe even in front of it, probably left or right of it, depending on the shape of the green. The compact turf bounds the ball forward a hop or two, at which point we see how gifted you really are. Shots clipped with a lot of spin will bite into the turf and just trickle forward while others with less spin tumble. It's dealer's choice on what the situation calls for—trickling or tumbling—but it's little shots like these that can make you look like a genius…an artist…or a fraud.

The room for error on these shots is measured in millimeters but when you find the sweet spot, there may not be a more fulfilling sensation. Close your eyes and you can tell by the sound. The best shots are just a *click* of contact. When I pulled one off mid-summer for a closing par at Cruden Bay, I was so overcome with euphoria that I actually shouted out loud. "That's it! *That* shot. I'm so glad I have *that* shot! I am *obsessed* with that shot." My host was nonplussed. "Ah, uh yeah…. That's great. Good shot." He grew up on shots like that. And he spent all day proving it, hitting it shorter than me with every club and waxing me by five.

I was clearly learning, just not fast enough. I had spent two months adapting to the linksy short game, but those lessons bore fruit only a few times per round. I had not learned how to play in the wind, an important facet considering I left the Windy City and moved to the Windy Country. I hadn't learned how to hit the ball low. Like, *really* low. To use the fairways like bowling alleys and hit a 5-iron that travels as far as a 5-wood. I remember joking to young James Colgan at Cruden Bay, "Man, downwind I'm a 2 handicap. And into the wind I'm a 20."

There was the one harrowing, breezy night at the Duke's where the wind grabbed my tee shot on the 10th and threw it over a bunker smack into the thick of a gorse bush. Gorse bushes, with their thousands of thorny leaves, should be renamed Don't Bother Bushes. Don't bother searching in there. Unfortunately for me, it was the fourth ball I had lost that evening and the last ball left in my bag. I was out of bullets, just like Tom Kenmack's golfing debut. The pro shop was closed. Luckily,

I was playing alone, so it was less embarrassing when I dragged my clubs to the range, tail between my legs. It was 8 PM and the range was technically closed. But if you want it badly enough, any driving range is always technically open. I spent 90 minutes alternating between whacking balls into the field and then scouring the dry, weedy patch to pick them up by hand. Every time I ran out of balls, I told myself, *This is what Tiger Woods means by "dig it out of the dirt."* Until the last time I ran out and cursed Tiger's name, that absurd golfing genius. Whatever *it* was, I didn't find it that night, and I let it get the best of me. I was a horrible customer for Nigel. Untalkative and unappreciative. He did his typical Nigel thing, cheery as hell, but I couldn't stop thinking about how much of a phony I would be when my friends arrived and I hadn't learned anything. Golf can do this to us if we let it. It was the perfect time for Pete Couhig to enter my life.

Pete was a 50-year-old father of three, born and raised in Louisiana. Before I heard his Cajun accent, I figured him for Pacific Northwest. He had a two-month beard that was well kept but covered most of his face. His hair up top was much scragglier, flowing out the back of his hat and to the sides, scraping the top of his shoulders. He played college soccer at Georgetown but took to golf in his mid-thirties, restless, competitive, and wanting to get *good* at something again.

On the first night of his first visit to St. Andrews—somewhere in the early 2010s—he met an American property owner in one of the pubs, who rented out a flat for 10 months and kept it to himself during the summer. "First chance I got I replicated that business plan as a semi-retirement plan," Pete told me. He spent years researching the local market—there are a lot of fixer-uppers in St. Andrews, if you're interested, just not a lot of people acting as fixers—before earning his wife's approval on a flat on the west end of Market St. He's summered in St. Andrews for a decade now.

Pete saw the video that coworker Dylan stitched together of my tour through St. Andrews and slid into my DM's to offer the eighth spot of a two-group, 36-hole day at Crail, about 10 miles down the coast from St. Andrews. "I'm the only American with a bunch of Scots in the group, so would appreciate the backup," Pete said. I loved his vibe.

The invite was for an official outing he set up for the Royal and Ancient Company of Dishonorable Golfers, also known as RACDG. Yes, you read that correctly. *Dis*honorable golfers, a witty play on the name of the uppity membership at Muirfield, known as The Honorable Company of Edinburgh Golfers. The RACDG describes itself as a "global golf society for people who take their on-course game seriously and their off-course game somewhat less so," and it exists to "bring together golf obsessives to enjoy the game and everything about it." My kinda people.

A couple of them drove up from Newcastle. That's in another country, three and a half hours away. Another drove down from Inverness, in the Scottish Highlands (which might as well be another country), three hours away. We teed off on the Craighead course at 11 AM, bounded into the clubhouse around 3 PM for a pint and a burger, then rushed back out onto the Balcomie course for 18 more holes, all of them on foot, just as it's supposed to be. It poured on us that afternoon, so much that I found myself squeezed into a one-stall bathroom with five strangers taking cover. Pete was among the few standing outside, now head-to-toe in navy blue rain gear, calling us wimps. He was one of those people who thrived on the existence of daylight. If there was time to do things, he had things to do. On our 20-minute ride back to town that night, I was so exhausted I nearly fell asleep. Pete was ready to get beers. Our summers were not the same.

We agreed to meet for those beers in a couple days, hoping to sit inside the bay windows of the St. Andrews Golf Club and gamble a few pounds on the amateurs putting on the 18th. This is the real divider between local and visitor. Visitors watch from behind the hole, on the pavement. Locals watch from inside one of the clubs. But true to form, Pete had too much energy for that. He visited the club early and weaseled our way into the last two spots of another 6 PM Dark Time. We'd be joining a fellow member, some guy named Rich, and his buddy Andy. Rich and Andy.

I paid my fee at the starter shack at 10 minutes to 6 and began peering around the putting green, searching for the kind of Rich and Andy characters that Pete might attract. Probably some younger guys. Some RACDG-worthy 35-year-olds with game. Probably wearing Jordans and well-fitting jumpers. Probably *not* the shlubby guy in the hospital boot who had just moseyed his way out to the 1st tee. That was my tee time donor, though. That was Rich Halliday.

"Which one of you is my teammate?" I asked, cutting the silence on the tee. Pete bounded down the steps with a sixer of Tennent's squeezed into his bag.

"Agh, you don' wan' that one," Rich's pal Andy said, pointing to Rich. "Less you wan' crazy."

I didn't want crazy. I just wanted to hit my ball straight and finally put together a good round on this vexing, fiddly course. I chose Andy, and we were off. It was a quiet start, like a lot of the starts on the Old. There are nerves out there. Rich played his first shot nearly out of bounds up the right and left his second shot short of the burn. I wouldn't have to take him seriously.

But then on the 2nd, he cut his approach to a horrible, far right corner of the green. There was maybe 50 feet between him and the hole and an absurd hump to climb and *halt* his ball on top of. But he pulled the putter back and tossed his lag putt up to five feet like it was nothing. When he made the par putt, it went into the scorecard as a 4-for-3 (four strokes counting as three, thanks to his handicap) and a won hole.

"Yes! *Thaaat's* Rich Halliday," he said with a little fist pump.

Excuse me?

"I'm Rich Halliday, baby."

Okay then.

On the 4th hole, he topped his tee shot maybe 40 yards, reiterating what I thought on the 1st, that this man wasn't a threat. But then on the 5th, when seemingly everyone was out of the hole but me, Rich drained a 30-footer for par, 5-for-4. It beat my casual 5-for-5.

"I mean, I don't know how they're gonna get over losing to a guy in a *boot*," he said to Pete, but not really to Pete at all. It was announced loudly enough for me, Andy, and even the group ahead of us to hear.

"I'm Rich Freaking Halliday."

The hospital boot was for a broken right foot Rich had suffered two months ago. He wouldn't explain how, but the mind wanders. He wore a soft-spike shoe on his left. He displayed impressive body control on the full swings, his toes grazing the grass through the boot opening as it slipped backward. His daughters were adamant that he rest, rest, rest, but they weren't here to keep watch over their old man, and he had grown tired of sitting around. Sitting around isn't easy to do in St. Andrews. This was his happy place, he said. A miniature patch of the Scottish flag was fastened to the boot's Velcro strap.

Rich was in his early sixties, stood about 5'9", and weighed maybe 150 pounds. I suppose that makes him similar to Rory McIlroy. He had a sizable gap between his two front teeth and grey hair peeking out the back of his St. Andrews Golf Club hat. The same club logo was on the chest of his quarter-zip, too. He and Andy had spent the afternoon at the club inhaling beers, but you couldn't tell just yet. They were hovering at a functionally operative level of drunkenness. The only abnormality was that Rich was a 16 handicap and putting like a scratch. On the 6th tee, I tried poking him out of magician mode. "Okay, Andy is clearly from here," I said. "I can hear it in his voice. But Rich, you don't have much of an accent. So where the hell are you *from?*"

"I'm a professional tourist. I'm from all over, baby," he said. "I've been working as a flight attendant for 40 years. American Airlines."

He grew up in Hawaii, 11 time zones from St. Andrews, on the island of O'ahu. He spent his college years in California (UC–Santa Barbara) and then joined a crew at American, setting up home base in LA. The job took him everywhere. London, Rio, Tokyo, Barcelona, Shanghai, often chasing whichever rock concert or football match was in town. What an incredible way to see the world, I thought. He was a professional tourist, a professional shit-talker, and taking swigs from a flask every few holes like a professional drinker.

On the 7th, he got up and down from 60 yards for par and a win. This time he didn't say anything, though. Perhaps because Andy and I were already out of the hole. On the drivable 9th, he putted from 40 yards away, off the green, trickling his Callaway across the flattest terrain on the course. I stood next to the pin shaking my head. It curled inside my ball (four feet) and inside the gimme zone (two feet). "*Oooops,*" he said with intended flair. "Little ol' Rich Halliday ruined your berrr-die. That's what Rich Halliday *does.*" Pete was lapping it up, and why wouldn't he? Pete carries two putters around in his Scotland bag. One for putts on the greens and a second, massive mallet for the linksy putts from 20 to 50, even 100 yards away. He calls it The Monstrosity.

Andy was quiet, in part because his putts were burning edges all evening, but also because he had seen these theatrics before. It's hard to talk when you're busy rolling your eyes. And what can you say when you're losing to a man playing with a backup set of clubs, draining putts with a dinged-up mallet, and finding fairways with a 15-year-old driver? Andy and I battled best we could. He sandwiched my par on 13 with a couple net pars of his own on 12 and 14. All of which brought us squarely level with Pete and Rich Halliday. Depressingly level. Concernedly level, imagining the Irish jig Rich Halliday would pull out on the 18th green if he won.

I stood there on the 15th tee shaking my head again. Maybe I'd been shaking it ever since that 40-yard two-putt that won Rich and Pete the 9th hole. Maybe even longer than that. This really was the silliest game in the world. In front of me stood a man not sober enough to drive, not fit enough for doctor's approval, not interested in humility, and definitely not good enough to be tied with me. But the ghost of Cam Smith had lingered in town long enough to possess this man's broken body. Everything was going in. I pulled out my phone to record Rich slap another loopy drive. He pirouetted back to us with a shit-eating grin on his face.

How...the hell...is he tied with us? More importantly, how did I get here? That's what I was thinking.

Most of my golf back home had become predictable. The annual matches with my three best friends from high school. The 7 AM starts with my Chicago muni friends, playing as many holes as possible before work hours. Even the rambunctious bachelor parties are predictable in nature. You might end up playing shirtless in the rain, but at least you knew that was plausible when the group of 16 arrived armed with a collective 192 High Noons. There was nothing predictable about this moment. Here on the 15th hole of one of the oldest golf courses in the world, I was doing battle against the CFO of a professional soccer team. (Pete's day job is balancing the roster of the Wycombe Wanderers.) My teammate was a local taxi driver who scorned the work load he had during Open Week, his most profitable week this decade. And the biggest thorn in my side, other than the scores I was making, was this live wire twirling around in front of us, obsessed with his full name, responding with, "Fuck youuuu, man" when we said his ball was headed for the sand. There isn't another sport on the planet that could put you outdoors, in a foreign country, at 9:47 PM, competing against this wicked collection of humans. But that's exactly the thing. St. Andrews promotes this. Golf promotes this.

It finally crystallized for me that Tuesday night: no course in the world mandates playing with strangers like the Old Course does. The ballot system only rewards a few full foursome entries per day. Maybe one tee time per hour, on average. Why? Think of it like selling tickets at a movie theater ahead of that year's blockbuster hit. The line is out the door, around the corner, down the street. In the theater, you've got 30 rows of 20 seats. If the customer experience goal is to see the movie and sit with your friends, the bigger groups will struggle to find seats together as the theater fills up. Couples who need just two adjacent seats have no problem squeezing in on the end, in the middle, or in those undesired seats up front. Couples are easy. The ballot system loves couples. So you end up with a lot of twosomes winning ballot times at the Old Course—unsurprisingly, about twice as many as foursomes— and getting paired with other twosomes or solo artists from the singles queue. Thus, it is more likely your round on the Old begins by learning the names of new playing partners than taking a group photo with three of your best mates. The extended takeaway here? I wasn't unique. I was not the first person to ride the Rich Halliday Roller Coaster. He'd no doubt given this experience to other innocent souls before. Maybe they realized on the 15th tee, too.

The next hour was not kind to Rich Halliday, but I don't think he much cared. Whatever strained sobriety remained in him when he pipped my birdie on No. 9 faded by the time he reached the 15th green. My par there was a winner. On the 16th, with honors, I hit the best drive of my summer, cutting over the left edge of the fairway, avoiding the Principal's Nose bunkers (noted round-ruiners) and rolling out about 315 yards. Another par, and another win. The sun had completely set now, and we relied on the latent light reflecting off the clouds.

We teed off 17 at 10:04 PM, the definition of Hit and Hope. *Feel* the spin of the ball off your club face and guesstimate where it ended up. When Rich took a phone call walking up the 17th, I knew it was over. (Our match, at least, not his performance.) The hanging lamps of the Jigger Inn helped illuminate the right side of the fairway, where my 3-wood left the yellow ball I was now playing. A well-lubricated crowd of 30 stood on other side of the out-of-bounds wall, chanting *Tiger, Tiger, Tiger* as we hit our approaches. I smoothed a 5-iron that I knew, if played with the perfect little cut, would bounce and roll up that same hill Cam Smith putted up during The Open. About two minutes after contact, I was stunned to see the ball waiting for me on the green, 20 feet away from the hole. Maybe that was something else I had learned here—*visualization*, a Scottish golf asset. Two putts later, I had made a third straight par, winning a third straight hole and closing out Rich Halliday and Pete for good, 3 and 1. A par in the darkness on the Road Hole is as good as golf gets. My prize for winning, according to Rich, was a private viewing of his secret party trick.

"Watch this shit," he said, pulling out maybe his sixth cigarette of the round. "Well, first of all…hang on."

He turned away and bent over slightly, cupping his hands to his face. When he whipped around, his hands were at his side and the cig wedged into that gap between his front teeth.

"When I, when I, when I told you watch this shit, I fuckin' meant it, okay?"

Pete went to his knees in laughter. Rich swung his arms around for emphasis, begging for us to be impressed.

"Yes, that's what I'm talking about. 'Cause I'm Rich Halliday."

Of all the astonishing things he did that day, this was the least impressive and somehow the most memorable. The no-hands heater. No wobble during inhale and exhale. Just a toothy vise grip on a dart. He stuck his right index finger in the air. No. 1. The No. 1 entertainer in all of Fife. He tipped his chin back, held his hands out wide, and sucked in the fumes. Only once I brought my phone camera closer did he exhale and smile wide like a tobacco-crazed Cheshire Cat.

Once again, *How did I get here?* To the 18th tee box of the Old Course, at 10:22 PM, getting light-headed at this peak of stupidity. We still had one more hole to play.

I called Pete up months later to see what he remembered about that late-July night. The selfie we took on the Swilcan Bridge makes us look like two friends who'd known each other forever. "I feel like I had a lot of birdies," he said immediately. I didn't have the guts to tell him that just wasn't the case. He didn't remember his score. I didn't remember mine, either. Eighty-seven strokes is what I took, according to the handicap app on my phone. Another disappointing result, I suppose, unhelpful to my index. But what Pete said next told the story.

"I just remember Rich told about 58 stories about himself in the third person." *That's it*, I thought. Because that was my answer, too. The answer to those "How did I get here?" questions is just a string of golfers doing things for other golfers. It wouldn't have happened if St. Andrews sold its tee times strictly to foursomes of the highest bidder, selling out in the name of capitalism. It wouldn't have happened if Rich stiff-armed Pete when he asked to join his Dark Time. Pete never would have invited me to Crail if Dylan hadn't made his video. Dylan wouldn't have been around to make his video if I hadn't offered a bed for him to crash in and a free round at the Duke's. It's often small stuff that golf connections lead to, but it's always something. Golf people always give you something. Sometimes the result is just as dumb as it is everlasting. A video or two on my phone that make me giggle every time I watch. That's what Rich Halliday *does*.

Chapter 15

People Behind the People

I'm doing that walk-jog thing we all do when we're late for a flight. We don't want to be that person outright sprinting, in pants and a peacoat, hoisting a duffel in the air, dodging families and senior scooters and the line snaking away from Starbucks. Rather than deal with *all that*, we walk-jog. It feels right. It feels safe. It feels necessary.

So I'm walk-jogging, duffel in hand, backpack filled with equipment to the point that its zippers may fail if I walk-jog any faster. I'm not late for a flight, but I am tardy. I'm back in East Lothian, rushing to the 1st tee of North Berwick Golf Club. Mel Reid is about to tee off, and if I'm not quick, I will miss the scene I was desperate to capture. My train was scheduled to arrive at 10:14 AM, but didn't do so until 10:16, which is to say it severely cut into the amount of time I had. From the end stall of the North Berwick train station to the 1st tee is precisely five minutes. I now had about three and a half. Mel was teeing off at 10:19.

Yes, I could have trained down to North Berwick the night prior, not leaving my timeliness to the whims of the ScotRail conductor, but that would have meant surrendering my Sunday afternoon in St. Andrews. And what a Sunday it was. A seagull swooped down that morning and smacked its flabby, webbed feet on top of my head while it stole a bite of my bacon roll. The other patrons at Con Panna sure thought it was funny, but neither the seagull nor I were laughing. I then watched canines take over the Old Course—a weekly Sunday tradition when the course is closed for play and reopened as a public park—turning the Swilcan Bridge into one of those ramps dogs bound over at the Westminster Dog Show. I then took in the women's European Championship football final between England and Germany. I was eager to see how the Scots would support England's best footballing women.

On the telly in the Dunvegan? The Celtic-Aberdeen game. That's men's football.

How about in Hams Hame, down the street? The Celtic-Aberdeen game.

Okay, well maybe the One Under Bar? The Celtic-Aberdeen game. The Scotland-England rivalry, decided by channel changers.

Back in the Dunvegan, after the Lionesses won, I found Sean Crocker, that week's champion on the DP World Tour. More specifically, that *day's* champion on the DP World Tour. Crocker made a 5-foot putt on the 72nd hole to win by one at the Fairmont St. Andrews, located just outside of town, and brought his after-party straight to the Dunny. "I just can't walk by this place," he told me Sunday night. In fairness, his name was written in a congratulatory message on the chalkboard out front. It would be tough to walk by that. Crocker has spent too many nights in the Dunny over the years and he was about to take it deep once again. "Not wasting time on this one," he said in a selfie on his Instagram story, a mostly empty Corona bottle pushed up to his lips. "Thanks to everyone who messaged or called, I will get back to [you] as soon as the hangover is gone."

He was doing a decent job at remaining anonymous in the bar, with his black Miami Marlins hat pulled down tight, working through Corona No. 3 or 4. But everyone around him was buzzing. Their man had won for the first time as a pro. His first win anywhere other than a Tuesday money game in more than five years, a reminder that golf constantly gives its best actors a criminally low chance at victory. I wanted to know if he could allow himself to think about what was next. "Wales, next week," he blurted out before taking another swig. "But that might be a rough week. Expectations are *low*."

Four hours later, you could find him spinning around the room, holding up Corona No. Whatever with both hands, high above his head, like it was the trophy he ever wanted. The entire bar serenaded him with Queen's "We are the Champions." When the Dunny began to close down, the Crocker Party headed to The Vic. Ol' reliable. Sometime the next day, Crocker dragged his hungover self to Wales for that week's Cazoo Open, about 400 miles away. The show goes on in pro golf. There is always a next event. It can get delayed by a win, but not much else. Which is part of why I needed to watch Mel Reid tee off on the 1st at North Berwick.

Mel is a friend first and an LPGA winner second, though she'd probably reverse the order if you asked her. If she spoke earnestly, she'd agree she shouldn't be playing in the Monday qualifier for that week's Women's Open at Muirfield. She should be *in* The Open already, by virtue of winning the 2020 ShopRite LPGA Classic just 20 months earlier. If you can summit the mountaintop to win on the LPGA Tour, you're probably going to be in the major championships for the next few years. But technically Mel wasn't. She notched just two top 10s in 40 starts since that win, dropping from 30th in the world ranking to outside the top 125. She missed the cut at the Women's Scottish Open and then zoomed over to North Berwick to prep for qualifying because, well, there's always another tournament. The show goes on. She woke up to good news, though: a last-minute exemption into the event. She was happy, of course, but slightly peeved. Couldn't the R&A have informed her Sunday night? Pro golfers like a defined path forward, and practice schedules were already getting scrunched over at Muirfield.

There were 12 more spots available in The Open that would be claimed from this qualifier, and it was evident who the locals were behind. Mel's taxi driver Sunday afternoon had told her one thing: *Keep an eye out for that Clara Young.*

That Clara Young was supposed to be in Mel's group, so my walk-jog to the 1st tee was not for nothing. I had a new story to cover. It seemed all of North Berwick had come out to watch.

I've caddied in U.S. Open qualifiers before. They are not attended by any discernible group of fans. Maybe Mom and Dad, but that's it. These events on the lower rungs of pro golf are extra lonely. Many times players don't even have a caddie. It's just them, their diary of thoughts, and the bag that holds their clubs, which may or may not be obeying command.

Clara Young had no fewer than 40 people surrounding that 1st tee at North Berwick. When she reached her ball in the 1st fairway, the mini flock crowded in behind and splayed out wide, creating a massive semi-circle. Somewhere floating about that chaos were her two playing partners. We know this was a crowd of locals because we have eyes and we looked down at their ankles. The temp was in the upper 50s and the breeze was ratcheting up but nearly every single one of them wore shorts or capris. "Ah, you've got to," said Alan Love, a West Links caddie who manages a local bed-and-breakfast. "You don' know how many good days ye'll have."

The townfolk were paying respect to one of their favorite golfing families. Clara's caddie was her father, Alan, who retired from his day job years ago but still loops twice a week on the West Links. Clara caddies on the West Links, too, for some side money when she isn't grinding on her own game. She was a rookie on the LET Access

Series, the equivalent of single-A baseball in the States. You may recall Scott Young, the assistant pro who drank beers with me, Joel Dahmen, Luke List, and others during that Missed Cut Saturday of the Scottish Open. Scott is Clara's younger brother and plenty good enough to take money off her any given night. But he was being humbled by the popularity contest he had to endure: a weekend's worth of inquiries over the phone and from visitors to the pro shop. *How's Clara feeling about her game? When's Clara's tee time? Think she'll make it to Muirfield?*

What started with a nervy par was quickly undone by dropped shots on the ensuing par-3s. Clara found a fried-egg lie in the cavernous front bunker on the 6th, left her second shot in the sand, and made double from there. Four over in a flash.

Scottish golf legend Catriona Mathew and her husband (who caddies on the West Links, too) watched along from their front yard. It's always fascinating to watch pro golfers watch golf, even if all you see is them nodding along sternly. Residents brought their Labs along for the walk, but held them quiet on a leash, which must have been confusing for the pups. Normally they roam freely across the West Links, a massive doggy playground among the dunes. But today was serious business. Tournament officials had sent a walking marshal out with the group, the only walking marshal on the course. She very earnestly held up a blue and white placard before every shot: QUIET. That was a first for me at a qualifying tournament.

I walked a few holes with brother Scott, and a few holes with Jane Nelson, former secretary of the East Lothian Ladies County Golf Association. I could only serve to offend by guessing her age, but Jane was not south of 60. She may have been north of 70. More relevant were the years she served as an ambassador for women's golf in the area. Jane has been a longtime planner for the Babe Zaharias, a local tournament for female amateurs. It costs just £25 to enter, all the proceeds going to local cancer research, and it sells out every single year. All 150 spots, ladies only.

Scotland has more people like Jane than we do in America. There were a couple Janes in this crowd alone. She's petite but not frail. She's aging like we all are but stays in incredible shape. Golf is what keeps her young. She plays off a 17 handicap and still dreams of becoming a 15. She's retired but works as secretary at the East of Scotland Girls Golf Association, nurturing opportunities for the next local kid to come through just as Clara Young did—from the Wee Course to the big course to winning county championships and then playing for Scotland's national teams. Jane even competed in the same group as Clara in local comps. "She probably doesn't remember that," Jane said fondly, "but I do." Most every pro golfer has a Jane Nelson in their history. Probably many of them. The people behind the people— sometimes literally, at qualifying events.

As Clara made the turn at North Berwick, where you literally turn around and start playing downwind, it was clear she wasn't going to be one of the 156 competing at Muirfield. She had found the burn that snaked across the 7th fairway and then found fairway bunkers on the par-5 8th and par-5 9th, ruining birdie chances.

Even though Jane was dismayed and Clara was frustrated and Scott headed back to the pro shop and there was only so much caddying Dad could do, only a few stragglers left the watch party. And frankly, if 92-year-old Grandma Valerie was out there walking all 18 holes, everyone else should finish the job, too. Clara finally eased the tension when she made her first birdie on 14, that same hole where Luke List missed that four-footer in his chase for the course record. It all felt like one big extended family out for a walk after Christmas dinner. Some moved along solo and silent. Others in groups of two or three, making plans for the upcoming music festival. Every single one of them a golfer of some sort.

It was a little odd, Clara told me after, playing this course she knows so well, but now with this ever-present cluster clinging to every shot. "I just tried to make it feel like a *fun* round," she said, hoping to feel as loose as the matches she played against her brother. It never quite worked. She signed for six-over, 78. "That's just golf," Dad said. "Sometimes it goes your way, sometimes it doesn't."

That's a healthy mindset and an easy one for Dad to have. He wasn't hitting the shots. He also wasn't rushing home to pack his bags for a flight to Sweden in the morning. Clara was off to compete in something called the Västerås Open Presented by PadelPitch, where first place would receive £6,400. The first round was kicking off in about 40 hours. "No practice round this week will be...fun," she said, forcing out a chuckle. The show goes on in pro golf. It always does.

You could not arrange a more historic summer than the R&A did, sending the men to St. Andrews and the women to Muirfield. Muirfield is home to the second-oldest club in the world—The Honorable Company of Edinburgh Golfers.

Besides Royal Burgess, which chewed me up and spit me out all sickly, no other club in the world is older than the Honorable Company. They held the first-ever golf competition, an 11-player affair won by a surgeon named John Rattay. To govern the comp, they created the first 13 Rules of Golf.

No. 12: *He whose ball lyes farthest from the hole is obliged to play first.*

No. 10: *If a ball be stopp'd...the ball so stop'd must be play'd where it lyes.*

No. 5: *If your ball come among water, or any watery filth* [aka cow manure] *you are at liberty to take out your ball and bringing it behind the hazard...you may play it with any club and allow your adversary a stroke for so getting out your ball.*

Sound familiar? All of that was decided in 1744. Back when golf was often referred to as "goff."

Here in 2022, to couple St. Andrews in a golf summer with Muirfield, about 90 minutes away by car, was almost too much. The

R&A was tipping the scales. Perhaps purposefully. Because mixed in with all that history at Muirfield was some baggage.

For the first 275 years of its existence, the Honorable Company was a club consisting entirely of men. Women were allowed to visit, and even play as guests, but for nearly three centuries there wasn't a single woman in the membership of more than 600. The golf world turned a blind eye to this for a long time, obviously, but Augusta National had recently been pressured into admitting women to its membership. It hosts the grandest golf tournament in the world. How could Scottish golf royalty get away with not doing the same?

The Honorable Company put it to a vote in early 2016. *Shall we allow women into this club or shall we not?* It's rarely that simple but this *was* that simple. The result was a majority of yesses, to the tune of 64 percent. Just not the supermajority of two-thirds required to change club policies. The R&A responded swiftly, with Martin Slumbers issuing a statement: "The Open is one of the world's great sporting events and going forward we will not stage the Championship at a venue that does not admit women as members."

You want our championship? Join us in the 21st century.

This was a big deal. Muirfield had hosted 16 Opens, more than any course not named St. Andrews. But the world was demanding change. Slumbers had been CEO for only a few months. This was an organizational directive, not some campaign promise. The R&A didn't single out Muirfield, either, because it was far from alone in this issue. But if Muirfield ever wanted to host an Open again, it had one very simple action to take. Admit women. So the next time the club voted, in the spring of 2017, 80 percent voted yes. The Honorable Company officially entered the 21st century with 20 percent of its members kicking and screaming. Two years after the vote, 12 female members joined the club, and one year after that, the R&A delivered some sweet irony. It granted Muirfield another Open: the 2022 *Women's* Open. That week had finally arrived.

What I couldn't figure out was how to handle all that context. It felt like we were nearing the end of a long, bumpy road where women were treated like secondary citizens in the sport. Female golf attire has always been criticized more than men's. Access to tee times hasn't always been equitable. Until 2021, Pine Valley, annually praised as the no. 1 course in the world, only allowed female guests to play on Sunday afternoons. As for Muirfield, horror stories arrived in my email inbox during Open week. Tales about female guests being ushered into the clubhouse through side entrances instead of the front door. Another story involved a foursome of mid-handicap female guests who were stopped after nine holes by a screaming club official who said, "They need a man to make sure they move along." Little did he know their husbands were two holes behind, trudging through the rough and struggling to keep pace. But the club official got his wish that day. The women waited for the husbands to catch up, eager to not displease anyone because, well, *Muirfield is Muirfield.*

And yet, this was the same club that often said yes to Jane Nelson and the East Lothian women's events she organized. Change *was* happening. Muirfield *was* changing. Its female membership had grown north of 20 now. The club produced new history books for the week, in which it is stated, "Our Women Members [notice the caps] now form a key part of the Club and have been seamlessly integrated into all its activities." The club held a gala Monday evening, welcoming the field to learn about club history, hopeful they'd become a part of it. Muirfield wanted to move forward.

So...how much do you talk about that? Should the Honorable Company be afforded the same pat on the back Augusta National received? Or should we wait until the next Women's Open for that? I didn't have a good answer.

What I did know was no players were going to bring it up. Female pros have a tendency toward deference, thankful for whatever they're given. They've grown accustomed to wage gaps and little to no time on network TV. They've ascended in sport where male management inhibits their clothing decisions, hiring practices, even the opinions they feel they can express. They may have opinions on Muirfield's membership, but that wasn't a battle for this week. Rather, we talked about the most unanimous opinion female golfers *do* share publicly: wanting their major championships hosted at clubs where the men have shined. They want their piece of that history, too. A women's U.S. Open has never been held at Shinnecock, where some of the best men's championships have been held. The R&A has never brought a Women's Open to Royal St. George's, where the men have played 15 times.

I asked Minjee Lee if, while she was growing up in Western Australia, there was ever a course she wanted to play a tournament at one day. Pebble Beach was one, she said. The other was St. Andrews.

"Why those courses?" I asked.

"Because they had a lot of events," she said. "And I watched it on TV."

It doesn't have to be any more complicated than that. When junior golfers watch golf on TV, they take note of the trophies, the players lifting them, and the holes where greatness happened. "Prestigious events and obviously a lot of prestigious winners" were her other reasons for wanting to play Pebble and St. Andrews. Muirfield has that as much as any host. Mickelson, Els, Faldo, Watson, Trevino, Nicklaus, Player, Hagen—they're all winners at Muirfield.

Pros ask themselves, *Could I do what they've done?* Women just want the opportunity. Thankfully, the Women's U.S. Open visited Pebble for the first time in 2023. Minjee's first Open at St. Andrews is coming in 2024. We're getting this thing right, slowly but surely. Muirfield included.

The best news of the week came a day after that chat with Minjee Lee, when Slumbers informed the media that this year's purse was bumped up to $7.3 million, a 26 percent increase. It was the third-biggest purse of the year, thanks to a partnership with AIG. Money is always on the mind of pros, but it was a trickier topic than ever that week. About 10 days earlier, LPGA Commissioner Molly Samaan Marcoux told Golfweek that if LIV Golf approached her with the kind of money Saudi Arabia was throwing around the men's game, she would absolutely take the phone call. As commissioner, she considered that her duty to the LPGA membership. This was momentum building for Greg Norman, who paraded the idea to the local south Florida newspaper. Samaan Marcoux said it would be irresponsible *not* to take the call. And she was probably right. But that quote elevated the discourse once again about what is good business, what is shady business, and what a commissioner owes to a 200-player membership.

LIV Golf launching a separate women's league would decimate the LPGA Tour. That's what women's golf legends Juli Inkster and Annika Sorenstam were saying, again in a report from Golfweek. And that's what was being whispered on the grounds, too. Wherever the most money is, pro golfers will follow. Mel Reid told me the same thing Wednesday afternoon. Her caddie that week, Jamie Longman, is the boyfriend of Carlotta Ciganda. He knows what women's golf financing looks like, and agreed wholeheartedly. So did Meghan MacLaren, even if begrudgingly so. The English pro competes on the Ladies European Tour and has to think about money as much as anyone. She makes enough to sustain the pursuit of her dreams, but not enough to live a comfy lifestyle. About £300,000 over six years for one of the 300 best players in the world.

Meghan also happens to be a Newcastle Football supporter. I could see the strain in her face when she rolled her eyes at a LIV Golf Women's League but acknowledged her football club is benefitting from Saudi money more than any other sports entity on the planet. "At some point, you can't ignore it," she said. Saudi Aramco, the state-owned petrol company worth $2 trillion, uses pocket change to sponsor the biggest purses on the Ladies European Tour. For a while, MacLaren refused to play in them, but eventually she had to give in with a promise to herself that she'd use the money to grow her platform, elevate her career, and speak out confidently about what she believes in. At some point, you can't ignore it.

Her dilemma and Samaan Marcoux's dilemma were different. Maybe that's what we learned in the summer of LIV Golf—that none of this was the same for everyone. And the golf world was having a really hard time deciding who was most important in this ecosystem. Was it the players? Was it the fans? Was it the organizations that govern the game? Was it the hope that headlines in 2035 would read "Worldwide Golf Participation Reaches Record High?" The best way to describe it all on August 3 was *blurry*. And getting blurrier. That day, on the eve of the Women's Open, 11 LIV golfers filed a lawsuit against the PGA Tour, alleging anti-competitive practices that barred them from freely plying their trade as LIV Golf entered the competitive landscape. *Mickelson et al. vs. PGA Tour, Inc.* was its name, the biggest lawsuit in professional golf history. In less than six months, Mickelson had gone from a career-defining public relations blunder to suing the organization he built his career on. Maybe Sorenstam and Inkster had reason to be wary. All of this stuff can move quickly.

I worked until 3 AM that night analyzing the juiciest details of the 105-page complaint. Turns out, Mickelson had been suspended by the PGA Tour in March for recruiting players to leave with him. Turns out, Bryson DeChambeau had signed a contract with LIV months before joining the circuit. Tiny tokens buried in the legalese.

In the few hours between when I filed the story and when I woke up, multiple TV and radio stations were begging me to join their show as some sort of legal analyst, which I very much was not. LIV was once again all-consuming, ensuring that when the Women's Open would start, the golf world would not be looking in the direction of Muirfield and the good happening in the women's game. Rather, it would be looking nine time zones west to a district court in Northern California.

On Thursday, I treated myself. I deserved it after slaving away all night for some lawsuit that Mickelson was going to yank his name off in a matter of months. Thursday, I decided, I would work to actually *get* something for the effort. So I walked all 18 holes with Nelly Korda, the No. 3 player in the world and owner of the prettiest, smoothest, most technically sound swing on the planet. If I watched intently enough, used my inside-the-ropes badge to get close enough, I'd hear things, see things, and learn why this course is really as good as everyone says it is.

First, an ode to simplicity. The 1st at St. Andrews is named "Burn," as we've discussed. The 12th at North Berwick is named "Bass," for the island Bass Rock, covered in gannet shit, as we've discussed. The 3rd at Muirfield? It's called Hole 3. No reason to overcomplicate things. Nelly birdied it to dip into red figures. Off and running. When she made eagle on 5, I thought I was going to learn that Muirfield isn't as hard as everyone says it is.

But 5 is right around the time that Muirfield decides to make you work. The stretch of 3, 4, and 5 is the longest stretch on the property of consecutive holes played in the same direction. Open hosts like St. Andrews and Troon are lauded for bringing golfers out for nine holes and then back with nine more, but Muirfield loops you around the property in one big clockwise circle and then reverses course with a counter-clockwise medley of chaos tucked into the middle. The wind is constant, but the way you set up to it is constantly changing. The 6th hole is a 90-degree turn from the 5th. The 7th is a 135-degree turn from the 6th. The 8th is a 155-degree pivot from 7. The 9th is 130 degrees off the 8th. We need not continue, s'long as ye get the point. Before she stepped into each shot, Nelly's caddie Jason McDede shouted the wind direction to her one final time. It couldn't hurt.

"You think [the holes] all run in the same direction, but they're *just* a little different," McDede told me after the round. I was up on my tippy-toes, speaking through the wickets that separate the press from player scoring.

"Look, it's a great golf course," he continued. "I think it's the best one."

It wasn't clear if he meant best course in the world, best in Scotland, or just best Open course, but he was comfy with the honorific.

"There really aren't any pars," he said. "I know that sounds weird, but you've got an 8-iron into a par-5 and then you turn around and you've got a par-4 playing 600. I know it's cliché, but you just have to take it as it comes."

What he means is that there is no normalized idea of what a par should look like. So often in pro golf par looks like a driver, a wedge to 20 feet, and two putts. But thanks to the wind, which you'd prefer to avoid, and the firmness of the ground, which can be unpredictable, and the 145 hellholes of sand waiting to gobble up your ball, there is no comfortable sense of how to acquire your par at Muirfield. Players have to detach themselves from what's normal and react to what the course is giving them that day. That's entertaining golf.

On the 17th, Nelly was in the wispy right rough and between clubs. It's either a full 6-iron in the air or something longer, running on the ground. She went with the "chippy 5" that couldn't have reached an apex of 40 feet. *Low-low.* The ball was in the air for four seconds, enough to fly past the cross bunkers, then bouncing for four seconds on a fairway that McDede likened to a bowling alley. Then it rolled out for another 12 seconds. Feel free to count that out in your head. Two-hundred and twenty-five yards—four seconds, four seconds, and 12 seconds. That is the rhythm of links golf. You can't fully appreciate it until you've played it or stood there in the rough like I was, 20 feet from Nelly, in awe of the physics. She cleaned up her two putts for birdie and added a par on 18 for a round of 70, one under. When she arrived in the flash zone, she received seven questions, all from me.

"It's pretty mentally draining, for sure," she said. "You have to play a round with a lot of different swings. I mean, I hit an 8-iron 190 [yards] and then I hit a 4-iron 180 today. That's British Open. But I think it's fun. It's nice to do once a year or a couple times a year. I wouldn't do it every week, but I think it's a lot of fun."

I wanted to rip my credential off and start a debate right there. *That's the difference between you and me, Nelly.* One of the differences at least. I *would* do it every week. Fifty-two weeks a year if I could. That's thinking man's golf. I know only a sliver of the mental grind it is to compete in a professional tournament and can only assume with a game like hers how relaxing it must be to switch the brain off and just hit drivers into wedges into putts for birdie. There's something about her game that's made to be robotic, so repeatable. We'll attribute that to growing up on Florida golf courses and attending school at the IMG Academy. But this—this is *invigorating* golf. *Fun golf.* She said it herself. Just like Scottie Scheffler did at the Scottish Open. You're not supposed to switch your brain off, and if you do, you get what she got on 13.

The 13th played downwind but uphill. The cup was cut in the front left, requiring a draw shot, but Nelly made her weakest swing of the day, leaving her approach out to the right and weak. Where does Muirfield have a bunch of perfectly placed bunkers? Out to the right and weak. She had no play but to chop a wedge onto the edge of the green and two-putt for bogey. When her 4-iron into the breeze on 15 leaked into the back of another bunker, she had to chop again, this time with one foot in the sand, one cranked backward on the rim of the trap. Another bogey.

This push and pull of what a course offers in return for the shots you give it called to mind what the previous champion at Muirfield said after his win in 2013.

"It gave a player like myself, that hit shots exactly how I was wanting to, to make birdies and to pull away," a 43-year-old Phil Mickelson said. "And I also saw a lot of guys where they hit less-than-perfect shots and made bogeys and doubles and fall back. I think that's what you're looking for."

Muirfield was doing that again. Nelly's perfect shots were rewarded while less-than-perfect shots were repelled. Good bounces? Yes. Bad breaks? Sure. Mentally draining? Sure, Nelly. Let's use the word *stimulating*.

I pinched myself later that night, knowing the rarity of the experience. One of the best players in the world at this finicky game just shot under par at one of the trickiest courses on the planet. My view was so intimate that I heard Nelly drop a clean "Fuck" underneath her breath on 18 when she thought she drove into the bunker. And then I was the only person in Scotland who talked to her *and* her caddie about everything they just did. Apply that to other sports and you're talking about sitting on the bench next to Steve Kerr as Steph Curry scores 28 on five threes…and then chatting with each of them 1-on-1 afterward. What a gig.

Sportswriters can get stuck trying to treat these everyday moments in our work casually, hellbent on describing it exactly as we saw it, being a professional ourselves. The ramifications for everything circle in our heads. But rarely do we ever acknowledge what watching the action actually does to enliven us as students of the game. That round was just another 70 for Nelly but it felt like a personal lecture to me. It was office hours with free tuition.

A real clarity arrives for writers on the Sunday of a major championship when one player has built, say, a five-shot lead. At that point, the field has been trimmed from 156 to single digits, and the field of storylines trimmed down to just two:

1. They win by coronation, up eight at the turn, waltzing to victory without much pressure.

2. They choke away that lead and at some point will cry about it. Probably right in front of you.

It may be ruthless to see the world this way, but that's how we see the world. The earlier the storylines crystallize, the deeper the reporting can get. The better the storytelling gets. Those impending tears after squandering a five-shot lead? That's just emotion. We'll record it appropriately. We love emotion.

As for a choke-job at Muirfield, it didn't seem possible. Ashleigh Buhai (B'yew-high) was so loose.

Buhai shot 65 in the second round Friday, a preposterous score on its own, and then followed it with 64 on Saturday. Preposterous times two. With a score of 13 under and that five-shot lead, she played UNO on Saturday night and did laundry on Sunday morning. In the precious minutes before the biggest tee time of her life, she…took a phone call? From who, we don't know. She signed autographs, too, and posed for photos. Most pros wouldn't want to talk to anyone, let alone strangers or whoever the hell was calling the leader of the Women's Open right before her tee time. The wind was whipping—gusting up to 28 mph— the hardest it had blown all week. But Ashleigh was relaxed. I suppose that comes with the five-shot cushion. Make a bunch of casual pars and you'll be walking up 18 in no time. Golf is rarely that simple, though. She knows better than anyone.

Born in Johannesburg, South Africa, she was one of the most successful amateurs the country has ever seen. Then, a few weeks after turning pro, she nabbed her first win on the Ladies European Tour at 18. She signed deals with Nike, IMG, and Golf Digest. South African legend Gary Player waxed on about her talents. She seemed destined to be an LPGA force.

It just didn't happen. Ashleigh occasionally picked off a win in Europe, but never in America. Never on the LPGA Tour, where the best players play. She was 33 now, the 84th-ranked player in the world wondering if her best golf was in her past, or somehow still in her future.

She stood 5'5" but with naturally slumped shoulders. She was not a long hitter. Fifteen years had passed since her shining debut and there wasn't a ton to show for it. She kept the same coach the entire time, through seasons where she made $400,000 and others where she made $40,000. "This game has a way of giving you a hard time," she says.

But on that Sunday, we appeared destined for Storyline No. 1: the coronation. Ashleigh was one over par for the day, holding a three-shot lead with just four holes to play. I had spent the last 20 minutes memorizing the face of her husband, David, on my phone, knowing that, in the absence of intel on Ashleigh herself, I could always lean on the reactions of her family. I found him just in time.

David was most of the way up the hole, between Ashleigh and where she wanted to go. He was easy to spot, a 6'4" jolly giant, wearing shorts that revealed the tree-trunk legs of a caddie. He had already looped the course that morning, on the bag for Jeongeun Lee, the 35th-ranked player in the world. The only thing he carried now was a half-empty cup of beer and a concerned look on his face. Ashleigh was in the fairway bunker left on 15. She had avoided bunkers phenomenally all week, but her tee ball kicked left when it very easily could have kicked forward. The kind of bounce that 72-hole tournaments are whittled down to on a Sunday evening. David's beer cup quickly became three-quarters empty when Ashleigh splashed out into knee-high rough. Bad lie into a bad lie. The rough grabbed the hosel of her wedge on the next swing, turning the face. She advanced it forward maybe 30 yards. Bad lie times three. Golf can be the slowest game in the world until moments like this where it gets *really fast*.

David had grown to nine feet now as he watched his wife pitch onto the green. He had climbed onto the back of a golf cart for a better view over the growing crowd in front of him. Everyone wanted to watch this slow-motion car crash. In that moment, it was time for a break. A break from the nerves, the view, or maybe just a potty break. Only David knows. But he stormed up the hill to the 16th green right then, while his wife read a 20-foot putt for double bogey. For

200 yards he took those bounding, outstretched caddie strides, then turned around, hands on his hips, to watch Ashleigh's body language from afar. Miss. Triple bogey. David was off to the loo.

The coronation was dead, the five-shot lead fully squandered, and I stood there next to a nervous husband who had lightened himself in the porta-john. This was a role I had long been curious about. What's it like to be the nervous husband? The wife? The significant other who has been there for...*ever.* How about the aunt? Ashleigh's aunt Mandy had driven seven hours that morning—across most of England—to see her niece win The Open. She tied a South African flag around her neck like a cape. Like the North Berwickians who tracked Clara Young's every shot, these are the people behind the people. Their experience is fascinating, too. It was going to be triumph or tears and potentially both.

By the time his wife reached the 18th, needing a par 4 to make the playoff, David had ascended and descended two more golf carts, unintentionally drawing enough attention that the TV broadcast crew stuck a cameraman at his side. #HusbandCam. He didn't seem to mind. The beer and his nerves were at equilibrium. We made a lovely train, the three of us. Husband Cam stepping in rhythm with David up the 18th, me stepping in the same footprints as Husband Cam. None of us knew how long the next 90 minutes was going to feel, once Ashleigh made a 4-footer for par. It was playoff time, against In Gee Chun, the No. 11 player in the world, who had just won the Women's PGA Championship in June. Ashleigh was definitely the underdog.

Earlier in the day, a caddie named John Pavelko told me all about the Buhais. How they're too beloved to travel alone. They go on safari vacations with other Tour pros and rent houses on the road with Carlotta Ciganda. "She'll be a popular winner on Tour," Pavelko said. "She's someone people *want* to see win."

His phrasing stuck with me as Team Buhai assembled behind the green. Every few minutes it grew larger and larger. There was American pro Marina Alex, along with her parents, who walked the last three holes with worried faces. Same for Danish pro Nicole Brock Estrup and her husband Kasper. Nicole missed the cut but hung around all weekend to watch Ashleigh. It was good vibes until an hour ago. There was the lovable Swede Madelene Sagström and her soon-to-be fiancé, Jack Clarke. Team Buhai was about 30 strong.

She's someone people want to see win.

Ashleigh and In Gee both parred the first playoff hole, making it look easier than it really was. The wind whipped from the right, slipping over the hospitality tent and playing tricks on their approach shots. They traded nervy bogeys on the second playoff hole.

I passed the time chatting with Baylor assistant coach Carly Ludwig. She had caddied for a former Baylor Bear that week and was headed to Carnoustie Monday morning to meet with recruits at the Boys and Girls Junior Amateur Championship. Her upcoming roster had players from five different continents. The only problem with Ludwig's recruiting schedule is she was staying with the Buhais. "This could be a really long night," she said.

Husband David would have a long morning, win or lose. Between every playoff hole, his caddie brethren returned with beers. Husband Cam stayed locked on his face. His exhales used his entire face, as though he were blowing out a candle.

"How you doin', husband?" asked Marina Alex's mother, Marissa.

"Not good at all," he said.

"Do you need wet wipes?" someone asked.

"I've been needing to go to the toilet for a while now," he said, racing off to relieve himself. His responses were short, emotional, genuine. All he could muster. He was showing himself, and doing it out loud, folding up little reporting nuggets and tucking them in my notebook like a valet tip. *Hey, here you go, Sean. Use this in that story later.* He grabbed beers for himself on his trip back from the bathroom, returning in time to watch another pair of pars.

Remember when I said, "Don't ever let a golf writer tell you they don't care who wins" and that "playoffs are the bane of a deadline's existence," but they make for better stories? There's a limit to all that and we were rapidly approaching mine. The clouds hung low that night, like neat little pillows overlapping each other out toward the coast. They were only getting darker. An R&A official told me we would *not* be playing another hole tonight after this one.

"Dave, this is like Le Mans, but times a hundred," shouted Jason McDede, Nelly Korda's caddie. That's the annual sports car race held in France, created for the sickest of sickos. For 24 hours, racers drive and drive and drive and drive. Whoever has finished the most laps after a full day of driving is the champion. I wasn't sure how much this was *like Le Mans, but times a hundred,* but it sure was intense. These people standing in front of me were either going to rage into the night or end up consoling each other with hugs and kisses and tears just like Rory McIlroy in St. Andrews.

Both players trudged back to that same tee box about 440 yards away. It was the fifth time they'd been here in the last two hours. Maybe that's what McDede meant. We're doing the same thing over and over and over. Who will survive through the final lap? None of the fans stood by the tee anymore. Everyone was pulled toward the green. Only a couple lonely marshals with their hands in their pockets and an audio tech whose arms were getting tired. Those gents had the view none of us had. One final roller-coaster turn. Chun blocked her tee shot out to the right, sending it up against the revetted wall of a fairway bunker. She would not be reaching the green in two. Ashleigh had a chance, but then she did just as Chun did, blocking her approach into a greenside trap that was unlike most greenside traps.

They call it an Island Bunker. There's a grassy knoll in the middle, with a four-foot-wide strip of sand surrounding the knoll like a moat. All together it's shaped like an upside-down pear. If your ball lands too close to the knoll, it'll deflect your next shot. If it lands too close to the outline of the moat, you won't be able to deliver the club face to the ball. But therein lies another example of the inherent luck in this stupid, stupid game. Just like McIlroy's approach that bounced too soft on the 14th at St. Andrews or Cam Smith's drive on 15 that found an alleyway through jail, Ashleigh's ball landed splat in the center of the moat. There was just enough room behind her ball to hit it clean and just enough in front of it to clear the knoll. She played it perfectly, splashing halfway onto the green, letting the firm turf and wind at her back do the rest. It rolled for a full seven seconds before stopping two feet from the hole. The Ground Game, as Scotland has forever intended it. David's eyes got big. Nicole Brock Estrup spoke for everyone: "What a fucking *shot*."

The greatest shot of her life. It earned her a mini coronation after all. Maybe five minutes' worth. When Ashleigh tapped in for par, the sea of cameras parted, Husband Cam included. David dipped beneath the ropeline and bull-rushed the green before anyone else could reach his wife. He threw his arms around her, hoisted her off the ground, and planted a kiss on her cheek.

I couldn't help but laugh at the juxtaposition. A goliath of a man releasing all his anxious energy while his embattled wife stoically— and mostly silently—let it all wash over her. She buried her face in her hands a few times, always looking like she was pinching herself. *Is this a dream?* Only during her acceptance speech, when she thanked her family watching back home in South Africa, did her voice crack. I stood over by David, who had thrown his arm around Michael Paterson, Ashleigh's caddie's hubby.

"Our life's changing," David said with the widest grin of the night. "Our lives are changing, I'll tell you that."

Both of them missed the beginning of Ashleigh's press conference, about 15 minutes later, clearly caught up in the hoopla of chanting "How high? Buhai!" When David finally found his way to the media center, he ducked below cameras and squeezed into the second row of reporters. I thought he might be bold enough to ask a question. *Why'd you have to do that to us?!* The evening had to be so dizzying, between the beers and the bogeys and the camera flashes and the threat of having to return Monday morning…hungover.

He leaned back in his chair and snapped a few photos with his phone. One vertical, then a few horizontal. You can never be too sure. When Ashleigh was whisked away on the endless train of champion engagements, he sat there shaking his head and smiling, arm up on the seatback next to him, absolutely awestruck by his wife. "It's always harder for those watching," Ashleigh said during the presser, glancing at him. David knew it better than anyone. The people behind the people.

Chapter 16

Love

I cannot tell you how many times in my life I've heard these six words in this exact sequence: *Oh, so you must love golf…*

The emphasis was occasionally on *you*, and sometimes on *must*, but mostly it was on the fifth word. *Love.* I cannot tell you how many times I've heard that sequence because it would be hard to keep track.

The sentence normally comes in conversations with acquaintances. One of my dad's cousins. Or maybe one of my brother's coworkers. One of my pals' pals. You write about golf, you watch a lot of golf, you play a lot of golf. You want to spend a summer in the Home of Golf?

Oh, you must love golf…

The inference arrives so naturally it's sometimes issued as a statement. An agreed-upon fact. But whenever it comes as a question, followed by a pause, I have always felt a weird pit in my gut. Lying to them would mean lying to myself. That was a mental block. So I never answered, *Yes.* Of course, I really *liked* golf, at 29 going on 30, but I did not love it. I felt there was a difference —a chasm that had grown over time.

I loved golf when I was 10 years old, riding shotgun in Grandpa's Buick sedan out to Lake Breeze Golf Course in Winneconne, Wisconsin. Golf was innocent then. Maddening, but innocent for me. Grandpa worked eight-hour shifts as a ranger and let me do whatever I wanted. I hit hundreds of balls on the range. I went hunting for lost balls in the cornfield next door. I played golf alone for the first time. I grew obsessed with the pursuit of par. And trying to beat Grandpa.

I loved golf as a high schooler, working for but mostly *with* members like Bash. It was one helluva summer job, and the golf was free. Mom always worried about my energy levels, and she had good reason. I ran myself ragged working 10-hour shifts in the morning before playing 18 holes in the afternoon. Twice a summer I'd become so worn down I'd get sick, and she'd be stuck taking care of me. But we never blamed golf. It made me too happy.

Like any relationship, the further along you go, the good stuff becomes great, but the bad stuff begins to feel worse. The longer I worked in golf, the more homogenous the sport seemed. I hated that the PGA Tour locker room looked nothing like the locker rooms of other sports. I hated that golf's reputation was an old, rich, white man's sport. I repeated those qualifiers so many times to explain myself on first dates—another *Oh, you must love golf* social interaction—that they seemed to morph into a single idiom: Oldrichwhitemanssport.

It depressed me that the sport's leaders aligned with that demo. And that change to these institutions was nauseatingly slow. That obvious moves required two-thirds supermajorities, and not just one membership vote but two. I hated that so many corners of the game demanded invites from insiders. And I hated how complicit I was, playing more private golf than ever before, cringing every time I had to carry my shoes into the clubhouse rather than change them in the parking lot, because that's a rule. I hated that many of golf's most famous entrances were guarded by literal gates with security staffers asking, "Who are you? Who do you know here?"

I felt all these things whenever people made that implication, *Oh, so you must love golf.* It was posed to me once again in the final days before flying to Scotland, by a group of fathers during cocktail hour at a wedding. My brain churned faster, maybe a bit more anxiously, at that time. I was about to belly flop into Fife. Why was I leaving home for something I wasn't helplessly in love with?

I think it was because I was seeing if I could be *more* intimate with golf. To know all that I knew and still have that desperate craving to be *around* the game, in any capacity. Or to hit a wall once again and maybe back away from it entirely. I went to Scotland to see if I could feel the same bliss of those summers in high school, or at Lake Breeze with Grandpa. The St. Andrews documentary sold me on that intimacy. And the first two months of summer let me live it. It existed in full force. But it was the month of August, when all the tournaments had ended and there was little left to write about for our website, when the *people* of golf pushed me over the edge.

Astute readers will have noticed something in the previous chapter. The third round of the Women's Open at Muirfield—Moving Day! Nary a mention of it. That's because I didn't want to go to Muirfield that day.

I woke up that morning at 6A North Berwick, my bed-and-breakfast for the week, and knew this would be one of my last mornings in the most underrated enclave of the country. I had booked my summer to be in St. Andrews and had slowly, secretly fallen for North Berwick, too. We can blame Simon Holt for that. Joel Dahmen as well. He's the one who asked me to research local home prices on Zillow.

For a prospective buyer, North Berwick rivals St. Andrews in so many ways. Both are about two square miles. St. Andrews is near an estuary but is located on the sea. North Berwick is near the sea but is located on an estuary. Coastal walking paths wind right through both towns. The main businesses are cafes, pubs, and bed-and-breakfasts. They each have bowling clubs and caravan parks on the outskirts of town. There is no shortage of stone fences or seagulls—*that* I am confident in. And then, of course, they each have rip-roaring golf courses with drivable finishing holes that bring you back toward town.

To compare the two courses feels a touch overzealous, and it might take a summer to realize that. There is no true match for St. Andrews, the undisputed Home of Golf, but North Berwick feels like its sister. The Old Course is world famous, but the West Links is more hipster. An *If you know, you know* kinda place. That's why I wanted to soak it up one last time. Who knows when I'd be back?

I snapped photographs of the little things we often stare right past, like tee markers, warning signs, or the nameplates screwed into the backs of benches. This country is littered with those nameplates, dedicated to people who once sat there but have passed on. Photographing those things is easy. Their simplicity fits in the frame. Capturing the contours of a golf course is much trickier, as evidenced by the 15 minutes I spent on top of and circling the 16th green. Golf photographers think they can write and golf writers think they can take photos, but the gap between those skill sets is pretty wide for a reason.

My struggles were interrupted when two children lugging golf bags over their shoulders darted through the doorway in the nearby rock wall. A woman in a beige trench coat paced quickly ahead of them. They were headed to the Wee Course.

If there exists a golfing bone in your body, there is desire to play the Wee Course. It runs alongside the big course but is just nine holes, where the North Berwick Ladies Club played their first matches in the late 1800s. Just like the big course, it is split by one of those centuries-old stone walls, too. Three holes south of the wall, six holes to the north. The holes measure anywhere from 60 to 100 yards with perfectly circular greens, like they were manicured by one massive protractor. Luke List couldn't help himself during Scottish Open week and occasionally took laps around the Wee Course.

Today, there would be no adult play. Just adult chaperones—about 20 of them. It was Malcolm Cup day, and thus a very important day. "This is one of their, uh, majors. There are five of them," Tom Halliburton said sheepishly, aware that he was calling a 14-and-under tournament a major. But this is where Clara Young grew up playing. She calls them "the real majors." Tom's 11-year-old son, Aedan, won the Malcolm Cup in 2020. All five Wee Major trophies were spread out on a foldable table, out of arm's reach but close enough to dream about. The names of junior golfers from decades ago were engraved on them, just like the Claret Jug.

The two brothers and the trench-coated woman were the Lane-Fox family. Walker, Harold, and mother Chrissy, who still spoke with a twinge of the Kansas accent of her youth, despite living in the U.K. for years. Walker and Harold were spending a couple summer weeks with Grandma and Grandpa—who lived just off the 9th green—and arrived just in time to squeeze into the field. Nine threesomes became seven threesomes and two foursomes, and one jam-packed 9-hole course. I had wondered what junior golf looked like in Scotland. Apparently, it's a town gathering, marked down on the calendar for months. I was already well aware what I looked like, a hovering father of none, 30 years old, with a three-day beard and a camera around my neck. So I made friendly with Tom and Chrissy.

When the horn sounded for play, balls were in the air immediately, like these tikes were a firing squad waiting for orders. Harold sniped the first green and made a lovely par. Mom followed behind, playing scorekeeper, caddie, and maybe most importantly, rules official.

I saw a version of my former self in little Harold, tailing behind his big brother, not skilled enough to keep up, always half-jogging to keep pace. He had caught my attention in the minutes before the Cup started, when he nearly hit his mom with a line-drive 9-iron. That's something nine-year-old Sean would have done. I asked him who his favorite golfer was, but he couldn't tell me one. All he could tell me was his favorite course was Gullane No. 3, about five miles west. That's where he plays with his grandparents.

In Harold's group was Aedan, chasing after his second Malcolm Cup trophy, as well as another boy named Luke. They were the tallest of the whole bunch. Then there was little Harvey, a nine-year-old like Harold, maybe half their size. He wore a hat from the Scottish Open, the day he met his favorite golfer, Rickie Fowler.

I couldn't believe the mannerisms of these kids. They plumb-bobbed just like the pros and marked their balls meticulously, but when it was their turn, they didn't dally. They swung with every ounce of their 60-pound frames but with plenty of finesse, too. In 75 minutes, all 29 boys and girls whipped around the Wee Course in orderly fashion.

I loitered behind, smiling so much my cheeks started to hurt. Someone, somehow, had taken the tormenting game and shrunk it perfectly to bite size. The Malcolm Cup had a trophy to play for and an order to play in. It even had a £2 entry fee. Players clapped for each other's pars and comforted bogeys with "Ohhh, unlucky" when a putt rolled by. They ran over to check in on how their friends were playing. There was stroke play to establish a cut, just like professional events, and then match play for one of those trophies on the table. These kids didn't know a game rankled by money. They just knew the game was fun. Genuine fun. They tallied up their scores by counting with their fingers and when they turned in their scorecards, they felt the same nerves that keep adults coming back to this game, week after week after week. Eight players would advance. Now was the moment of truth.

Aedan was announced as a finalist first. Luke came next. Then a few more names, followed by Harold and, immediately after him, Harvey. They hugged each other like Olympians on the medal stand. Somehow, all four boys from the group I walked with had made it to match play. Their nerves about missing out turned to elation and then quickly back into nerves since they were now the center of attention. They had 10 minutes to gather themselves, talk with Mom and Dad, and hit a couple putts. Then they were announced on the 1ˢᵗ tee, extra official, and then it was time for more. I turned away feeling buoyant but a bit dismayed. My taxi had arrived to bring me to Muirfield.

The way I found Iona Stephen was exactly how I imagined she would be. She was smiling, her blonde hair flapping in the wind as it blew across the car park between the Old Course and the North Sea. Absolutely in her element. A rambunctious brown Lab leapt out the trunk door of her SUV and yanked Iona in my direction. That was Las, and exactly what I had hoped for as well. Back in May, Iona promised me I'd get to meet her dogs at some point this summer. She handed me the leash and a couple ProV1 golf balls. Truly, what more could a boy want?

"This'll be great, even better than the Joob,'" she said. We had considered playing nine holes on St. Andrews' Jubilee course. "I'd just like to get to know ya a bit better," she continued. The feeling was mutual.

Iona and I were the same age, both worked in golf media, and had spent the summer narrowly missing each other. When I was in town, she'd be on the road. When she was coming through town, I'd be too busy. Occasionally, we'd be right next to each other at work, her trudging through the rough as an on-course reporter for Sky Sports, and me filing through the same long grasses in search of a story. Our attempts to get a game never worked out in the big golf sense, but once the end of my summer came into focus, we finally got serious about it—3:15 on a Friday afternoon, putting at the Himalayas. "We'll have a blether," Iona said. In Scottish, she told me, that means "a cozy chat."

Everyone in St. Andrews will tell you there are seven courses in town, but the Himalayas is the eighth wonder of this golfy world. It's an 18-hole putting course laid out over heaving waves of land. Some holes measure 25 feet and require you to putt over a sidewalk. Others measure just five paces but require all the touch you possess to climb up a boulder of turf. Staked into the ground near every cup is a cute little blue arrow: THIS WAY NEXT TEE.

As we reached the tiny cottage that is the Himalayas clubhouse, I was reminded of a very important thing: it is owned by the St. Andrews Ladies' Putting Club and has been ever since 1867. They take that ownership seriously. Three elderly ladies walked by in classic golf attire, putters in hand. The sign on the clubhouse said CLOSED, and we expressed our frustration. "Well, it *is* a match day," one of the ladies said as she crossed us. The sun was shining for another six hours on this technically private patch of grass, but…their course, their rules.

"Soo, what does that mean for us?" I asked out of desperation.

"You will have to ask the man in the window," she said, turning to leave. We knew how she felt.

Only there was no man in the window. A shadowy figure rummaged about deeper inside the hut, only opening the gate once we knocked.

"Is thaarre…any chance you could let us out today?" Iona asked.

"Ahhhhh, humph." He made a big exhale, looking at the clock behind him and then succumbed. "Give me about 15 minutes."

When you need some sympathy, always have the lady ask. We grabbed a cup of coffee, took Las to the beach for 10 minutes of fetch, and returned to play an absolute pillow-fight of a putting match. The stakes: a sleeve of golf balls.

I went 2 up early, but she came back in the middle. We got lost in chat about our careers and work aspirations. Iona was sketching out a big interview series with Titleist and was curious for my thoughts. I was brainstorming how this day might fit into a book and was curious for hers. Iona's other Lab, Ghillie, had been golf trained, but Las was still learning, diving after our putts as they neared the hole. I really missed my dog back home.

I went 2 up again on the second nine but left the door ajar. The 17th was a downhill 30-footer, a turf bank on the left before the hole and another one on the right as you neared the cup. You had to funnel it through this valley, biting off just enough of the left hill and just enough of the right. I smashed my putt right through, leaving a depressing 10 feet on the comeback. It didn't matter, because for the first time all day, Iona made a putt of length. We were all square. She waved her putter into the air as it dropped. With her knit maroon sweater and wide-rimmed glasses, she looked like a Hogwarts student finally in control of her wand. We both two-putted the 18th and shook hands. A spirited, gentle draw.

At this late stage of my summer, I had acquired new digs: a 1,500-square-foot sandstone house with a baby-blue front door on the east side of town. A few visitors were coming, and Lorraine's elephant-adorned one-bedroom wasn't going to cut it. She sent me on my way across town in the most motherly way—with a fresh load of clean laundry and advice to get some rest. Iona offered to drive me home from the Himalayas, but as we approached the vicinity of the AirBnb, I found it funny Iona never asked for the exact address. We drove down North Street, toward the cemetery, in the right direction for sure. I was about to interject with the address when she said, "Ahh, I've got to show yeh some stuff," whipping another right turn onto South Street.

Inching along well below the speed limit, Iona pointed out every place in town that mattered to her. The cheese shop I had blindly ignored all summer; the dormitory she used to live in. We made a pit stop at the Sproson Art Gallery, where artwork from her mother, Rona, was on display. For 10 minutes we stopped by the house Iona owns on the west side of town, which she rents out to university students. She casually clipped a few pieces of sage from the garden and handed them to me.

"Take these home, melt a stick of butter in a pan, drop the sage in there, and let it cook," she said. "Get yarrself a fresh salmon filet from one of the fish shops and pour the butter over it. It will be the best-tasting fish you've ever had." *Ahem*—where was this advice all summer?!

I'm not sure what it was, exactly. Perhaps the aggregation of time around someone that helps you feel comfortable. But something seemed to click in our conversation after that drive through town. We had discussed golf in the professional sense all day, but when we got back in the car, we dug a layer deeper.

"Golf became so vital to my mental health," Iona said. "Courses became my sanctuary. Not just being outside but being in *nature*. Slowing down. A feeling of disconnecting. Not being on the end of emails and phones and questions and pressure."

Maybe that's why she smiled so wide when I met her that afternoon. Setting foot in St. Andrews reminds her of *the* moment in her life. Not just *a* moment. *The* moment. Where everything changed. She had gone to art school in Glasgow for two years, studying architecture and following in her family's professional footsteps. Her great-grandfather had helped build the Forth Bridge that connects Fife to West Lothian. She was a gifted athlete, playing field hockey at an international level, but knew there was a ceiling on that career. She attended the Women's Open in 2011 at Carnoustie and, as she described it, it was as though the sport reached out and grabbed her.

"I thought, 'This is the game that I need to play. Why am I not playing *this* game?'"

She gave up architecture, gave up Glasgow, and transferred to the one place in the world that made the most sense for a golfing life: St. Andrews.

"Some people thought it was crazy, but my gut feeling was so strong," she said. "I felt so *aligned* with golf. It felt like a big bright light I had to go toward. I knew somewhere deep in my soul that it would work out okay."

Her stop in St. Andrews led her to Wentworth, in London, where she broke the ladies course record, amassed a plus-3 handicap, and eventually launched a professional playing career. All of that in just four years.

As golf would have it, that playing career came to a screeching halt with a mysterious injury in her right wrist. The type doctors couldn't diagnose and that steroids and surgeries and stem-cell injections couldn't fix. But chasing the game at the highest level made her adept as anyone at talking about it on camera. She has one of those soothing voices you don't want to go quiet. Our conversation had only a few more street turns in it. This felt like a podcast I didn't want to end.

The bizarre injury—that she still struggles to explain—forced her to pivot, but in a way that makes every golfing moment feel a bit more wholesome now. Nine holes is often enough to fill up her spiritual tank, athletic tape wrapped tight around her wrist. She can't practice like she used to. It still hurts to play. But it heals to play, too. Golf for her can be as simple as a three-hole loop with the doggos. We wove back through campus again and made the same right turn at the cemetery, this time coasting downhill with no detours. She put the car in park and then turned the spotlight on me.

"Sean, tell me. What was *yorr* simplest, happiest moment in golf?"

I had been thinking about the way she used the word *sanctuary*. That word feels so religious to me, and maybe that's the point. Golf was her religion.

I told her about this one Friday evening during my senior year of college, when I worked in the pro shop at a club for beer money. My phone was filled with unread texts from roommates wondering when I'd return home for our typical Friday festivities. I wasn't playing. I didn't hit any shots. I tidied up the range, parked all the carts, buttoned up the course for the next morning, and drove around in a maintenance cart slowly enough that I could watch the sun sink down over distant fairways. An odd feeling rushed over me that night. It was something akin to ownership, and even of belonging, which was so odd because I was completely alone. But when Iona described golf being a "bright light" that was exactly what I thought of. Simply existing on a golf course filled up my tank.

As the details tumbled out, it was clear that fall 2013 evening in a funny town named Oregon, Wisconsin, was just as vivid as any of my evenings in St. Andrews. It was a moment where I deeply *loved* golf. Weirder yet was that I hadn't discussed it with anyone in… years? I wasn't sure I had *ever* talked to anyone about it. But Iona's own vulnerability pulled it right out of me. The mark of a good interviewer, I guess. Or some sort of golf psych. We hugged goodbye and promised to stay in touch, but I wasn't holding my breath. Life gets busy, especially when there's an ocean in between. I promised her I would cook the hell outta that sage. Then I shut the door and promised myself: *Make more time for blethers.*

The email began,

> Sean, good morning,
>
> Jim and I would be delighted if you could join us for coffee about 10 AM on Tuesday in the Golf Museum Cafe.
> Kind regards,
> Ronald

What a message to wake up to! Two months after eavesdropping led to a free cup of coffee, my friends from the Cottage Kitchen were still thinking about me.

That Tuesday kicked off my final week in St. Andrews. I found Jim and Ronald seated next to the floor-to-ceiling windows at the cafe above the R&A Museum. Ronald on my left, Jim on my right, and golfers playing down the 1ˢᵗ hole of the Old Course in the background. Golf Disney chugged along like always.

Jim cut to the chase the instant I sat down. "Has yorr trip been worthwhile?"

"Best trip of my life, I think?" I replied. Then Ronald jumped in.

"Are ye going to write a bouk about it?"

My fear of commitment went into overdrive and made me say I wasn't sure, but that was a lie. I had made up my mind at the Women's Open. There was something in the inebriated joy of David Buhai and his silent admiration of his champion wife that looked a lot like golf *love.*

We only had an hour, but Jim and Ronald wanted to break down the entire summer. We debated if the next Open would really be in 2030. I received a tip that the R&A would likely take Tiger's prediction as a call for help and rather than wait to see if he could get around at 54, they would force another St. Andrews Open into the calendar earlier, maybe in 2027. The 155ᵗʰ.

Jim and Ronald wanted to share some thoughts on Rory McIlroy. Mainly, Ronald thought he played too defensively on Sunday, calling Cam Smith not by his name but rather "a blizzard of bar-dies ahead of Rory." Jim was a Rory skeptic in general.

"He's always talking about his opennyins of things," Jim said. "You don't know the opennyins of Scohtee Schefflar or all these people. They're just worken on their game. Rory, I think, is just too *vocal.*

[pause]

"Perhopps you don't agree with me?"

Of course not! Rory was pulling the game forward by being vocal. He just happened to get chased down on the final stretch of the final day. He beat every Tom, Dick, and Harry in the field. Just lost to two of the three Camerons. I didn't fight Jim on it because his opinion also wasn't unique. McIlroy not winning that Open was a bit of a rain cloud hanging over the goodwill he'd built up. At some point, you just have to *do it.*

Lastly, it seemed, they wanted to share the juicy details they learned this summer, too. Scotland's Summer of Golf, as it was stated in *The Scotsman,* one of the biggest newspapers in the country.

"Some of the older Open winners played Crail the week before The Open," Ronald said. "Not all together. But [Gary] Player, [John] Daly, Bob Charles. [Tom] Watson and [Lee] Trevino. They all went down there to play. Player had a 67 with four birdies on the Balcomie. Tom Watson thought it played longer than it louked. He loved the two holes along the water. He said it was a long time since he's taken driver on a par-3. That was the 13th into the wind, up the hill."

This. *Now* we were getting to the good stuff.

"Trevino, bless him," Ronald continued. "And his view is shared by Peter Dawson—whom I spoke to on Saturday—Balcomie is better than Pebble Beach."

There was a pause.

"Quote, unquote," he said, lifting his eyebrows above an impish smile. *Sean, are you going to argue with the thoughts of golfing legends?*

I knew better than to believe every word Jim and Ronald had heard secondhand from other Jims and other Ronalds across Fife. It would take months to verify some of these tales. I just sat back and smiled into my latte knowing that 1. The 150th Open was already adding to Scottish folklore. And 2. Golf chats were keeping these old boys young.

As we said our farewells that day, it felt a lot like my goodbye to Iona, with that overwhelming sense of finality. Who knows if I'd ever see them again? I was annoyed with myself for how much time I spent working *alone* in cafes this summer. Coffee visits with Jim and Ronald should have been a weekly occurrence. But now I had officially run out of time. My ride to Carnoustie pulled up.

I didn't think much about Jim and Ronald for the next three months. But then one day, another email arrived. Subject line: "Winter's Day at Balcomie," *Sent from my iPad*. Six photos were attached, of a piercing yellow sun, the peachy haze surrounding it, the calm blue sea and the charcoal, rocky shore. The yellow-green turf, and the pin with its simple, golden flag hanging limp. A white ball rested two feet from the cup, casting a long afternoon shadow.

A week later, another email: "Stunning morning in St. Andrews," *Sent from my iPad*. Six photos attached, a similar scene in a different location. "Lots of eyes on the forthcoming England vs. France World Cup Match on Sunday evening."

A week after that, another email: "First snow," *Sent from my iPad*. Three photos attached. The 1st and the 18th at the Old Course, blanketed in a thin coat of white. Tiny, green, joyful footsteps all over.

I'm not sure I deserved it, but I had weaseled my way onto Ronald's exclusive Golf Updates distribution list. Among the two dozen recipients was Gil Hanse, the preeminent golf course designer on the planet. There was Michael Bonallack, a member of the World Golf Hall of Fame. There were numerous former captains of the R&A, even a member of Augusta National. There was also George Peper, an American author who once bought a two-bedroom flat in St. Andrews in 1983, maybe 1,700 square feet, renting to students in the fall and spring and keeping it to himself in the summer. Pete Couhig before Pete Couhig. Me before me. Peper was once an editor at *GOLF Magazine*, too, and in response to his time in the Auld Grey Toon, he felt compelled to write a book about it. It's called *St. Andrews Sojourn*. I was thrilled to be on the same email chain as him. St. Andreans at heart, knighted as such by Ronald Sandford, a certified golf lover who enjoyed nothing more than connecting with other certified golf lovers. He was a lot like Bash, I thought. Ronald entered my life just days after Bash departed. Absolutely a coincidence. Unless it's not.

We gazed out over the Old Course from the private balcony of
the R&A clubhouse, right where R&A CEO Martin Slumbers
entertained his VIPs during Open week. The only way to access this
terrace is to tiptoe through his office, perhaps the best workspace in
all of sport.

A few days earlier, we were sternly advised that an invite for lunch
at the R&A was not to be skipped. "You've goht to get yerselves a coat
an' tie," Laurie Watson told us from the clubhouse at Royal Aberdeen.
I had convinced myself that living up to the formal dress code wasn't
worth our hassle, but Laurie doubled down: "You dohn't pass up lunch
at the R&A. The wine cellar is out of this world."

So there we stood on Mr. Slumbers' epic veranda, geeking like
goobers in front of the most famous backdrop in golf. College pals
of mine, Adam and Max, had flown in from America for an eight-
courses-in-eight-days boondoggle, and this was Day 8, August 27,
the 88th day of my trip. We were all going home soon, back to the
comforts of everything we're used to, but for now, Max and Adam
looked like out-of-place security guards, having thrifted coats and
ties upon Laurie's recommendation. These Wisconsin boys squeezed
into boxy, navy blue suits, and each fastened the top two buttons,
looking even more like amateurs. Adam's shoes *shined* but his pants
were at least one size short, exposing athletic socks instead of dressier
ones. Max's shoes were too big, his sleeves too long, and his tie knot
too small and too crooked. We did the best we could with £50, but I
just couldn't get Max to lighten up. Every photo shows him standing
upright and rigid, like a statue, with his hands linked behind his back.
I think he was worried we may get the boot if anyone could smell the
scent of obviously used clothes from the Salvation Army on Church
Street. This was the final Know Somebody Who Knows Somebody
box on the summer bucket list. I met our host, Craig, during that
blurry June afternoon at Royal Burgess, and much like everyone in
this country, he insisted we share in his golf club.

The Scots have created some of the greatest golf courses on the planet, but instead of keeping them walled from the world—as is custom in America—they open their doors to visitors on one condition: it's going to cost a bit more. Visitor rounds are typically priced around £200 to £250—and they're absolutely worth it. That tourist premium props up every club's operating budget, and since the ownership structure is not singularly focused on increasing property values, or deriving dividends for a conglomerate, and because maintaining golf courses isn't some exorbitant, 20-person daily quest for the perfect shade of green grass, the windfall of money serves a simple purpose: to keep membership dues at a minimum.

The annual cost to be a member at Cruden Bay, a course that seems to transplant you to across the U.K. to the dunes of Ireland, is about £700. Royal Aberdeen, just down the coast, charges its members £1,500. Scotscraig, located in between St. Andrews and Carnoustie, is a delightful little romp through the trees that costs just £700. And the beloved West Links at North Berwick? £900. They'll have my money in an instant if I ever get serious about buying a cottage in town.

When I informed Joel Dahmen of these consumer-friendly golf economics, his jaw basically dragged on the turf. He knows how broken the club structure is in America. Joel lives in Scottsdale, where initiation fees of clubs extend comfortably into the six digits. After that, annual dues start around $15,000 per year.

"How many clubs in the States would you belong to if membership was $1,000?" I asked Joel.

"Uh, one in every city the Tour stops in, for starters," he said. "So that's 26." He was dead serious, and I never doubted him. Though the visual of 26 bag tags clanking around on his golf bag did make me chuckle.

Golf is not treated like a profit-desperate commodity in Scotland. Different people in a different country have different incentives and dreams and ideas about capitalism. The supply and demand of the game is in such equilibrium here that "good" doesn't need to be great. Good can be *good enough,* especially when it is so intertwined with its natural surroundings. The pubs in these tiny towns are golf pubs. The bed-and-breakfasts are golf houses. The actual clubs are named after the towns in which they reside. The handful of street signs that catch your eye as you drive through Crail and Carnoustie and Anstruther and Aberdeen—they all point you in the direction of the city's main attraction: its course. Many of the courses are public land. And if not, public paths often carve throughout them. Scotland's national economy runs on sales of petroleum and whisky and machinery and fishing, but its greatest export is this game, and they know it. A cautious member from North Berwick knew what I was up to all summer and told me, "Happy to have you out at *any* time. Just don't tell the world how good we've got it here. I don't want my dues going up."

I thought about that quote a good bit during my final week in Scotland. The man who delivered it wasn't a Scot, a Brit, or even European. He was an American who had taken up residency in Edinburgh. But because an invigorating golfing life is so attainable in Scotland, he now owned a piece of it. I did too. That is the Scottish way. Everyone generally owns the piece of the game that they want to own, and there aren't many barriers keeping them from doing so.

So when my two friends from college visited for that final, weeklong golf bender, I acted like I owned the place. Because I sort of did. The Scotland we toured was *my* Scotland. We didn't sprint around in a shuttle van trying to play 36 holes a day. It was one course per day, nothing more. I had arranged five different sherpas to guide us around their home tracks, offering us the discounted rates that come when you play with members. Craig was our sixth chaperone, guiding us through Martin Slumbers' office, the R&A beef roast, encouraging us into a second glass of the red, then zipping us down through the countryside to our final tee time, at Dumbarnie.

It only started to sink in, during those last few days, that what made my summer was not so much the experiences or the courses or the history of Open No. One-Fifty. Rather, it was the names and faces that the game placed in front of me. People like Craig who gleefully drove out of his way to host three frugal foreigners for lunch, pay for it all, and not hit a single golf shot with us. But that's one thing this sport does best. Through the people come the experiences. Commit to this game just enough and the golf people you cross at 16 years old are different than the ones you find at 24. Different than those at 30 and 47 and 62 and 91. As I played tour guide that week, the list of names I rattled off grew longer and longer, and the more it all felt like Parents' Weekend at college. *I did this with these people, and I did that with those people, and this summer wouldn't be the same without them.*

Euan Smith and the 21-year-olds jamming to Counting Crows during a dark time? They paid for my first beer in town. They arranged my first round of seaside golf. They were my academic parents. We'll call Nigel Snow my academic grandparent then. I never quite got to say goodbye to him—always convinced he would be there at the end of the telephone line when I called for my final ride to the airport— but I trust there's a reader or two of this book who might be able to say hi for me.

Joel Dahmen at Renaissance Club? He was like a teaching assistant pursuing grad school. Damnit, did he know how to golf his ball. Damnit, did he have a golfer's mind. But he was still learning the links life, too, albeit at a higher frequency than mortals like me. He'll make the cut in his next Scottish Open. I'm sure of it. Probably with a better caddie.

Every round at North Berwick felt like playing frisbee in the university quad, not a care in the world. Simon Holt and Iona Stephen were guest lecturers. Tom Kenmack too. His 30-minute class in Anstruther Hall retaught me that golf is a behemoth of a game that can be whittled down to simple derivatives. Golf derivatives were the bedrock of my amusement as a 13-year-old. That a 91-year-old can have the same experience should tell you something.

I feel like I earned a philosophy certificate in morality and ethics during my week at LIV London. Golf is far from perfect and a life in golf will present you with some squirrelly things. How you handle them will always say something about you. How you attack opportunities says a lot about you, too. Pete Couhig was my counselor for that, urging me in directions (local real estate) that would test my inner desires. Maybe it was his Louisiana accent contrasting with our Scottish surroundings, but him promising *It'll be the best decision you ever make* still rings in my head months and months later.

My last week felt a lot like college, too. We lay around in the mornings and took leisurely strolls through campus. Adam created a power ranking of the best vanilla lattes in town, because why not? Max fell in love with Tennent's, as one does. I spent a fortune on ice cream. We stayed up late watching *Love Island* and drinking red wine, picking away at a block of Parmesan cheese from the store Iona recommended. Everywhere we wanted to be, we could get to on foot, via taxi, or by train. And quickly. We reveled in our thin itinerary— one course per day means one obligation per day—phones (and the real world) tucked away in our bags. The long birdie Max made on 18 at the Old Course, as the setting sun lit the clouds on fire behind us, and as Old Tom Morris' great-great granddaughter sat watching in her windowsill, is a memory that will never fade.

The competitive, covetous part of me would prefer that part of my summer would be remembered by the courses I played and the scores I shot. But I think it was telling that the only scorecard that came home with me was the last one in my pocket. It was a 76 at Dumbarnie, the newest course in Fife, during the immediate hours after our boozy R&A lunch. (They hand you a shooter of whisky on the 1st tee, which made our initial tee balls even more wobbly.) I polished off the round by executing one of those Artist or Fraud shots. With 30 yards between me and the final hole of my trip, I made the wedge go *click*, launched the ball 15 yards in the air, watched it spin into the ground and roll out to six feet. My putter did the rest. Golf felt so easy in that moment. Probably like Cam Smith felt during the final round. I felt like a wizard. Or maybe just a graduate.

It was a romantic way of wrapping the trip—my lowest career round in my final Scotland days—but Dumbarnie really wasn't a token of my summer in the slightest. It's the newest course in Fife—having opened in 2020—so its greens were much too soft and its dunes too pointy. Neither had been weathered into form by decades of wind and rain. What *was* a token of my summer came an hour later. One final cab ride. Our driver's name was James White, a Scot.

"How had the greens grown in?" James asked when we piled into his van, exposing himself as a golfer. As it turns out, he was a really good golfer. The kind good enough to have a cup of coffee on the European Tour in the late '80s and early '90s. He played eight events, made two cuts, and bankrolled about £6,000. Enough to tell customers, as long as he wanted, that he had done it. His proudest moment came when he qualified into the 1988 Open at Royal Lytham and St. Annes. His scores of 77 and 79 didn't matter. His name was in the field and on the leaderboard. A 99.99th-percentile achievement. Only in Scotland do the cabbies play in Open Championships. Only in Scotland could you spend 90 days basking in all its glory and still feel like you've only scratched the surface.

The jumbo jet from Edinburgh descended into Boston Logan International Airport around 3 PM. I was back on American soil almost 90 days to the hour since I'd left Chicago. The network connection on my phone finally flipped back to AT&T—5G, at last. We deboarded the plane on the tarmac and I couldn't help from groaning out loud.

The American summer was wet and hot—87 degrees, with 83 percent humidity, feeling like 104. You're not in Fifeland anymore, Seano.

The international baggage claim was just as upsetting. Pure, rampant chaos. Bags were stacked in lines on the ground like sandbags trying to control a flood. I was one of the lucky ones, able to secure my suitcase with ease, sidestepping through the madness over to the oversized baggage area. And that's when I saw him, a face I hadn't seen since London. Fresh off an eight-hour flight from Frankfurt, eyes scanning the room for his baggage carousel, was German LIV golfer Martin Kaymer. Of course.

How cyclical of my summer, I thought. LIV at the beginning, getting its footing, and LIV at the end, in its fourth major city, pushing toward normalization. What happened in between? Everything, really. Kaymer slid through the foot traffic, pulled ahead by his fiancée.

In some ways he was just like all the other LIV pros I had rolled my eyes at all summer. He was 37 years old, a former world No. 1. He won two major championships and the 2014 Players Championship. His résumé will be analyzed for years by future voters of the World Golf Hall of Fame. To LIV or not to LIV is a battle they'll be working through.

Kaymer committed to LIV early, a personal acknowledgement that his best days were behind him. The last time I had seen him, he squeezed into the back of a London Black Cab at Centurion Club, headed to a tee box thousands of yards away. In that early LIV moment, I watched him apologize to his fiancée for the fact they wouldn't be riding together. There wasn't enough room. She'd have to figure it out on her own. Play goofy games, win goofy prizes, they say. Well, he played well enough in the first three events to make the easiest $1 million of his life. We'll always remember pro golf's summer of 2022 for things like that. *Money, money, money.*

I was growing impatient, knowing I needed to get the oversized bag my clubs traveled in, sprint to recheck it, and then zoom to another airport terminal just to catch my connecting flight home. The soothing pace of Scotland was already fading in my memory. But there was nothing to do but wait. So we waited. Me and the former best golfer on the planet, for about 15 minutes, doing exactly the same thing: day-dreaming as we wait for the silly sticks we use to play the game we love.

When the metal curtain rose up, my bag was shoved out first—a badly needed victory for my time constraints. I grabbed the handle and dragged my barge of things his way. He woke up from a trance and moved to grab his own. We crossed paths and locked eyes for a moment, and I wished him good luck on the week. He nodded thank you, grabbed his clubs, and headed in the opposite direction. He was off to wherever golf was taking him. No doubt it would be interesting. You could say the exact same for me.

Acknowledgments

For the people who helped inspire this thing into existence, those who made life abroad feel like home, and the many others who impacted my summer, thank you. Especially:

Bob Harig, Kevin Van Valkenburg, Laurie Watson, Lorraine Bayne, Graylyn Loomis, Jamie Kennedy, Nigel Snow, Michael Bamberger, my patient coworkers, Jamie Weir, David Romilly, Ru Macdonald, Mike Stoneman, Iona Stephen, Jim Rait, Ronald Sanford, Alan Shipnuck, Simon Holt, Craig Brodie, Charlie Lane Fox, Alan Smith, Paul Mullan, RACDG, Pete Couhig, Jamie Hall, Jake Fischer, the coffee shops in Chicago, Tamara Allen, Joel Dahmen, Geoff Shackleford, Kyle Porter, Shane Ryan, my Titleist 3-wood, Michael Rosenberg, Euan Smith, Teddy Wallace, Nick Whalen, Michael McEwen, The Deeyooks, Joe Perry, Marshall Lund, Jess Allison

And to the many others I am surely forgetting—thank you, too.